W9-DIV-026

SAMS
Teach Yourself

XML

in 24 Hours

Michael Morrison

SECOND EDITION

SAMS 201 West 103rd St., Indianapolis, Indiana, 46290 USA

Sams Teach Yourself XML in 24 Hours, Second Edition

Copyright © 2002 by Sams Publishing

International Standard Book Number: 0-672-32213-7

Library of Congress Catalog Number: 2001088015

Printed in the United States of America

First Printing: December 2001

05 04 03 02   5 4 3 2

Trademarks

Warning and Disclaimer

ACQUISITIONS EDITOR
Betsy Brown

DEVELOPMENT EDITOR
Heather Goodell

MANAGING EDITOR
Charlotte Clapp

PROJECT EDITOR
Michael Kopp,
Publication Services, Inc.

COPY EDITORS
Meg Griffin,
Jason Mortenson,
Publication Services, Inc.

PRODUCTION EDITOR
Theodore Young, Jr.,
Publication Services, Inc.

INDEXER
Richard Bronson,
Publication Services, Inc.

PROOFREADER
Publication Services, Inc.

TECHNICAL EDITOR
Kevin Flanagan

TEAM COORDINATOR
Amy Patton

INTERIOR DESIGNER
Gary Adair

COVER DESIGNER
Aren Howell

PAGE LAYOUT
Michael Tarleton,
Jim Torbit,
Publication Services, Inc.

Contents at a Glance

Contents

Lead Author

MICHAEL MORRISON is a writer, developer, toy inventor, and author of a variety of books, including *HTML and XML for Beginners*, *The Unauthorized Guide to Pocket PC*, *XML Unleashed*, and *The Complete Idiot's Guide to Java 2*. He is the instructor of several Web-based courses and also serves as a technical director for ReviewNet, a company that provides Web-based staffing tools for information technology personnel. He is also the creative lead at Gas Hound Games, a toy company he co-founded that is located on the Web at `http://www.gashound.com/`. When not risking life and limb on his skateboard or mountain bike, trying to avoid the penalty box in hockey, or watching movies with his wife, Masheed, Michael enjoys daydreaming next to his koi pond.

Contributing Authors

RAFE COLBURN designs and builds Web applications for Alerts, Inc. in Raleigh, North Carolina. He contributed Part IV, "Processing and Managing XML Data." He's also the author of *Special Editon Using SQL* from Que Publishing and *Sams Teach Yourself CGI in 24 Hours*. His personal site is `http://rc3.org/`.

VALERIE PROMISE is a writer and designer living in Santa Cruz, California. She has been involved with technical writing for nine years, with special interests in Web, wireless, interactive TV, and other emerging technologies. She contributed Chapters 21 and 22.

- Part III, "Formatting and Displaying XML Documents"—In this part, you learn how to format XML content with style sheets so that it can be displayed. XML formatting is explored using two different style sheet technologies—CSS and XSLT.

- Part IV, "Processing and Managing XML Data"—In this part, you find out how to process XML documents and manipulate their contents. You learn all about the Document Object Model (DOM) and how it provides access to the inner workings of XML documents. You also learn how databases fit into the XML landscape.

- Part V, "XML and the Web"—In this part, you explore XML's relationship to HTML and the Web. You learn about XHTML, which is the merger of XML and HTML, along with advanced XML linking technologies. You also learn how XML is being used to provide a means of creating Web pages for wireless devices via a language called WML.

- Part VI, "A Few Interesting XML Languages"—In this part, you examine some practical applications of XML that allow you to do some pretty interesting things. You learn how to draw vector graphics using a language called SVG, design multimedia experiences with a language called SMIL, and create virtual worlds with a language called 3DML.

What You'll Need

This book assumes you have some familiarity with a markup language, such as HTML. You don't have to be an HTML guru by any means, but it definitely helps if you understand the difference between a tag and an attribute. Even if you don't, you should be able to tackle XML without too much trouble. It will also help if you have experience using a Web browser. Even though there are aspects of XML that reach beyond the Web, this book focuses a great deal on using Web browsers to view and test XML code. For this reason, I encourage you to download and install the latest release of one of the two big Web browsers—Internet Explorer or Netscape Navigator.

In addition to Web browsers, there are a few other tools mentioned throughout the book that you may consider downloading or purchasing based upon your individual needs. At the very least, you'll need a good text editor to edit XML documents. Windows Notepad is sufficient if you're working in a Windows environment, and I'm sure you can find a suitable equivalent for other environments. That's really all you need; a Web browser and a trusty text editor will carry you a long way toward becoming proficient in XML.

How to Use This Book

In code listings, line numbers have been added for reference purposes. These line numbers aren't part of the code. The code used in this book is also on this book's Web site at `http://www.samspublishing.com`

This book uses different typefaces to differentiate between code and regular English. Text that you type and text that appears on your screen is presented in monospace type.

`It will look like this to mimic the way text looks on your screen.`

Placeholders for variables and expressions appear in *monospace italic* font. You should replace the placeholder with the specific value it represents.

In addition, the following elements appear throughout the book:

Notes provide you with comments and asides about the topic at hand.

A Caution advises you about potential problems and helps you steer clear of disaster.

XML's relationship with HTML doesn't end with XHTML, however. Although XHTML is a great idea that may someday make Web pages cleaner and more consistent for Web browsers to display, we're a ways off from seeing Web designers embrace XHTML with open arms. It's currently still too convenient to take advantage of the freewheeling flexibility of the HTML language. Where XML is making a significant immediate impact on the Web is in Web-based applications that must shuttle data across the Internet. XML is an excellent transport medium for representing data that is transferred back and forth across the Internet as part of a complete Web-based application. In this way, XML is used as a behind-the-scenes data transport language, whereas HTML is still used to display traditional Web pages to the user. This is evidence that XML and HTML can coexist happily both now and in the future.

XML and Web Browsers

One of the stumbling blocks to learning XML is figuring out exactly how to use it. You now understand how XML complements HTML, but you still probably don't have a good grasp on how XML data is used in a practical scenario. More specifically, you're probably curious about how to view XML data. Since XML is all about describing the content of information, as opposed to the appearance of information, there is no such thing as a generic XML viewer, at least not in the sense that a Web browser is an HTML viewer. In this sense, an "XML viewer" is simply an application that lets you view XML code, which is normally just a text editor. To view XML code according to its meaning, you must use an application that is specially designed to work with a specific XML language. If you think of HTML as an XML language, then a Web browser is an application designed specifically to interpret the HTML language and display the results.

Another way to view XML documents is with style sheets using either XSL (eXtensible Stylesheet Language) or CSS (Cascading Style Sheets). Style sheets have come into vogue recently as a better approach to formatting Web pages. Style sheets work in conjunction with HTML code to describe in more detail how HTML data is to be displayed in a Web browser. Style sheets play a similar role when used with XML. The latest versions of Internet Explorer and Netscape Navigator support CSS, and Internet Explorer also supports a portion of XSL. You learn a great deal more about style sheets in Part III, "Formatting and Displaying XML Documents."

In addition to Internet Explorer and Netscape Navigator, the W3C offers a Web browser that can be used to browse XML documents. The Amaya Web browser supports the editing of Web documents and also serves as a decent browser. However, Amaya is intended more as a means of testing XML documents than as a commercially viable Web browser. You can download Amaya for free from the W3C Web site at http://www.w3c.org/Amaya/.

In addition to style sheets, there is another XML-related technology that is supported in the latest major Web browsers. I'm referring to the DOM (Document Object Model), which allows you to use a scripting language such as JavaScript to programmatically access the data in an XML document. The DOM makes it possible to create Web pages that selectively display XML data based upon scripting code. You will learn how to access XML documents using JavaScript and the DOM in Hour 15, "Understanding the XML Document Object Model (DOM)."

One last point to make in regard to viewing XML with Web browsers is that Internet Explorer allows you to view XML code directly. This is a neat feature of Internet Explorer because it automatically highlights the code so that the tags and other contents are easy to see and understand. Additionally, Internet Explorer allows you to expand and collapse sections of the data just as you expand and collapse folders in Windows Explorer. This reveals the hierarchical nature of XML documents. Figure 1.1 shows the virtual pets XML document as viewed in Internet Explorer 5.5.

FIGURE 1.1

You can view the code for an XML document by opening the document in Internet Explorer.

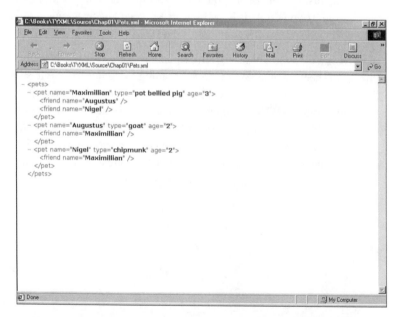

HOUR 2

Creating XML Documents

Tell a man that there are 300 billion stars in the universe, and he'll believe you. Tell him that a bench has wet paint on it, and he'll have to touch it to be sure.

—Anonymous

Similar to HTML, XML is a technology that is best understood by working with it. I could go on and on for pages about the philosophical ramifications of XML, but in the end I'm sure you just want to know what you can do with it. Most of your XML work will consist of developing XML documents, which are sort of like HTML Web pages, at least in terms of code. Keep in mind, however, that XML documents can be used to store any kind of information. Once you've created an XML document, you will no doubt want to see how it appears in a browser. Since there is no standard approach to viewing an XML document according to its meaning, you must either find or develop a custom application for viewing the document or use a style sheet to view the document in a Web browser. This hour uses the latter approach to provide a simple view of an XML document that you create.

In this hour, you'll learn

- The basics of XML
- How to select an XML editor
- How to create XML documents
- How to view XML documents

A Quick XML Primer

You learned in the previous hour that XML is a markup language used to create other markup languages. Seeing as how HTML is a markup language, it stands to reason that XML documents should in some way resemble HTML documents. In fact, you saw in the previous hour how an XML document looks a lot like an HTML document, with the obvious difference that XML documents can use custom tags. So, instead of seeing `<head>` and `<body>` you saw `<pet>` and `<friend>`. Nonetheless, if you have some experience with coding Web pages in HTML, XML will be very familiar. You will find that XML isn't nearly as lenient as HTML, so you may have to unlearn some bad habits carried over from HTML. Of course, if you don't have any experience with HTML then you probably won't even realize that XML is a somewhat rigid language.

XML Building Blocks

Like some other markup languages, XML relies heavily on three fundamental building blocks: elements, attributes, and values. An *element* is used to describe or contain a piece of information; elements form the basis of all XML documents. Elements consist of two tags, an opening tag and a closing tag. Opening tags appear as words contained within angle brackets (`<>`), such as `<pet>` or `<friend>`. Closing tags also appear within angle brackets, but they have a forward-slash (`/`) before the tag name. Examples of closing tags are `</pet>` and `</friend>`. Elements always appear as an opening tag, optional data, and a closing tag:

```
<pet>
</pet>
```

XML doesn't care too much about how white space appears between tags, so it's perfectly acceptable to place tags together on the same line:

```
<pet></pet>
```

single element in an XML document that contains all other elements in the document. Every XML document must contain a root element, which means that only one element can be at the top level of any given XML document. In the "pets" example that you've seen throughout this hour and the previous hour, the `pets` element is the root element because it contains all of the other elements in the document (the `pet` elements). To make a quick comparison to HTML, the `html` element in a Web page is the root element, so HTML is similar to XML in this regard. However, technically HTML will let you get away with having more than one root element, whereas XML will not.

> Since the root element in an XML document must contain other elements, it cannot be an empty element. This means that the root element always consists of a pair of opening and closing tags.

Special XML Symbols

There are a few special symbols in XML that must be entered differently than other text characters. The reason for entering these symbols differently is because they are used in identifying parts of an XML document such as tags and attributes. The symbols to which I'm referring are the less than symbol (<), greater than symbol (>), quote symbol ("), apostrophe symbol ('), and ampersand symbol (&). These symbols all have special meaning within the XML language, which is why you must enter them using a symbol instead of just using each character directly. So, as an example, the following code isn't allowed in XML because the ampersand (&) and apostrophe (') characters are used directly in the `name` attribute value:

```
<movie name="Bill & Ted's Excellent Adventure"/>
```

The trick to referencing these characters is to use special predefined symbols known as entities. An *entity* is a symbol that identifies a resource, such as a text character or even a file. There are five predefined entities in XML that correspond to each of the special characters you just learned about. Entities in XML begin with an ampersand (&) and end with a semicolon (;), with the entity name sandwiched between. Following are the predefined entities for the special characters:

- Less than symbol (<) — `&lt;`
- Greater than symbol (>) — `&gt;`
- Quote symbol (") — `&quot;`
- Apostrophe symbol (') — `&apos;`
- Ampersand symbol (&) — `&amp;`

To fix the movie example code, just replace the ampersand and apostrophe characters in the attribute value with the appropriate entities:

```
<movie name="Bill &amp; Ted&apos;s Excellent Adventure"/>
```

Admittedly, this makes the attribute value a little tougher to read, but there is no question regarding the usage of the characters. This is a good example of how XML is willing to make a trade-off between ease of use on the developer's part and technical clarity. Fortunately, there are only five predefined entities to deal with, so it's pretty easy to remember them.

The XML Declaration

One final important topic to cover in this quick tour of XML is the XML declaration, which is not strictly required of all XML documents but is a good idea nonetheless. The *XML declaration* is a line of code at the beginning of an XML document that identifies the version of XML used by the document. Currently there is still only one version of XML (version 1.0), but eventually there will likely be additional versions that add new features. The XML declaration notifies an application or Web browser of the XML version that an XML document is using, which can be very helpful in processing the document. Following is the standard XML declaration for XML 1.0:

```
<?xml version="1.0"?>
```

This code looks somewhat similar to an opening tag for an element named xml with an attribute named version. However, the code isn't actually a tag at all. Instead, this code is known as a *processing instruction,* which is a special line of XML code that passes information to the application that is processing the document. In this case, the processing instruction is notifying the application that the document uses XML 1.0. Processing instructions are easily identified by the <? and ?> symbols that are used to contain each instruction.

Selecting an XML Editor

In order to create and edit your own XML documents, you must have an application to serve as an XML editor. Since XML documents are raw text documents, a simple text editor can serve as an XML editor. For example, if you are a Windows user you can just use the standard Windows Notepad or WordPad applications to edit XML documents. If you want XML-specific features such as the ability to edit elements and attributes visually, then you'll want to go beyond a simple text editor and use a full-blown XML editor. There are several commercial XML editors available at virtually every price range. Although a commercial XML editor might prove beneficial at some point, I recommend

Although this may appear to be a lot of code at first, upon closer inspection you'll notice that most of the code is simply the content of the trivia questions and answers. The XML tags should all make sense to you given the earlier explanation of the Tall Tales trivia data. You now have your first complete XML document that has some pretty interesting content ready to be processed and served up for viewing.

Viewing Your XML Document

Short of developing a custom application from scratch, the best way to view XML documents is to use a *style sheet,* which is a series of formatting descriptions that determine how elements are displayed on a Web page. In plain English, a style sheet allows you to carefully control what content in a Web page looks like in a Web browser. In the case of XML, style sheets allow you to determine exactly how to display data in an XML document. Although style sheets can improve the appearance of HTML Web pages, they are especially important for XML because Web browsers typically don't understand what the custom tags mean in an XML document.

You learn a great deal about style sheets in Part III, "Formatting and Displaying XML Documents," but for now I just want to show you a style sheet that is capable of displaying the Tall Tales trivia document that you created in the previous section. Keep in mind that the purpose of a style sheet is to determine the appearance of XML content. This means that you can use styles in a style sheet to control the font and color of text, for example. You can also control the positioning of content, such as where an image or paragraph of text appears on the page. Styles are always applied to specific elements. So, in the case of the trivia document, the style sheet should include styles for each of the important elements that you want displayed: tt, question, a, b, and c.

Later in the book, in Hour 15, "Understanding the XML Document Object Model (DOM)," you learn how to incorporate interactivity using scripting code, but right now all I want to focus on is displaying the XML data using a style sheet. The idea is to format the data so that each question is displayed followed by each of the answers in a smaller font and different color. The code in Listing 2.3 is the TallTales.css style sheet for the Tall Tales trivia XML document:

LISTING 2.3 A CSS Style Sheet for Displaying the Tall Tales XML Document

```
1: tt {
2:    display: block;
3:    width: 750px;
4:    padding: 10px;
5:    margin-bottom: 10px;
6:    border: 4px double black;
```

continues

LISTING 2.3   Continued

```
 7:   background-color: silver;
 8: }
 9:
10: question {
11:   display: block;
12:   color: black;
13:   font-family: Times, serif;
14:   font-size: 16pt;
15:   text-align: left;
16: }
17:
18: a, b, c {
19:   display: block;
20:   color: brown;
21:   font-family: Times, serif;
22:   font-size: 12pt;
23:   text-indent: 15px;
24:   text-align: left;
25: }
```

Don't worry if the style sheet doesn't make too much sense. The point right now is just to notice that the different elements of the XML document are addressed in the style sheet. If you study the code closely, you should be able to figure out what many of the styles are doing. For example, the code color: black; (line 12) states that the text contained within a question element is to be displayed in black. If you create this style sheet and include it with the TallTales.xml document, the document as viewed in Internet Explorer 5.5 appears as shown in Figure 2.3.

FIGURE 2.3

The TallTales.xml *document is displayed as XML code since the style sheet hasn't been attached to it.*

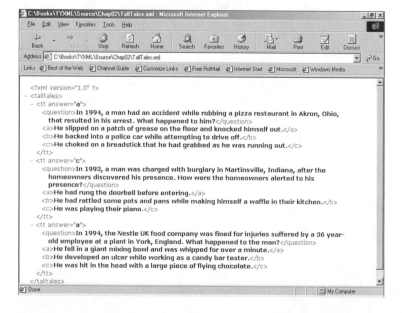

The page shown in the figure probably doesn't look like you thought it should. In fact, the style sheet isn't even impacting this figure because it hasn't been associated with the XML document yet. So, in the absence of a style sheet Internet Explorer just displays the XML code. To attach the style sheet to the document, add the following line of code just after the XML declaration for the document:

```
<?xml-stylesheet type="text/css" href="TallTales.css"?>
```

If you've been following along closely, you'll recognize this line of code as a processor instruction, which is evident by the <? and ?> symbols. This processor instruction notifies the application processing the document (the Web browser) that the document is to be displayed using the style sheet TallTales.css. After adding this line of code to the document, it is displayed in Internet Explorer in a format that is much easier to read (Figure 2.4).

FIGURE 2.4

A simple style sheet provides a means of formatting the data in an XML document for convenient viewing.

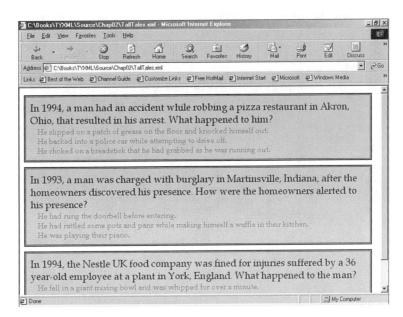

That's a little more like it! As you can see, the style sheet does wonders for making the XML document viewable in a Web browser. You've now successfully created your first XML document, along with a style sheet to view it in a Web browser.

If you're concerned that I glossed over the details of style sheets in this section, please don't be. I admit to glossing them over, but I just wanted to quickly show you how to view a Web page in a Web browser. Besides, you'll get a heavy dose of style sheets in Part III of the book, so hang in there.

Summary

As you learned in this hour, the basic rules of XML aren't too complicated. Although XML is admittedly more rigid than HTML, once you learn the fundamental structure of the XML language, it isn't too difficult to create XML documents. It's this consistency in structure that makes XML such a useful technology in representing diverse data. Just as XML itself is relatively simple, the tools required to develop XML documents can be quite simple—all you really need is a text editor such as Windows Notepad.

This hour began by teaching you the basics of XML, after which you learned about how XML documents are created and edited using XML editors. After covering the fundamentals of XML, you were then guided through the creation of a complete XML document that stores information for a Web-based trivia game. You then learned how a style sheet is used to format the XML document for viewing in a Web browser.

Q&A

Q How do I know what the latest version of XML is?

A The latest (and only) version of XML to date is version 1.0. To find out about new versions as they are released, please visit the World Wide Web Consortium (W3C) Web site at http://www.w3c.org/. Keep in mind, however, that XML is a relatively stable technology, and isn't likely to undergo version changes nearly as rapidly as more dynamic technologies such as Java or even HTML.

Q What happens if an XML document breaks one or more of the XML commandments?

A Well, of course, your computer will crash immediately. No, actually nothing tragic will happen unless you attempt to process the document. Even then, you will likely get an error message instead of any kind of fatal result. XML-based applications expect documents to follow the rules, so they will likely notify you of the errors whenever they are encountered. Fortunately, even Web browsers are pretty good at reporting errors in XML documents, which is in sharp contrast to how loosely they interpret HTML Web pages.

Q Are there any other approaches to using style sheets with XML documents?

A Yes. The Tall Tales trivia example in this hour makes use of CSS (Cascading Style Sheets), which is used primarily to format HTML and XML data for display. Another style sheet technology known as XSL (eXtensible Style Language) allows you to filter and finely control exactly what information is displayed from an XML document. You learn about both style sheet technologies in Part III, "Formatting and Displaying XML Documents."

The question you might now be asking yourself is how exactly do you create a markup language? In other words, how do you specify the set of elements and attributes for a markup language, along with how they relate to each other? Although you could certainly create genealogical XML documents using the elements and attributes, there really needs to be a set of rules somewhere that establishes the format and structure of documents created in the language. This set of rules is known as the *schema* for a markup language. A schema describes the exact elements and attributes that are available within a given markup language, along with which attributes are associated with which elements and the relationships between the elements. You can think of a schema as a legal contract between the person who created the markup language and the person who will create documents using that language.

> Although I describe a schema as a "legal contract," in reality there is nothing legal about schemas. The point is that schemas are very exacting and thorough, and leave nothing to chance in terms of describing the makeup of XML documents—this degree of exacting thoroughness is what we all look for in an ideal legal contract.

Schemas and XML Data Modeling

The process of creating a schema for an XML document is known as *data modeling* because it involves resolving a class of data into elements and attributes that can be used to describe the data in an XML document. Once a data model (schema) is in place for a particular class of data, you can create structured XML documents that adhere to the model. The real importance of schemas is that they allow XML documents to be validated for accuracy. This simply means that a schema allows an XML developer (or an application) to process a document and see if it adheres to the set of constraints laid out in the schema. If not, then you know the document could prove to be problematic. A *valid* XML document is kind of like a stamp of approval that declares the document suitable for use in an XML application.

To help clarify the role schemas play in XML, let's consider a practical real-world analogy. Pretend you just met a friend whom you haven't seen in years and she gives you her e-mail address so that you can get in touch with her later. However, she lists her e-mail address as `lucy*thetribe.com`. You know that all e-mail addresses consist of a name followed by an "at" symbol (@), followed by a domain name, which means that something is wrong with her e-mail address. The `name@domainname` format of e-mail addresses is actually a simple schema—you used this schema to "validate" your friend's e-mail address and determine that it is in error. The obvious fix is to replace the asterisk (*) in her e-mail address with an "at" symbol (@).

You now understand how schemas are used to determine the validity of XML documents, but you don't entirely know why. The main reason schemas are used in XML is to allow machine validation of document structure. In the invalid e-mail example, you were easily able to see a problem because you knew that e-mail addresses couldn't have asterisks in them. But how would an e-mail application be able to make this determination? The developer of the application would have to write specific code to make sure that e-mail addresses are structured to follow a given syntax, such as the name and domain name being separated by an "at" symbol. Whereas an e-mail application developer writes code to check the validity of an e-mail address, an XML document creator uses a schema. This schema can then be used by XML applications to ensure that documents are valid; schemas provide a mechanism to automate the process of validating XML documents.

When it comes to creating schemas, there are two different approaches you can take:

- Document Type Definitions (DTDs)
- XML Schemas (XSDs)

These two schema approaches represent different technologies that make it possible to describe the data model of an XML-based markup language. The next two sections explain each approach in more detail.

Document Type Definitions (DTDs)

Warning, I'm about to roll out a new acronym! You'll eventually get the idea that XML is all about new acronyms. The new acronym I want to introduce you to now is DTD, which stands for *Document Type Definition*. *DTDs* represent the original approach of creating a schema for XML documents. I say "original approach" because DTDs did not originate with XML; DTDs originated with XML's predecessor, SGML (Standard General Markup Language). DTDs made their way into XML because it eased the transition from SGML to XML—many SGML tools existed that could be used for XML. Things have changed since the early days of XML, however, and now there is a more powerful approach to establishing schemas than DTDs. Even so, DTDs still are currently considered the de facto standard schema technology for XML.

 You learn about the more powerful schema approach, XML Schema, in the next section, "XML Schemas."

The main drawback to DTDs is that they are based upon a somewhat cryptic language. When XML provides a highly structured approach to formatting data, why should you have to learn an entirely new language to describe XML schemas? I don't have a good answer to this question except to say that DTDs still play an important role in XML, so you should therefore learn how to work with them. The good news is that DTDs are actually quite simple for most markup languages. This is due to the fact that the DTD language is extremely compact, which is why it has a cryptic appearance. Rather than continue to describe DTDs in words, let's just look at an example in Listing 3.1.

LISTING 3.1 A Simple DTD for the Tall Tales XML Document

```
 1: <!ELEMENT talltales (tt)+>
 2:
 3: <!ELEMENT tt (question, a, b, c)>
 4: <!ATTLIST tt
 5:   answer (a | b | c) "">
 6:
 7: <!ELEMENT question (#PCDATA)>
 8:
 9: <!ELEMENT a (#PCDATA)>
10:
11: <!ELEMENT b (#PCDATA)>
12:
13: <!ELEMENT c (#PCDATA)>
```

I warned you it was kind of cryptic. However, if you take a moment to read through the DTD code you can actually start to make some sense of it. You might even recognize that this DTD is for the Tall Tales trivia document that you saw in the previous hour. By studying the code, you can see that the word ELEMENT precedes each element that can be used in a TTML (Tall Tales Markup Language) document. Also the attributes for the tt element are listed after the word ATTLIST (line 4); in this case there is only one attribute, answer (line 5). Also notice that the three possible values of the answer attribute (a, b, and c) are listed out beside the attribute (line 5). Although there are a few strange looking pieces of information in this DTD, such as the <! at the beginning of each line and (#PCDATA) following each element, it's pretty apparent that DTDs aren't overly complex.

You learn a great deal more about DTDs in the next hour, so I won't go into more detail here. Instead, we'll move on and learn about the other approach to data modeling that uses a syntax that should be very familiar to you.

XML Schema (XSDs)

XML Schema is a new technology that is designed to replace DTDs with a more powerful and intuitive approach to creating schemas for XML-based markup languages.

Schemas created using XML Schema are coded in the XSD (XML Schema Definition) language, and are therefore referred to as XSDs. XML Schema and the XSD language were created by the W3C (World Wide Web Consortium), and although they represent a considerably more powerful and flexible approach to schemas than DTDs, they are still emerging as an XML schema standard. The idea behind XML Schema is to use XML as the basis for creating schemas. Although this may sound strange, it really makes a lot of sense to use XML as a means of coding schemas for custom XML markup languages. So, instead of using the special DTD language to create a schema, you can use familiar XML elements and attributes that are defined in the XSD language.

An XSD is very similar in purpose to a DTD in that it is used to establish the schema of a class of XML documents. Similar to DTDs, XSDs describe elements and their content models so that documents can be validated. However, XSDs go several steps further than DTDs by allowing you to associate data types with elements. In a DTD, element content is pretty much limited to text. An XSD is more flexible in that it can set the data type of elements to specific types, such as integer numbers and dates.

Of course, the most compelling aspect of XSDs is the fact that they are based upon an XML vocabulary (XSD). This means that you create an XSD as an XML document. So, the familiar tag approach to encoding XML documents is all you need to know to code an XSD document. You still have to learn the specific elements and attributes that comprise the XSD language, but it isn't too terribly difficult to learn. To give you an example, the code in Listing 3.2 is for an XSD that describes the familiar Tall Tales document:

LISTING 3.2   An XSD Document That Serves as a Schema for the Tall Tales XML Document

```
 1: <?xml version="1.0"?>
 2:
 3: <xsd:schema xmlns:xsd="http://www.w3.org/2000/10/XMLSchema">
 4:
 5: <xsd:element name="talltales" minOccurs="1" maxOccurs="1">
 6:   <xsd:complexType>
 7:     <xsd:element name="tt">
 8:       <xsd:complexType>
 9:         <xsd:sequence>
10:           <xsd:element name="question" type="xsd:string" maxOccurs="1"/>
11:           <xsd:element name="a" type="xsd:string" maxOccurs="1"/>
12:           <xsd:element name="b" type="xsd:string" maxOccurs="1"/>
13:           <xsd:element name="c" type="xsd:string" maxOccurs="1"/>
14:         </xsd:sequence>
15:         <xsd:attribute name="answer" type="answerType" use="required"/>
16:         <xsd:simpleType name="answerType">
```

continues

Element content is very unconstrained and is better suited for storing long strings of text and other child elements. Consider the following list of advantages that attributes offer over elements:

- Attributes can be constrained against a predefined list of enumerated values.
- Attributes can have default values.
- Attributes have data types, although admittedly somewhat limited.
- Attributes are very concise.

Attributes don't solve every problem, however. In fact, they are limited in several key respects. Following are the major disadvantages associated with attributes:

- Attributes can't store long strings of text.
- Attributes can't contain nested information.
- White space can't be ignored in an attribute value.

Given that attributes are simpler and more concise than elements, it's reasonable that you should use attributes over child elements whenever possible. Fortunately, the decision to use child elements is made fairly straightforward by the limitations of attributes: if a piece of information is a long string of text, requires nested information within it, or requires white space to be ignored then you'll want to place it in an element. Otherwise, an attribute is probably your best choice. Of course, regardless of how well your document data maps to attributes, it must have at least a root element.

Digging Deeper into Elements

To declare an element in a DTD, you must use an *element declaration,* which takes the following form:

```
<!ELEMENT ElementName Type>
```

The name of the element determines the name of the tag(s) used to mark up the element in a document and corresponds to *ElementName* in the element declaration. This name must be unique within the context of a DTD. The type of the element is specified in *Type*; XML supports four different types of elements, which are determined by the content contained within the element. Following are the different types of content that can be contained within an element:

- Empty—the element doesn't contain any content (it can still contain attributes)
- Element-only—the element only contains child elements
- Mixed—the element contains a combination of child elements and character data
- Any—the element contains any content allowed by the DTD

The name of an element must not contain the ampersand character (&) or begin with the sequence of letters X, M, and L in any case combination (XML, xml, XmL, and so on).

The next few sections explore the different element types in more detail.

Empty Elements

An *empty element* is an element that doesn't contain any element content. An empty element can still contain information, but it must do so using attributes. Empty elements are declared using the following form:

```
<!ELEMENT ElementName EMPTY>
```

Following is an example of declaring an empty element using this form:

```
<!ELEMENT clothing EMPTY>
```

Once an empty element is defined in a DTD, you can use it in a document in one of two ways:

- With a start-tag/end-tag pair
- With an empty-tag

Following is an example of an empty element defined using a start-tag/end-tag pair:

```
<clothing></clothing>
```

Notice that no content appears between the tags; if any content did appear, even a single space, the document would be invalid. A more concise approach to defining empty elements is to use an empty tag. Following is an example of using an empty tag to define an empty element:

```
<clothing/>
```

As you can see, an empty-tag is somewhat of a combination of a start-tag and end-tag. In addition to being more concise, empty-tags help to make it clear in a document that an element is empty and therefore can't contain content. Remember that empty elements can still contain information in attributes. Following is an example of how you might use a few attributes with an empty element:

```
<clothing type="t-shirt" color="navy" size="xl"/>
```

Element-Only Elements

An *element-only* element contains nothing but child elements. In other words, no text content is stored within an element-only element. An element is declared element-only by simply listing the child elements that can appear within the element, which is known as the element's *content model*. Following is the form expected for declaring an element's content model:

```
<!ELEMENT ElementName ContentModel>
```

The content model is specified using a combination of special element declaration symbols and child element names. The symbols describe the relationship between child elements and the container element. Within the content model, child elements are grouped into sequences or choice groups using parentheses (( )). A sequence of child elements indicates the order of the elements, whereas a choice group indicates alternate possibilities for how the elements are used. Child elements within a sequence are separated by commas (,), whereas elements in a choice group are separated by pipes (|). Following are the different element declaration symbols used to establish the content model of elements:

- Parentheses (( ))—encloses a sequence or choice group of child elements
- Comma (,)—separates the items in a sequence, which establishes the order in which they must appear
- Pipe (|)—separates the items in a choice group of alternatives
- No symbol—indicates that a child element must appear exactly once
- Question mark (?)—indicates that a child element must appear exactly once or not at all
- Plus sign (+)—indicates that a child element must appear at least once
- Asterisk (*)—indicates that a child element can appear any number of times

Although I could use several paragraphs to try and explain these element declaration symbols, I think an example is much more explanatory. Following is the declaration for an element named resume that might be used in a resume markup language:

```
<!ELEMENT resume (intro, (education | experience+)+, hobbies?, references*)>
```

The resume element is pretty interesting because it demonstrates the usage of every element declaration symbol. The resume element is element-only, which is evident in the fact that it contains only child elements. The first child element is intro, which must appear exactly once within the resume element. The education or experience elements must then appear at least once, which is indicated by the plus sign just outside of the

4

parentheses. Within the parentheses, the `education` element must appear exactly once, whereas the `experience` element must appear at least once but can also appear multiple times. The idea is to allow you to list part of your education followed by any relevant work experience. The `hobby` element can appear exactly once or not at all; all of your hobbies must be listed within a single `hobby` element. Finally, the `references` element can appear any number of times.

Mixed Elements

Mixed elements are elements that contain both character data (text) and child elements. The simplest mixed element is also known as a *text-only element* because it contains only character data. Text-only elements are declared using the following form:

```
<!ELEMENT ElementName (#PCDATA)>
```

The content model for text-only elements consists solely of the symbol #PCDATA contained within parentheses, which indicates that an element contains Parsed Character DATA. Following is an example of a simple text-only element declaration:

```
<!ELEMENT hobbies (#PCDATA)>
```

> The word "parsed" in Parsed Character DATA (PCDATA) refers to the fact that PCDATA within a document is processed (parsed) by an XML application. Most of the text content in an XML document is considered PCDATA. The alternative to PCDATA is CDATA (Character DATA), which is text that isn't processed by an XML application. Later in the book you learn why it is sometimes useful to include CDATA in a document.

This element might be used to mark up a list of hobbies in an XML document that helps to describe you to other people. Following is an example of how you might define the `hobbies` element in a document:

```
<hobbies>juggling, unicycling, tight-rope walking</hobbies>
```

In reality, a text-only element is just a mixed element that doesn't contain any child elements. Mixed elements that contain both text data and child elements are declared very much like element-only elements, with the addition of a few subtle requirements. More specifically, the content model for a mixed element must contain a repeating choice list of the following form:

```
<!ELEMENT ElementName (#PCDATA | ElementList)*>
```

If this looks a little confusing at first, don't worry. Let's break it down. The symbol #PCDATA at the start of the choice list indicates that the mixed element can contain character data. The remainder of the choice list contains child elements, and resembles a regular element-only content model. Additional #PCDATA symbols may be interspersed throughout the content model to indicate that character data appears throughout the child elements. An asterisk (*) must appear at the end of the content model's choice list to indicate that the entire choice group is optional—this is a requirement of mixed elements. Also, although a mixed element declaration constrains the type of child elements allowed, it doesn't constrain the order of the elements or the number of times they may appear.

> In the content model for a mixed element, the character data (#PCDATA) must always be specified first in the choice group, and the choice group itself must be declared as repeating by following it with an asterisk (*).

Although mixed elements provide a considerable amount of flexibility, they lack the structure of element-only elements. So, with the exception of text-only elements, you're better off using element-only elements instead of mixed elements whenever possible; you can often get the equivalent of a mixed element by declaring attributes on a text-only element.

Any Elements

The *any element* is the most flexible element of all because it has virtually no structure. The any element is declared using the symbol ANY, and earns its name by being able to contain any declared element types, character data, or a mixture of both. You can think of the any element as a mixed element with a wide-open content model. Following is the form used to declare an any element:

```
<!ELEMENT ElementName ANY>
```

Not surprisingly, the lack of structure associated with the any element makes it something you should avoid at all costs in a production DTD. I mention a production (completed) DTD because the any element is typically used only during the development of a DTD for testing purposes.

Putting Attributes to Work

Attributes go hand in hand with elements and are incredibly important to the construction of DTDs. Attributes are used to specify additional information about an element. More specifically, attributes are used to form a name/value pair that somehow describes a particular property of an element. Attributes are declared in a DTD using attribute list declarations, which take the following form:

```
<!ATTLIST ElementName AttrName AttrType Default>
```

This form reveals that an attribute has a name (`AttrName`) and a type (`AttrType`), as well as a default value (`Default`). The default value for an attribute refers to either a value or a symbol that indicates the usage of the attribute. There are four different types of default values you can specify for an attribute in *Default:*

- `#REQUIRED`—the attribute is required.
- `#IMPLIED`—the attribute is optional.
- `#FIXED` *value*—the attribute has a fixed value.
- default—the default value of the attribute.

The `#REQUIRED` value identifies a required attribute, which means the attribute must be set if you use the element. The `#IMPLIED` value identifies an optional attribute, which means the attribute is optional when using the element. The `#FIXED` attribute is used to assign a fixed value to an attribute, effectively making the attribute a constant piece of information; you must provide the fixed attribute value after the `#FIXED` symbol when declaring the attribute. The last option for declaring attribute defaults is to simply list the default value for an attribute; an attribute will assume its default value if it isn't explicitly set in the element. Following is an example of an attribute list for an element that specifies the units for a duration of time:

```
<!ELEMENT distance (#PCDATA)>
<!ATTLIST distance
  units (miles | kilometers | laps) "miles"
>
```

In this example the element is named `distance` and its only attribute is named `units`. The `units` attribute can only be set to one of three possible values: `miles`, `kilometers`, or `laps`. The default value of the `units` attribute is `miles`, which means that if you don't explicitly set the attribute it will automatically take on a value of `miles`.

Although attribute lists don't have to be declared in a particular place within a DTD, it is common practice to place them immediately below the declaration for the element to which they belong.

In addition to the default value of an attribute value, you must also specify the type of the attribute in the attribute list declaration. There are ten different attribute types, which follow:

- CDATA—unparsed character data
- Enumerated—a series of string values
- NOTATION—a notation declared somewhere else in the DTD
- ENTITY—an external binary entity
- ENTITIES—multiple external binary entities separated by white space
- ID—a unique identifier
- IDREF—a reference to an ID declared somewhere else in the DTD
- IDREFS—multiple references to ID's declared somewhere else in the document
- NMTOKEN—a name consisting of XML token characters (letters, numbers, periods, dashes, colons, and underscores)
- NMTOKENS—multiple names consisting of XML token characters

To help in understanding these attribute types, it's possible to classify them into three groups: string, enumerated, and tokenized. The next few sections explore the meanings and usages of these different groups of attributes.

String Attributes

String attributes are the most commonly used attributes and are represented by the CDATA type. The CDATA type indicates that an attribute contains a simple string of text. Following is an example of declaring a simple CDATA attribute that must be defined in the education element:

```
<!ATTLIST education school CDATA #REQUIRED>
```

In this example, the school a person attended is a required character data attribute of the education element. If you wanted to make the school attribute optional, you could use the #IMPLIED symbol:

```
<!ATTLIST education school CDATA #IMPLIED>
```

Enumerated Attributes

Enumerated attributes are constrained to a list of predefined strings of text. The enumerated type is similar to the CDATA type except the acceptable attribute values must come from a list that is provided in the attribute list declaration. Following is an example of how you might provide an enumerated attribute for specifying the type of degree earned as part of the education element:

```
<!ATTLIST education degree (associate | bachelors | masters | doctorate)
  "bachelors">
```

When using the degree attribute in a document, you are required to select a value from the list. If you don't use the attribute at all, it will assume the default value of bachelors.

In addition to normal enumerated attributes, you can also create a *notation attribute* that represents a specific type of enumeration. Although you learn about notations in Hour 6, "Digging Deeper into XML Documents," for the moment I can simply describe them as references to external data. For example, a GIF image requires a notation in order for an XML application to know how to handle it. You declare a notation attribute by preceding the list of attribute values with NOTATION:

```
<!ATTLIST photo format NOTATION (gif | jpeg) #REQUIRED>
```

The #REQUIRED symbol is specified to indicate that the format attribute is required of the photo element. Enumerated attributes can also be optional, in which case you specify the #IMPLIED symbol as the default value.

Tokenized Attributes

Tokenized attributes are processed as tokens by an XML application, which means the application converts all contiguous white space to a single space character and eliminates all leading and trailing white space. In addition to eliminating the majority of white space in a tokenized attribute value, the XML application will also validate the value of a tokenized attribute based upon the declared attribute type: ENTITY, ENTITIES, ID, IDREF, IDREFS, NMTOKEN, or NMTOKENS.

A *token* is the smallest piece of information capable of being processed by an XML application. A tokenized attribute is simply an attribute that is processed into tokens by an XML application, which has the effect of eliminating extraneous white space (space characters, newline characters, and so on). Contrast this with a string attribute, which goes unprocessed, and therefore retains all of its white space.

The ENTITY and ENTITIES types are used to reference entities, which you learn about in Hour 6. As an example, images are typically referenced as binary entities, in which case you use an ENTITY attribute value to associate an image with an element type:

```
<!ATTLIST photo image ENTITY #IMPLIED>
```

The ENTITIES type is similar to ENTITY but it allows you to specify multiple entities. The ID, IDREF, and IDREFS attribute types all relate to unique identifiers. The ID type is a unique identifier that can be used to uniquely identify an element within a document:

```
<!ATTLIST part id ID #REQUIRED>
```

Only one attribute of type ID may be assigned to a given element type. The NMTOKEN and NMTOKENS attribute types are used to specify attributes containing name token values. A *name token value* consists of a single name, which means that it can't contain white space. More specifically, a name token value can consist of alphanumeric characters in addition to the following characters: ., -, _, and :.

Working with Multiple Attributes

I've only shown you examples of individual attributes thus far, but you'll likely create elements that rely on several attributes. You can list all of the attributes for an element in a single attribute list by listing the attributes one after the next within the attribute list declaration. Following is an example of declaring multiple attributes within a single attribute list:

```
<!ELEMENT photo (image, format)>
<!ATTLIST photo
  image ENTITY #IMPLIED
  photo format NOTATION (gif | jpeg) #REQUIRED
>
```

This example shows how the two attributes of the photo element, image and photo, are declared in a single attribute list declaration.

A Complete DTD Example

Admittedly, this hour has been pretty technical thus far. To help you get some perspective on how elements and attributes fit into a DTD for a new markup language, let's work through the design of a DTD for a sports training markup language. This markup language, which we'll call ETML (Endurance Training Markup Language), might come in handy if you decided to compete in a marathon or triathlon—it models training data related to endurance sports such as running, swimming, and cycling. Following are the major pieces of information that are associated with each individual training session:

- Date—the date and time of the training session
- Type—the type of training session (running, swimming, cycling, and so on)
- Heart rate—the average heart rate sustained during the training session
- Duration—the duration of the training session
- Distance—the distance covered in the training session (measured in miles or kilometers)
- Location—the location of the training session
- Comments—general comments about the training session

4

Knowing that all of this information must be accounted for within a training session element, can you determine which ones would be better suited as child elements and which would be better suited as attributes? There really is no correct answer but there are a few logical reasons you might separate some of the information into elements and some into attributes. Following is how I would organize this information:

- Attributes—Date, Type, Heart rate
- Child elements—Duration, Distance, Location, Comments

The date, type, and heart rate for a training session are particularly well suited for attributes because they all involve short, simple values. The type attribute goes a step further since you can use an enumerated list of predefined values (running, cycling, and so on). The duration and distance of a session could really go either way in terms of being modeled by an element or an attribute. However, by modeling them as elements you leave room for each of them to have attributes that allow you to specify the exact units of measure. The location and comments potentially contain more descriptive text, and therefore are also better suited as child elements.

 A golden rule of XML design is that the more constraints you can impose on a document, the more structured its content will be.

With the conceptual design of the DTD in place, you're ready to dive into the code. Listing 4.1 contains the code for the ETML DTD, which is stored in the file ETML.dtd.

LISTING 4.1 The ETML.dtd DTD That Is Used to Validate ETML Documents

```
 1: <!ELEMENT trainlog (session)+>
 2:
 3: <!ELEMENT session (duration, distance, location, comments)>
 4: <!ATTLIST session
 5:   date CDATA #IMPLIED
 6:   type (running | swimming | cycling) "running"
 7:   heartrate CDATA #IMPLIED
 8: >
 9:
10: <!ELEMENT duration (#PCDATA)>
11: <!ATTLIST duration
12:   units (seconds | minutes | hours) "minutes"
13: >
14:
15: <!ELEMENT distance (#PCDATA)>
16: <!ATTLIST distance
```

continues

LISTING 4.1 Continued

```
17:    units (miles | kilometers | laps) "miles"
18: >
19:
20: <!ELEMENT location (#PCDATA)>
21:
22: <!ELEMENT comments (#PCDATA)>
```

You should be able to apply what you've learned throughout this hour to understanding the ETML DTD. All of the elements and attributes in the DTD flow from the conceptual design that you just completed. The trainlog element (line 1) is the root element for ETML documents and contains session elements for each training session. Each session element consists of duration, distance, location, and comments child elements (line 3) and date, type, and heartrate attributes (lines 4–7). Notice that the type attribute of the session element (line 6) and the units attributes of the duration and distance elements (lines 12 and 17) are constrained to lists of enumerated values.

Of course, no DTD is really complete without an XML document to demonstrate its usefulness. Listing 4.2 shows an example document that is coded in ETML.

4

LISTING 4.2 The Training Log Example ETML Document

```
 1: <?xml version="1.0"?>
 2: <!DOCTYPE trainlog SYSTEM "ETML.dtd">
 3:
 4: <trainlog>
 5:    <session date="11/19/01" type="running" heartrate="158">
 6:       <duration units="minutes">45</duration>
 7:       <distance units="miles">5.5</distance>
 8:       <location>Warner Park</location>
 9:       <comments>Mid-morning run, a little winded throughout.</comments>
10:    </session>
11:
12:    <session date="11/21/01" type="cycling" heartrate="153">
13:       <duration units="hours">2.5</duration>
14:       <distance units="miles">37.0</distance>
15:       <location>Natchez Trace Parkway</location>
16:       <comments>Hilly ride, felt strong as an ox.</comments>
17:    </session>
18:
19:    <session date="11/24/01" type="running" heartrate="156">
20:       <duration units="hours">1.5</duration>
21:       <distance units="miles">8.5</distance>
22:       <location>Warner Park</location>
23:       <comments>Afternoon run, felt reasonably strong.</comments>
24:    </session>
25: </trainlog>
```

As you can see, this document strictly adheres to the DTD both in terms of the elements it defines as well as the nesting of the elements. The DTD is specified in the document type declaration, which clearly references the file `ETML.dtd` (line 2). Another two aspects of the document to pay attention to are the `type` and `units` attributes (lines 5, 12, and 19), which adhere to the lists of available choices defined in the DTD. Keep in mind that even though only three training sessions are included in the document, the DTD allows you to include as many as you want. So if you're feeling energetic, go sign up for a marathon and start logging away training sessions in your new markup language!

Summary

A document type definition (DTD) is responsible for describing the structure and format of a class of XML documents. Within a document, the DTD is referenced in the document type declaration. A DTD consists of markup declarations that determine the rules for a custom markup language. In addition to providing a formal set of rules for a markup language, DTDs form a critical part of XML in that they provide a means of validating documents for accuracy.

This hour explored DTDs and the role they play in XML. You first learned about the general structure of DTDs, including the meaning of entities, elements, and attributes. You then examined elements and attributes in more detail, including how to declare each of them using markup declarations. The hour culminated with the creation of a complete DTD for the Endurance Training Markup Language (ETML). You also saw an example XML document created in ETML.

Q&A

Q Why would you ever want to use an internal DTD?

A Since an internal DTD is declared directly in an XML document and not in an external file, it applies only to that particular document. Therefore, you should only use an internal DTD for markup declarations that apply to a specific document. Otherwise, all markup declarations should be placed in an external DTD so that they can be reused with other documents.

Q What's the difference between character data (CDATA) and parsed character data (PCDATA)?

A CDATA and PCDATA are both text—the difference between the two has to do with how an XML application treats them. An XML application doesn't process CDATA, which means the text is handled by the application exactly as it appears in an XML document. PCDATA, on the other hand, is processed by the application before it is handled and used in any meaningful way. This processing involves stripping out extraneous white space and replacing special XML symbols.

Q Why would you use an attribute over an element when designing a DTD?

A Attributes provide tighter constraints on data, can be constrained against a predefined list of possible values, and can have default values. Element content is much less constrained, and is better suited for housing long strings of text and other child elements. A golden rule of XML design is that the more constraints you can impose on a document, the more structured its content will be. Knowing this, you should attempt to fit data into attributes whenever possible.

Workshop

The Workshop is designed to help you anticipate possible questions, review what you've learned, and begin learning how to put your knowledge into practice.

Quiz

1. What is the difference between a document type definition (DTD) and a document type declaration?

2. What does the standalone status of a document determine?

3. What type of element is the trainlog element in the ETML DTD?

4. What kind of attribute would you use to constrain an attribute's value to a list of predefined strings of text?

4

Quiz Answers

1. A document type definition (DTD) contains the actual description of a markup language, whereas the document type declaration is a line of code in a document that identifies the DTD. In other words, the definition (DTD) describes your markup language, whereas the declaration associates it with a document.

2. The standalone status of a document determines whether or not a document relies on any external information sources, such as an external DTD.

3. The trainlog element in the ETML DTD is an element-only element because it contains only child elements.

4. To constrain an attribute's value to a list of predefined strings of text you would use an enumerated attribute.

Exercises

1. Modify the ETML DTD so that it includes a new attribute of the session element that stores a rating for the training session—the rating indicates how well you felt during the session on a scale of 1 to 10. Design the new rating attribute so that it is constrained to a list of numeric values between 1 and 10.

2. Modify the TrainLog.xml document so that it takes advantage of the new rating attribute.

HOUR 5

Using XML Schema

Any good strategy will seem ridiculous by the time it is implemented.

—Scott Adams (cartoonist, creator of *Dilbert*)

Fortunately for XML, XML Schema doesn't seem ridiculous even though it has been in the works for quite some time. The W3C (World Wide Web Consortium) initially set out to improve upon DTDs by developing a schema technology that was based on XML. The end result is known as the XML Schema Definition Language, or XSD, which is now an official W3C standard. XSD schemas are used similarly to DTDs in that they provide a means of defining a custom markup language and validating XML documents. However, XSDs are considerably more powerful than DTDs and give you much finer control over the design of markup languages. This hour introduces you to XSD and shows you how to create XSD schemas that can be used to validate your own documents.

In this hour, you'll learn

- The basics of XML Schema
- How to use elements and attributes in XSD schemas
- How to work with simple and complex data types
- How to build a complete XSD schema and use it to validate a document

XML Schema Construction Basics

In the previous hour you learned how to describe a custom markup language using a DTD. In a DTD you lay out the elements and attributes that can be used to describe a particular type of data. Similar to a DTD, XML Schema allows you to create markup languages by carefully describing the elements and attributes that can be used to code information. Unlike DTDs, schemas created with XML Schema are coded in XML, which makes them more consistent in terms of keeping everything in the XML domain; if you recall, DTDs use their own cryptic language. The language used to describe markup languages in XML Schema is XSD. Schemas created in this language are often referred to simply as XSDs.

The XSD language is an XML-based language, which means you use XML elements and attributes to describe the structure of your own custom markup languages. This means that XSD itself was created in XML. Although this might seem confusing at first, keep in mind that it is necessary for there to be a means of validating XSD documents, which means the XSD language must be spelled out in terms of XML. More specifically, the elements and attributes in the XSD language are described in none other than a DTD. This is because it isn't exactly possible to use XSD to describe the XSD schema. Admittedly, this is a "chicken and egg" kind of problem because we're talking about creating a schema for a schema language that is in turn used to create schemas. Which one comes first? To be honest, it really doesn't matter. Rather than confuse you further, I'd rather push on and learn how an XSD document comes together. The main point here is that XSD is an XML-based markup language, similar in many ways to any other custom markup language you might create.

Since XSD schema documents are really just XML documents, you must include the familiar XML declaration at the start of them:

```
<?xml version="1.0"?>
```

After entering the XML declaration, you're ready to start coding the XSD document. All of the elements and attributes in XSD are part of what is known as a namespace, which is essentially a grouping of elements and attributes used for a particular purpose. You learn much more about namespaces in Hour 7, "Putting Namespaces to Use." For now, just understand that a namespace is a way to formally organize elements and attributes together and also guarantee that they have unique names. You typically assign a namespace a prefix that is used throughout a document to reference elements and attributes within the namespace. In order to reference XSD elements and attributes, you must first declare the XSD namespace in the root element of the XSD document. The prefix of the XSD namespace is typically set to xsd, which means that all XSD elements and attributes are preceded by the prefix xsd and a colon (:). The root element of XSD documents is named xsd:schema. Following is an example of how you declare the XSD namespace in the xsd:schema element:

```
<xsd:schema xmlns:xsd="http://www.w3.org/2000/10/XMLSchema">
```

In this code, the xmlns:xsd attribute is used to set the XSD namespace, which is a standard URI made available by the W3C. Again, you learn all about namespaces and their significance in Hour 7. For the purposes of this hour, just understand that a namespace prefix is used with elements and attributes that are part of a namespace. In the case of XSD, it means that you must precede each element and attribute name with xsd:. So, to recap, the general structure of an XSD schema document has the following form:

```
<?xml version="1.0"?>
```

```
<xsd:schema xmlns:xsd="http://www.w3.org/2000/10/XMLSchema">
</xsd:schema>
```

Of course, this code has no content within the root element, so it isn't doing much. However, it lays the groundwork for the basis of all XSD schema documents.

XSD Data Types

The XSD language is defined by the elements and attributes that can be used within it, as well as their relationship to one another. At the heart of XSD are data types, which determine the type of data that can be represented by a particular piece of markup code. For example, numeric data in XSD is coded differently than text data and therefore has an associated data type that is used when creating a schema with XSD. There are two different general types of data used in XSDs: simple data and complex data. *Simple data* corresponds to basic pieces of information such as numbers, strings of text, dates, times, lists, and so on. *Complex data,* on the other hand, represents more involved information such as mixed elements and sequences of elements. Generally speaking, complex data types are built upon simple data types.

Simple data types can be used with both elements and attributes and provide a means of describing the exact nature of a piece of information. The xsd:element element is used to create elements of a simple type, whereas the xsd:attribute element is used to create attributes. Following are a few examples of each:

```
<xsd:element name="name" type="xsd:string"/>
<xsd:element name="title" type="xsd:string"/>
<xsd:element name="occupation" type="xsd:string"/>
<xsd:attribute name="birthdate" type="xsd:date"/>
<xsd:attribute name="weight" type="xsd:integer"/>
```

Although these examples show how simple data types enter the picture with elements and attributes, they don't reveal the relationship between elements and attributes, which is critical in any XSD document. These relationships are established by complex data types, which are capable of detailing the content models of elements. Following is an example of how simple data types can be used within a complex type to describe the content model of an element named person:

```
<xsd:element name="person">
  <xsd:complexType>
    <xsd:sequence>
      <xsd:element name="name" type="xsd:string"/>
      <xsd:element name="title" type="xsd:string"/>
      <xsd:element name="occupation" type="xsd:string"/>
    </xsd:sequence>

    <xsd:attribute name="birthdate" type="xsd:date"/>
    <xsd:attribute name="weight" type="xsd:integer"/>
  </xsd:complexType>
</xsd:element>
```

Keep in mind that this XSD code describes a custom markup language that is used to create XML documents. In order to fully understand how the schema code works, it's a good idea to take a look at what XML code might look like that adheres to the schema. Following is an example of some XML document data that follows the data structure laid out in the prior XSD schema code:

```
<person birthdate="1969-10-28" weight="160">
  <name>Milton James</name>
  <title>Mr.</title>
  <occupation>mayor, chef</occupation>
</person>
```

This code should look much more familiar to you as it is basic XML code with custom elements and attributes. It doesn't take too much analysis to see that this code adheres to the XSD schema code you just saw. For example, the person element includes two attributes, birthdate and weight, as well as three child elements, name, title, and occupation. Unlike a DTD, the schema is able to carefully describe the data type of each element and attribute. For example, the birthdate attribute is a date (xsd:date), not just a string that happens to store a date, and the `weight` attribute is an integer number (`xsd:integer`).

XSD Schemas and XML Documents

You now have a basic knowledge of how a schema is used to establish a markup language that in turn is used to create XML documents. What you don't know is how a schema is actually associated with such documents. If you recall, a DTD is associated with a document by way of a document type declaration. XSDs don't rely on a document type declaration and instead use a special attribute called `noNamespaceSchemaLocation`. To associate a schema with an XML document for validation purposes, you set this attribute to the location of the schema document. However, in order to use this attribute you must first declare the namespace to which it belongs. Following is how this is accomplished in XML code:

```
<contacts xmlns:xsi="http://www.w3.org/2000/10/XMLSchema-instance"
  xsi:noNamespaceSchemaLocation="contacts.xsd">
  <person birthdate="1969-10-28" weight="160">
    <name>Milton James</name>
    <title>Mr.</title>
    <occupation>mayor, chef</occupation>
  </person>
</contacts>
```

This code shows how to declare the appropriate namespace and then set the `noNamespaceSchemaLocation` attribute for the schema document. Assuming the schema for the contacts document is located in the file named contacts.xsd, this XML document is ready for validation. This brings up an important point regarding schema documents—they are coded in XML but they are stored in files with a `.xsd` extension. This makes it possible to quickly determine if a file is an XSD schema.

5

Working with Simple Types

XSD includes several different simple data types, or *simple types,* that make it possible to model a wide range of data in XML documents. These types can be classified according to the kind of data they represent. Following are the major categories of simple data types supported in the XSD language, along with the specific XSD elements associated with each category:

- String types—`xsd:string`
- Boolean types—`xsd:boolean`
- Number types—`xsd:integer`, `xsd:decimal`, `xsd:float`, `xsd:double`

- Date and time types—xsd:time, xsd:timeInstant, xsd:timeDuration, xsd:date, xsd:month, xsd:year, xsd:century, xsd:recurringDate, xsd:recurringDay
- Custom types—xsd:simpleType

These simple types are typically used to create elements and attributes in a schema document. In order to create an element based upon a simple type, you must use the xsd:element element, which has two primary attributes used to describe the element: name and type. The name attribute is used to set the element name, which is the name that appears within angle brackets (<>) when you use the element in XML code. The type attribute determines the type of the element and can be set to a simple or complex type. Following are the element examples you saw a little earlier in the hour that make use of the xsd:string simple type:

```
<xsd:element name="name" type="xsd:string"/>
<xsd:element name="title" type="xsd:string"/>
<xsd:element name="occupation" type="xsd:string"/>
```

Attributes are created in much the same manner as elements and even rely on the same two attributes, name and type. However, you create an attribute using the xsd:attribute element. Following are the attribute examples you saw earlier that use the xsd:date and xsd:integer simple types:

```
<xsd:attribute name="birthdate" type="xsd:date"/>
<xsd:attribute name="weight" type="xsd:integer"/>
```

Now that you understand how simple types enter the picture with elements and attributes, you're ready to learn more about the types themselves.

The String Type

The string type represents a string of text and is represented in the type attribute by the xsd:string value. The string type is probably the most commonly used type in XSD. Following is an example of how to use the xsd:string value to create a string element:

```
<xsd:element name="name" type="xsd:string"/>
```

In an XML document, this element might be used like this:

```
<name>Milton James</name>
```

The Boolean Type

The Boolean type represents a true/false or yes/no value and is represented in the type attribute by the xsd:boolean value. When using a Boolean type in an XML document, you can set it to true or false, or 1 or 0, respectively. Following is an example of an attribute that is a Boolean type:

```
<xsd:attribute name="retired" type="xsd:boolean"/>
```

In an XML document, this attribute might be used like this:

```
<person retired="false">
  <name>Milton James</name>
</person>
```

Number Types

Number types are used in XSD to describe elements or attributes with numeric values. The following number types are available for use in schemas to represent numeric information:

- xsd:integer—integer numbers (with no fractional part); for example, 3

- xsd:decimal—decimal numbers (with a fractional part); for example, 3.14

- xsd:float—single precision (32-bit) floating point numbers; for example, 6.022E23

- xsd:double—double precision (64-bit) floating point numbers; same as float but for considerably more precise numbers

If you'd like to exert exacting control over the sign of integer numbers, then you might consider using one of these additional numeric types: xsd:positiveInteger, xsd:negativeInteger, xsd:nonPositiveInteger, or xsd:nonNegativeInteger. The latter two types are zero-inclusive, whereas the first two don't include zero.

5

To create an element or attribute for a numeric piece of information, you simply select the appropriate number type in the XSD. Following is an example of a couple of attributes that are number types:

```
<xsd:attribute name="height" type="xsd:decimal"/>
<xsd:attribute name="weight" type="xsd:integer"/>
```

In an XML document, this attribute might be used like this:

```
<person height="5.75" weight="160">
  <name>Milton James</name>
</person>
```

Date and Time Types

XSD includes support for date and time types, which is very useful when it comes to modeling such information. Following are the different date and time types that are supported in XSD:

- `xsd:time`—a time of day; for example, 4:40pm
- `xsd:timeInstant`—an instant in time; for example, 4:40pm on August 24, 1970
- `xsd:timeDuration`—a length of time; for example, 3 hours and 15 minutes
- `xsd:date`—a day in time; for example, August 24, 1970
- `xsd:month`—a month in time; for example, August, 1970
- `xsd:year`—a year in time; for example, 1970
- `xsd:century`—a century; for example, 20th century
- `xsd:recurringDate`—a date without regard for the year; for example, August 24
- `xsd:recurringDay`—a day of the month without regard for the month or year; for example, the 24th of the month

To create an element or attribute for a date or time, you must select the appropriate date or time type in the XSD. Following is an example of an attribute that is a date type:

```
<xsd:attribute name="birthdate" type="xsd:date"/>
```

This attribute is of type `xsd:date`, which means that it can be used in XML documents to store a day in time, such as August 24, 1970. You don't just set the `birthdate` attribute to `October 28, 1969`, however. Dates and times are actually considered highly formatted pieces of information, so you must enter them according to predefined formats set forth by the XSD language. The format for the `xsd:date` type is *ccyy-mm-dd,* where *cc* is the century (19), *yy* is the year (69), *mm* is the month (10), and *dd* is the day (28). The following code shows how you would specify this date in the `birthdate` attribute using the CCYY-MM-DD format:

```
<person birthdate="1969-10-28" height="5.75" weight="160">
  <name>Milton James</name>
</person>
```

Other date and time types use similar formats. For example, the `xsd:month` type uses the format *ccyy-mm,* `xsd:year` uses *ccyy,* and `xsd:century` uses the succinct format *cc.* The `xsd:recurringDate` type uses *--mm-dd* to format recurring dates, whereas the `xsd:recurringDay` type uses *---dd.* Following is an example of the `xsd:recurringDate` type so that you can see how the dashes fit into things:

```
<person birthday="--10-28" height="5.75" weight="160">
  <name>Milton James</name>
</person>
```

In this example, an attribute named `birthday` is used instead of `birthdate`, with the idea being that a birthday is simply a day and month without a birth year. Notice that an extra dash appears at the beginning of the `birthday` attribute value to serve as a placeholder for the missing year.

The remaining time types are xsd:timeDuration, xsd:time, and xsd:timeInstant. The xsd:timeDuration type uses an interesting format to represent a length of time—to specify a value of type xsd:timeDuration you must enter the length of time according to the format P*yyYmmMddDThhHmmMssS*. The P in the format indicates the period portion of the value, which consists of the year (*yy*), month (*mm*), and day (*dd*). The T in the format begins the optional time portion of the value and consists of hours (*hh*), minutes (*mm*), and seconds (*ss*). You can precede a time duration value with a minus sign (-) to indicate that the duration of time goes in the reverse direction (back in time). Following is an example of how you would use this format to code the time duration value 3 years, 4 months, 2 days, 13 hours, 27 minutes, and 11 seconds:

```
<worldrecord duration="P3Y4M2DT13H27M11S">
</worldrecord>
```

The xsd:time type adheres to the format *hh:mm:ss.sss*. In addition to specifying the hours (*hh*), minutes (*mm*), and seconds (*ss.sss*) of the time, you may also enter a plus (+) or minus (-) sign followed by *hh:mm* to indicate the offset of the time from Universal Time (UTC). As an example, the U.S. Central Standard Time zone is six hours behind UTC time, so you would need to indicate that in an xsd:time value that is in Central Standard Time (CST). Following is an example of a CST time:

```
<meeting start="15:30:00-06:00">
</meeting>
```

UTC stands for Coordinated Universal Time and is the same as Greenwich Mean Time (GMT). UTC time is set for London, England, and therefore must be adjusted for any other time zones. Other time zones are adjusted by adding or subtracting time from UTC time. For example, U.S. Pacific Standard Time (PST) is UTC - 8, whereas Japan is UTC + 9.

5

Notice in the code that the hours in the time are entered in 24-hour form, also known as "military time," meaning that there is no AM or PM involved. The time specified in this example is 3:30pm CST.

The xsd:timeInstant type follows the type *ccyy-mm-dd* T*hh:mm:ss.sss* and is essentially an xsd:time type with the year, month, and day tacked on. As an example, the previous xsd:time type could be coded as a xsd:timeInstant type with the following code:

```
<meeting start="2002-02-23T15:30:00-06:00">
</meeting>
```

Custom Types

One of the neatest things about XSD is how it allows you to cook up your own custom data types. Custom data types allow you to refine simple data types to meet your own needs. For example, you can limit the range of numbers for a number type, or constrain a string type to a list of possible strings. Regardless of how you customize a type, you always begin with the xsd:simpleType element, which is used to create custom simple types. Most of the time your custom types will represent a constraint of a simple type, in which case you'll also need to use the xsd:restriction element. The restriction element supports a type named base that refers to the base type you are customizing. Following is the general structure of a custom simple type:

```
<xsd:simpleType name="onetotenType">
  <xsd:restriction base="xsd:integer">
  </xsd:restriction>
</xsd:simpleType>
```

This code merely sets up the type to be created; the actual restrictions on the custom type are identified using one of several different elements. To constrain the range of values a number may have, you use one of the following elements:

- xsd:minInclusive—minimum number allowed

- xsd:minExclusive—one less than the minimum number allowed

- xsd:maxInclusive—the maximum number allowed

- xsd:maxExclusive—one greater than the maximum number allowed

These types allow you to set lower and upper ranges on numeric values. Following is an example of how you would limit a numeric value to a range of 1 to 10:

```
<xsd:simpleType name="onetotenType">
  <xsd:restriction base="xsd:integer">
    <xsd:minInclusive value="1"/>
    <xsd:maxInclusive value="10"/>
  </xsd:restriction>
</xsd:simpleType>
```

It's important to note that this code only establishes a custom type named onetotenType; it doesn't actually create an element or attribute of that type. In order to create an element or attribute of a custom type, you must specify the type name in the type attribute of the xsd:element or xsd:attribute element:

```
<xsd:element name="rating" type="onetotenType">
```

Although this approach works fine, if you plan on using a custom type with only a single element or attribute, then you may want to declare the type directly within the element or attribute:

```
<xsd:element name="rating">
  <xsd:simpleType>
    <xsd:restriction base="xsd:integer">
      <xsd:minInclusive value="1"/>
      <xsd:maxInclusive value="10"/>
    </xsd:restriction>
  </xsd:simpleType>
</xsd:element>
```

In addition to controlling the bounds of simple types, it is also possible to control the length of them. For example, you might want to limit the size of a string of text. To do so, you would use one of the following elements:

- xsd:length—the exact number of characters
- xsd:minlength—the minimum number of characters
- xsd:maxlength—the maximum number of characters

Since the xsd:length element specifies the exact length, you can't use it with the xsd:minlength or xsd:maxlength elements. However, you can use the xsd:minlength and xsd:maxlength elements together to set the bounds of a string's length. Following is an example of how you might control the length of a string type:

```
<xsd:element name="password">
  <xsd:simpleType>
    <xsd:restriction base="xsd:string">
      <xsd:minLength value="8"/>
      <xsd:maxLength value="12"/>
    </xsd:restriction>
  </xsd:simpleType>
</xsd:element>
```

5

In this example, a password element is created that must have at least 8 characters but no more than 12. This shows how to control the length of strings, but it is also possible to control the length of numbers. More specifically, you can use the xsd:precision and xsd:scale elements to control how many digits appear to the left or right of a decimal point; this is known as the *precision* of a number. The xsd:precision element determines how many total digits are allowed in a number, whereas xsd:scale determines how many of those digits appear to the right of the decimal point. So, if you wanted to allow monetary values up to $9999.00 with two decimal places, you would use the following code:

```
<xsd:element name="balance">
  <xsd:simpleType>
    <xsd:restriction base="xsd:decimal">
      <xsd:precision value="6"/>
      <xsd:scale value="2"/>
    </xsd:restriction>
  </xsd:simpleType>
</xsd:element>
```

Keep in mind that the `xsd:precision` and `xsd:scale` elements set the maximum allowable number of digits for the total number and to the right of the decimal place, which means that all of the following examples are valid for the `balance` element:

```
<balance>3.14</balance>
<balance>12.95</balance>
<balance>1.1</balance>
<balance>524.78</balance>
```

One other customization I'd like to mention at this point has to do with default and fixed values. In the event that an element or attribute isn't specified in a document, you may want to declare a *default value* that is assumed. You may also want to limit an element or attribute so that it can have only one possible value, which is known as a *fixed value*. Default and fixed values are established with the `default` and `fixed` attributes of the `xsd:element` and `xsd:attribute` elements. Following are a few examples of default and fixed elements and attributes:

```
<xsd:element name="balance" type="xsd:decimal" default="0.0"/>
<xsd:element name="pi" type="xsd:decimal" fixed="3.14"/>
<xsd:attribute name="expired" type="xsd:boolean" default="false"/>
<xsd:attribute name="title" type="xsd:string" fixed="mr."/>
```

The `balance` element has a default value of `0.0`, which means it will assume this value if it isn't used in a document. The same thing goes for the `expired` attribute, which assumes the default value of `false` if it goes unused. The `pi` element is fixed at the value `3.14`, which means if it is used it must be set to that value. Similarly, the `title` attribute must be set to `mr.` if it is used. Notice that none of the examples are defined as having both default and fixed values; that's because you aren't allowed to define both a default and a fixed value for any single element or attribute.

In addition to customizing simple types as you've seen thus far, you can also do some other interesting things with custom types. The next few sections explore the following data types, which are considered slightly more advanced custom types:

- Enumerated types
- List types
- Patterned types

Enumerated Types

Enumerated types are used to constrain the set of possible values for a simple type and can be applied to any of the simple types except the Boolean type. To create an enumerated type, you use the `xsd:enumeration` element to identify each of the possible values. These values are listed within an `xsd:restriction` element, which identifies the base type. As an example, consider an element named `team` that represents the name of an NHL hockey team. Following is an example of how you might code this element with the help of enumerated types:

```
<xsd:element name="team">
  <xsd:simpleType>
    <xsd:restriction base="xsd:string">
      <xsd:enumeration value="Nashville Predators"/>
      <xsd:enumeration value="Detroit Red Wings"/>
      <xsd:enumeration value="St. Louis Blues"/>
      <xsd:enumeration value="Chicago Blackhawks"/>
      <xsd:enumeration value="Columbus Blue Jackets"/>
    </xsd:restriction>
  </xsd:simpleType>
</xsd:element>
```

This code obviously doesn't include every NHL team, but you get the idea. The important thing to note is that the schema won't allow an XML developer to use any value for the `team` element other than those listed here. Enumerated types therefore provide a very effective means of tightly defining data that is limited to a set of predefined possibilities.

List Types

Whereas enumerated types force an XML developer to use a value from a predefined set of values, list types allow an XML developer to provide multiple values for a given element. The `xsd:list` element is used to create list types, which are useful any time you need to allow for a list of information. As an example, you might want to create an element that stores rainfall totals for each month of the year. Following is code that carries out this function:

```
<xsd:element name="rainfall">
  <xsd:simpleType>
    <xsd:list base="xsd:decimal">
      <xsd:length value="12"/>
    </xsd:list>
  </xsd:simpleType>
</xsd:element>
```

This code allows you to list exactly twelve decimal numbers, separated by white space. Following is an example of what the XML code might look like for the `rainfall` element:

```
<rainfall>1.25 2.0 3.0 4.25 3.75 1.5 0.25 0.75 1.25 1.75 2.0 2.25</rainfall>
```

5

If you wanted to be a little more flexible and not require exactly twelve items in the list, you could use the xsd:minLength and xsd:maxLength elements to set minimum and maximum bounds on the list. You can also create a completely unbounded list by using the xsd:list element by itself, like this:

```
<xsd:element name="friends">
  <xsd:simpleType>
    <xsd:list base="xsd:string"/>
  </xsd:simpleType>
</xsd:element>
```

Patterned Types

Patterned types are undoubtedly the trickiest of all custom types, but they are also the most powerful in many ways. Patterned types allow you to use a regular expression to establish a pattern that tightly controls the format of a simple type. A *regular expression* is a coded pattern using a special language that describes an arrangement of letters, numbers, and symbols. The regular expression language employed by XSD is fairly complex, so I won't attempt a complete examination of it. Instead, I'd like to focus on the basics and allow you to investigate it further on your own if you decide you'd like to become a regular expression guru. Getting back to patterned types, you create a patterned type using the xsd:pattern element.

The xsd:pattern element requires an attribute named value that contains the regular expression for the pattern. Following are the building blocks of a regular expression pattern:

- .—any character
- \d—any digit
- \D—any nondigit
- \s—any white space
- \S—any nonwhite space
- x?—— one x or none at all
- x+—one or more x's
- x*—any number of x's
- (xy)—groups x and y together
- $x|y$—x or y
- [xyz]—one of x, y, or z
- [x-y]—in the range x to y
- $x\{n\}$—n number of x's in a row
- $x\{n,m\}$—at least n number of x's but no more than m

See, I told you regular expressions are kind of tricky. Actually, these regular expression symbols and patterns aren't too difficult to understand when you see them in context. So, let's take a look at a few examples. First off, how about a phone number? A standard U.S. phone number is of the form xxx-xxx-xxxx. In terms of patterned types and regular expressions, this results in the following code:

```
<xsd:element name="phonenum">
  <xsd:simpleType>
    <xsd:restriction base="xsd:string">
      <xsd:pattern value="\d\d\d-\d\d\d-\d\d\d\d"/>
    </xsd:restriction>
  </xsd:simpleType>
</xsd:element>
```

As you can see, the phonenum element is described by a pattern that consists of a series of digits separated by hyphens. Although this pattern works fine, it's important to note that regular expressions are extremely flexible, often offering more than one solution to a given problem. For example, the following xsd:pattern element also works for a phone number:

```
<xsd:pattern value="\d{3}-\d{3}-\d{4}"/>
```

In this example a phone number is described using curly braces to indicate how many decimal numbers can appear at each position in the pattern. The code \d{3} indicates that there should be exactly three decimal numbers, whereas \d{4} indicates exactly four decimal numbers.

Let's now consider a slightly more advanced regular expression pattern such as a pizza order. Our pizza order pattern must have the form *s-c-t+t+t+*, where *s* is the size (small, medium or large), *c* is the crust (thin or deep), and each *t* is an optional topping (sausage, pepperoni, mushroom, peppers, onions, and anchovies) in addition to cheese, which is assumed. Following is how this pizza order pattern resolves into an XSD regular expression pattern:

```
<xsd:element name="pizza">
  <xsd:simpleType>
    <xsd:restriction base="xsd:string">
      <xsd:pattern value="(small|medium|large)-(thin|deep)-(sausage+)?
        (pepperoni+)?(mushroom+)?(peppers+)?(onions+)?(anchovies+)?"/>
    </xsd:restriction>
  </xsd:simpleType>
</xsd:element>
```

Following is an example of how you might code a pizza element based upon this pattern:

```
<pizza>medium-deep-sausage+mushroom+</pizza>
```

5

Obviously, there is a great deal more that can be done with regular expression patterns. Hopefully this is enough information to get you going in the right direction with patterned types.

Digging into Complex Types

Complex data types represent a step up from simple types because they allow you to do more interesting things such as define the content model of elements. Complex types effectively build upon simple types, so your knowledge of simple types will come in quite handy as you work with complex types. All complex types are created using the xsd:complexType element. This element includes a tag named name that is used to name a complex type. You can also declare a complex type directly within an element, in which case it doesn't require a name.

Complex types can be broken down into four major classifications, as follows:

- Empty elements
- Element-only elements
- Mixed elements
- Sequences and choices

The next few sections explore these different complex types in detail.

Empty Elements

Empty elements contain no text content or child elements but are capable of having attributes. In fact, attributes are the only way to associate information with empty elements. You create empty elements using the xsd:complexType element in conjunction with the xsd:complexContent element. Following is an example of how you create an empty element:

```
<xsd:element name="automobile">
  <xsd:complexType>
    <xsd:complexContent>
      <xsd:extension base="xsd:anyType">
        <xsd:attribute name="vin" type="xsd:string"/>
        <xsd:attribute name="year" type="xsd:year"/>
        <xsd:attribute name="make" type="xsd:string"/>
        <xsd:attribute name="model" type="xsd:string"/>
      </xsd:extension>
    </xsd:complexContent>
  </xsd:complexType>
</xsd:element>
```

Although this may seem like a lot of work to simply create an empty element with a few attributes, it is necessary. The `xsd:complexType` and `xsd:complexContent` elements are necessary to establish that this is a complex type, whereas the `xsd:extension` element is used to declare that there is no specific base type (`xsd:anyType`) for the element. Finally, the attributes for the element are created using the familiar `xsd:attribute` element. Following is an example of how you would use the automobile element in an XML document:

```
<automobile vin="SALHV1245SA661555" year="1995"
  make="Land Rover" model="Range Rover"/>
```

Element-Only Elements

Element-only elements are elements that contain only child elements with no text content. They can also contain attributes, of course, but no text content is allowed within an element-only element. To create an element-only element, you simply use the `xsd:complexType` element. Following is an example of an element-only element that contains a single child element:

```
<xsd:element name="assets">
  <xsd:complexType>
    <xsd:element name="automobile" type="automobileType"/>
  </xsd:complexType>
</xsd:element>
```

This code presents a new wrinkle because the child element of `assets` is declared as type `automobileType`. This kind of named complex type is created much like the named simple types you saw earlier in the hour. Following is an example of how you might code the `automobileType` complex data type:

```
<xsd:complexType name="automobileType">
  <xsd:complexContent>
    <xsd:extension base="xsd:anyType">
      <xsd:attribute name="vin" type="xsd:string"/>
      <xsd:attribute name="year" type="xsd:year"/>
      <xsd:attribute name="make" type="xsd:string"/>
      <xsd:attribute name="model" type="xsd:string"/>
    </xsd:extension>
  </xsd:complexContent>
</xsd:complexType>
```

This is the same empty complex type you saw in the previous section, except in this case it has been created as a named type. Following is an example of XML code that uses the `assets` element, `automobile` element, and `automobileType` complex type:

```
<assets>
  <automobile vin="SALHV1245SA661555" year="1995"
    make="Land Rover" model="Range Rover"/>
</assets>
```

5

You might be wondering exactly how useful the assets element is since it can contain only a single automobile element. In reality, practically all element-only elements are capable of storing multiple child elements, sometimes of different types. However, in order to allow for multiple child elements you must use a special construct known as a sequence. You learn about sequences a little later in this hour in the section titled "Sequences and Choices."

Mixed Elements

Mixed elements contain both text and child elements and are the most flexible of all elements. Text-only elements are considered a type of mixed element and can contain only text with no child elements. You create text-only elements using the xsd:complexType element in conjunction with the xsd:simpleContent element. Following is an example of a text-only element:

```
<xsd:element name="distance">
  <xsd:complexType>
    <xsd:simpleContent>
      <xsd:extension base="xsd:decimal">
        <xsd:attribute name="units" type="xsd:string" use="required"/>
      </xsd:extension>
    </xsd:simpleContent>
  </xsd:complexType>
</xsd:element>
```

The distance element stores a distance traveled and is capable of using different units of measure to give meaning to the numeric content it stores. The actual distance is located in the element's content, whereas the units are determined by the units attribute, which is a string. It's important to notice the extra use attribute, which is set to required. This attribute setting makes the units attribute a requirement of the distance element, which means you must assign a value to the units attribute. Following is an example of how the distance element and units attribute might be used in an XML document:

```
<distance units="miles">12.5</distance>
```

Although text-only elements are certainly useful in their own right, there are some situations where it is necessary to have the utmost freedom in coding element content, and that freedom comes with the mixed element. Mixed elements are created similarly to other complex types but with the addition of the xsd:mixed attribute. Keep in mind that mixed types allow for text and child element content, as well as attributes. Following is an example of a mixed type:

```
<xsd:element name="message">
  <xsd:complexType mixed="true">
    <xsd:sequence>
      <xsd:element name="emph" type="xsd:string"/>
    </xsd:sequence>

    <xsd:attribute name="to" type="xsd:string" use="required"/>
    <xsd:attribute name="from" type="xsd:string" use="required"/>
    <xsd:attribute name="timestamp" type="xsd:timeInstant" use="required"/>
  </xsd:complexType>
</xsd:element>
```

In this example, a mixed element is created that can contain text, an emph element, and three attributes. Admittedly, I skipped ahead a little by placing the emph child element in a sequence, but that will be cleared up in the next section. Following is an example of how the message element might be used in an XML document:

```
<message to="you" from="me" timestamp="2001-03-14T12:45:00">
I hope you return soon. I've <emph>really</emph> missed you!
</message>
```

In this example the emph child element is used to add emphasis to the word "really" in the message.

Sequences and Choices

One powerful aspect of complex types is the ability to organize elements into sequences and choices. A *sequence* is a list of child elements that must appear in a particular order, whereas a *choice* is a list of child elements from which only one must be used. You create a sequence with the xsd:sequence element, which houses the elements that comprise the sequence. Following is an example of creating a sequence:

```
<xsd:element name="quiz">
  <xsd:complexType>
    <xsd:sequence>
      <xsd:element name="question" type="xsd:string">
      <xsd:element name="answer" type="xsd:string">
    </xsd:sequence>
  </xsd:complexType>
</xsd:element>
```

In this example, the quiz element contains two child elements, question and answer, that must appear in the order specified. By default, a sequence can occur only once within an element. However, you can use the xsd:minOccurs and xsd:maxOccurs attributes to allow for the sequence to occur multiple times. For example, if you wanted to allow the quiz element to contain up to twenty question and answer pairs, you would code it like this:

5

```
<xsd:element name="quiz">
  <xsd:complexType>
    <xsd:sequence minOccurs="1" maxOccurs="20">
      <xsd:element name="question" type="xsd:string">
      <xsd:element name="answer" type="xsd:string">
    </xsd:sequence>
  </xsd:complexType>
</xsd:element>
```

> You can set the maxOccurs attribute to unbounded to allow for an unlimited number of sequences. The maxOccurs attribute can also be used with individual elements to control the number of times they can occur.

Following is an example of how you might use the quiz element in an XML document:

```
<quiz>
  <question>What does XML stand for?</question>
  <answer>eXtensible Markup Language</answer>
  <question>Who is responsible for overseeing XML?</question>
  <answer>World Wide Web Consortium (W3C)</answer>
  <question>What is the latest version of XML?</question>
  <answer>1.0</answer>
</quiz>
```

If you want to allow an element to contain one of a series of optional elements, then you can use a choice. A choice allows you to list several child elements and/or sequences, with only one of them allowed for use in any given element. Choices are created with the xsd:choice element, which contains the list of choice elements. Following is an example of a choice:

```
<xsd:element name="id">
  <xsd:complexType>
    <xsd:choice>
      <xsd:element name="ssnum" type="xsd:string">

      <xsd:sequence>
        <xsd:element name="name" type="xsd:string">
        <xsd:element name="birthdate" type="xsd:date">
      </xsd:sequence>

      <xsd:element name="licensenum" type="xsd:string">
    </xsd:choice>
  </xsd:complexType>
</xsd:element>
```

In this example, an element named `id` is created that allows three different approaches to providing identification: social security number, name and birth date, or driver's license number. The choice is what makes it possible for the element to accept only one of the approaches. Notice that a sequence is used with the name and birth date approach since it involves two child elements. Following is an example of a few `id` elements that use each of the different choice approaches:

```
<id>
  <ssnum>123-89-4567</ssnum>
</id>
<id>
  <name>Milton James</name>
  <birthdate>1969-10-28</birthdate>
</id>
<id>
  <licensenum>12348765</licensenum>
</id>
```

 If you're looking to create content models with little structure, then you might consider using the `xsd:all` type, which is used to create complex types that can hold any number of elements in any order. The `xsd:all` element is used much like a sequence except that the child elements within it can appear any number of times and in any order.

One last topic worth covering before moving on to a complete XSD example has to do with how data types are referenced. With the exception of the root element, which is automatically referenced in an XSD, global components must be referenced in order to actually appear as part of a document's architecture. In most of the examples you've seen, the components have been declared locally, which means they are automatically referenced within the context that they appear. However, consider an element, such as the following one, which is declared globally:

```
<xsd:element name="password">
  <xsd:simpleType>
    <xsd:restriction base="xsd:string">
      <xsd:minLength value="8"/>
      <xsd:maxLength value="12"/>
    </xsd:restriction>
  </xsd:simpleType>
</xsd:element>
```

Although this element has been declared and is ready for use, it doesn't actually appear within the structure of an XSD until you reference it. You reference elements using the ref attribute, which applies to both elements and attributes. Following is an example of how the `password` element might be referenced in an element:

5

```
<xsd:element name="login" >
  <xsd:complexType>
    <xsd:sequence>
      <xsd:element name="userid" type="xsd:string"/>
      <xsd:element ref="password"/>
    </xsd:sequence>
  </xsd:complexType>
</xsd:element>
```

In this example the userid element is created and used locally, whereas the password element is referenced from the previous global element declaration. Whether or not you use elements and attributes locally or globally primarily has to do with how valuable they are outside of a specific context; if an element or attribute is used only in a single location then you might as well simplify things and keep it local. Otherwise, you should consider making it a global component and then referencing it wherever it is needed using the ref attribute.

A Complete XML Schema Example

You've covered an awful lot of territory in this hour and hopefully have a pretty good understanding of the XSD language and how it is used to create XSD schemas. To help pull everything that you've learned together, I thought it might be helpful for you to see a complete example. If you recall, in the previous hour you constructed a DTD for a sports training markup language known as ETML. Listing 5.1 contains the XSD equivalent for this markup language, which puts to use many of the XSD construction techniques you've learned about throughout this hour.

LISTING 5.1 The etml.xsd XSD Schema Used to Validate ETML Documents

```
 1: <?xml version="1.0"?>
 2:
 3: <xsd:schema xmlns:xsd="http://www.w3.org/2000/10/XMLSchema">
 4:   <xsd:element name="trainlog">
 5:     <xsd:complexType>
 6:       <xsd:sequence>
 7:         <xsd:element name="session" type="sessionType" minOccurs="0"
 8:           maxOccurs="unbounded"/>
 9:       </xsd:sequence>
10:     </xsd:complexType>
11:   </xsd:element>
12:
13:   <xsd:complexType name="sessionType">
14:     <xsd:sequence>
15:       <xsd:element name="duration" type="xsd:timeDuration"/>
16:       <xsd:element name="distance" type="distanceType"/>
```

continues

LISTING 5.1 Continued

```
17:        <xsd:element name="location" type="xsd:string"/>
18:        <xsd:element name="comments" type="xsd:string"/>
19:      </xsd:sequence>
20:
21:      <xsd:attribute name="date" type="xsd:date" use="required"/>
22:      <xsd:attribute name="type" type="typeType" use="required"/>
23:      <xsd:attribute name="heartrate" type="xsd:positiveInteger"/>
24:    </xsd:complexType>
25:
26:    <xsd:complexType name="distanceType">
27:      <xsd:simpleContent>
28:        <xsd:extension base="xsd:decimal">
29:          <xsd:attribute name="units" type="unitsType" use="required"/>
30:        </xsd:extension>
31:      </xsd:simpleContent>
32:    </xsd:complexType>
33:
34:    <xsd:simpleType name="typeType">
35:      <xsd:restriction base="xsd:string">
36:        <xsd:enumeration value="running"/>
37:        <xsd:enumeration value="swimming"/>
38:        <xsd:enumeration value="cycling"/>
39:      </xsd:restriction>
40:    </xsd:simpleType>
41:
42:    <xsd:simpleType name="unitsType">
43:      <xsd:restriction base="xsd:string">
44:        <xsd:enumeration value="miles"/>
45:        <xsd:enumeration value="kilometers"/>
46:        <xsd:enumeration value="laps"/>
47:      </xsd:restriction>
48:    </xsd:simpleType>
49:
50: </xsd:schema>
```

5

Admittedly, this is considerably more code than the DTD for the ETML that you saw in the previous hour. However, you have to consider the fact that XSDs provide a more exacting approach to data modeling by incorporating rich data types. A quick study of the XSD code for ETML reveals that this schema does a much better job of modeling ETML data than its DTD counterpart. This is primarily due to the data typing features of XSD. Additionally, because XSD is an XML-based language, the code should be a little more familiar to you than the more cryptic code used in DTDs.

The trainlog element is described first in the XSD as containing a sequence of session elements (lines 4–11). The sessionType data type is created to represent session elements (line 13) and contains child elements that store the duration, distance, location, and comments for a training session (lines 15–18). The sessionType data type also includes several attributes that store the date, type, and heart rate for the training session (lines 21–23). The remaining distanceType (line 26), typeType (line 34), and unitsType (line 42) data types model the remaining content in ETML documents.

Of course, no schema would be complete without an example XML document that puts it through its paces. Listing 5.2 contains the training log document from the previous hour, modified slightly to accommodate the needs of the XSD schema.

LISTING 5.2 The Training Log Example ETML Document

```
 1: <?xml version="1.0"?>
 2:
 3: <trainlog
 4:    xmlns:xsi="http://www.w3.org/2000/10/XMLSchema-instance"
 5:    xsi:noNamespaceSchemaLocation="etml.xsd">
 6:    <session date="2001-11-19" type="running" heartrate="158">
 7:      <duration>PT45M</duration>
 8:      <distance units="miles">5.5</distance>
 9:      <location>Warner Park</location>
10:      <comments>Mid-morning run, a little winded throughout.</comments>
11:    </session>
12:
13:    <session date="2001-11-21" type="cycling" heartrate="153">
14:      <duration>PT2H30M</duration>
15:      <distance units="miles">37.0</distance>
16:      <location>Natchez Trace Parkway</location>
17:      <comments>Hilly ride, felt strong as an ox.</comments>
18:    </session>
19:
20:    <session date="2001-11-24" type="running" heartrate="156">
21:      <duration>PT1H30M</duration>
22:      <distance units="miles">8.5</distance>
23:      <location>Warner Park</location>
24:      <comments>Afternoon run, felt reasonably strong.</comments>
25:    </session>
26: </trainlog>
```

Other than including the standard noNamespaceSchemaLocation attribute to identify the XSD schema document (line 5), the changes to the training log document have to do with the stricter data typing features of XSDs. For example, the date attributes and duration elements conform to the `xsd:date` and `xsd:timeDuration` simple types (lines 6, 7, 14, 15, 21, and 22). Beyond those changes, the document is the same as the one you saw in the previous hour. This version of the document, however, is considered valid with respect to the ETML XSD, whereas the previous version is considered valid with respect to the ETML DTD.

Summary

Although DTDs certainly represent a technology that is sufficient for modeling XML document data, XML Schema provides a much more advanced alternative that will likely replace DTDs at some point in the future. XSD schemas are constructed using the XSD markup language, which includes elements and attributes for describing the structure of custom XML-based markup languages. This means that you create XSD schema documents in the same manner as you create any other document, which makes XSD schemas immediately more accessible to XML developers than DTDs. The hope now is that XML tools will quickly support XSD and help usher it in as the new standard for XML schemas.

This hour explored the inner workings of XSD schemas and taught you the fundamental skills necessary to design and create them. After explaining the different types of XSD data and how to use each of them, the hour showed you a complete example schema created in XSD.

Q&A

Q Are there any other simple types other than the ones mentioned in this hour?

A Yes. In addition to the simple types you learned about in this hour, there are a few other types such as `binary` and `uriReference` that I didn't mention. These types were left out of the lesson primarily for the sake of brevity, as it is difficult to cover the entirety of the XSD language in a single hour. Besides, the aim of this hour is not to make you an XSD expert but to give you the essential knowledge required to design and create XSD schemas.

Q How do I find out more about regular expressions and how they are used to create patterned types?

A You can learn an immense amount about regular expressions from Stephen Ramsay's online regular expression tutorial, which is located at `http://etext.lib.virginia.edu/helpsheets/regex.html`. This tutorial is hosted by the University of Virginia's Electronic Text Center.

5

**Q I still don't quite understand the distinction between local and global compo-
nents in an XSD schema. What gives?**

A Elements and attributes are considered global if they are declared directly below
the xsd:schema element. If they are declared anywhere else, then they are considered local. Global elements and attributes are used differently in that they must be
referenced in order to factor into a schema. Contrast this with local elements and
attributes, which are automatically referenced simply by virtue of being local.

Workshop

The Workshop is designed to help you anticipate possible questions, review what you've
learned, and begin learning how to put your knowledge into practice.

Quiz

1. What file extension is used to identify XSD schema documents?

2. What two primary attributes are used with the xsd:element element to describe an
   element in an XSD schema?

3. What simple type would you use to represent a recurring monthly bill in an XSD
   schema?

4. What is the purpose of the xsd:precision and xsd:scale elements?

5. How do you control how many times an element may appear within an XSD
   schema?

Quiz Answers

1. XSD schema documents are stored with a file extension of .xsd.

2. The two primary attributes used with the xsd:element element to describe an element in an XSD schema are name and type.

3. Both the xsd:recurringDate and xsd:recurringDay types are sufficient to store
   the date of a recurring monthly bill. The xsd:recurringDate type would be better
   if you cared about knowing the month of the bill, whereas the xsd:recurringDay
   type would work fine if you were interested only in the day of the month.

4. The xsd:precision element determines how many total digits are allowed in a
   number, whereas xsd:scale determines how many of those digits appear to the
   right of the decimal point.

5. The xsd:minOccurs and xsd:maxOccurs attributes allow you to control how many
   times an element appears within an XSD schema.

Exercises

1. Using the pets.xml document from Hour 1, create a pets.xsd schema document that uses XSD to describe a virtual pet markup language.

2. Modify the pets.xml document so that it can be validated against the new pets.xsd schema document.

5

Hour 6

Digging Deeper into XML Documents

You can observe a lot just by watchin'.

—Yogi Berra (Hall of Fame baseball player)

If only this was true with XML, then you'd really never need to peer beneath the surface of XML documents. You can actually learn a lot about XML just by watchin', but at some point you have to go a step further and learn a little more about what is going on. For example, in addition to the logical structure of documents that is dictated by elements, there is also a physical structure that is very important. This physical structure of documents is determined by entities, which are units of storage that house content within documents. Closely related to entities are notations, which make it possible for XML applications to handle certain types of entities that aren't capable of being processed. This hour tackles entities and notations along with a few other important topics related to the inner workings of XML documents.

In this hour, you'll learn

- How to document your XML code with comments
- How characters of text are encoded in XML
- All about entities and how they are used
- Why notations make it possible to use certain kinds of entities

Leaving a Trail with Comments

Even though it doesn't really tie into anything else, I feel compelled to start out this hour with a bit of housekeeping. Any self-respecting XML developer would want to write clean XML code that is as easy to understand as possible. Part of the process of writing clean XML code is documenting the code whenever necessary. Comments are used in XML to add descriptions to code and include information that isn't part of a document's content. Comments aren't considered part of a document's content because XML processors ignore them.

> Technically speaking, it's possible for an XML processor to not ignore comments, which might make sense in an XML development tool. Such a tool might allow you to enter and modify comments through a graphical user interface, in which case it would need to process comments to some degree. Even so, the comments wouldn't be interpreted as document content.

Comments are specified in a document between the <!-- and --> symbols. The only limitation on comments is that you can't include double-hyphens (--) in the body of a comment because they conflict with XML's comment syntax. Following is an example of how you could use a comment to add information to a training session in the training log document from Hour 4:

```
<!-- This session was part of the marathon training group run. -->
<session date="11/19/01" type="running" heartrate="158">
  <duration units="minutes">45</duration>
  <distance units="miles">5.5</distance>
  <location>Warner Park</location>
  <comments>Mid-morning run, a little winded throughout.</comments>
</session>
```

The information contained within the comment isn't considered part of the document data. The usefulness of comments will naturally vary with the type of XML documents you are creating. Some documents tend to be relatively self-explanatory, whereas others benefit from comments that make them more understandable.

Characters of Text in XML

As you know, XML documents are made of text. More specifically, an XML document consists of a bunch of characters of text that have meaning based upon XML and the specific markup language dictated by a schema (DTD or XML Schema). The characters of text within an XML document can be encoded in a number of different ways to suit different human languages. The character-encoding scheme for a document is determined within the XML declaration in a piece of code known as the *character encoding declaration*. The character encoding declaration looks like an attribute of the XML declaration, as the following code shows:

```
<?xml version="1.0" encoding="UTF-8"?>
```

The UTF-8 value assigned in the character encoding declaration specifies that the document is to use the UTF-8 character-encoding scheme, which is the default scheme for XML. All XML applications are required to support the UTF-8 and UTF-16 character encoding schemes; the difference between the two schemes is the number of bits used to represent each character (8 or 16). If you don't expect your documents to be used in a scenario with multiple human languages, then you can probably stick to UTF-8. Otherwise, you'll need to go with UTF-16, which requires more memory but allows for multiple languages.

Regardless of the scheme you use to encode characters within an XML document, you need to know how to specify characters numerically. All characters in an encoding scheme have a numerical value associated with them that can be used as a character reference. Character references come in very handy when you're trying to enter a character that can't be typed on a keyboard. For example, the copyright symbol (©) is an example of a character that can only be specified using a character reference. There are two types of numeric character references:

- Decimal reference
- Hexadecimal reference (base 16)

A *decimal character reference* relies on a decimal number (base 10) to specify a character's numeric value. Decimal references are specified using an ampersand followed by a pound sign (&#),the character number, and a semicolon (;). So, a complete decimal character reference has the following form:

```
&#Num;
```

The decimal number in this form is represented by *Num*. Following is an example of a decimal character reference:

```
&#169;
```

6

This character reference identifies the character associated with the decimal number 169, which just so happens to be the copyright symbol. Following is the copyright symbol character reference used within the context of other character data:

```
&#169;2001 Michael Morrison
```

Even though the code looks a little messy with the character reference, you're using a symbol (the copyright symbol) that would otherwise be difficult to enter in a normal text editor.

> The actual decimal number associated with the copyright symbol is determined by a standard that applies to both XML and HTML. To learn more about special characters that can be encoded using character references, please refer to the following Web page: http://www.w3.org/TR/REC-html40/sgml/entities.html.

If you're coming from a low-level programming background, then you may opt for the second approach to specifying numeric characters: hexadecimal references. A *hexadecimal reference* uses a hexadecimal number (base 16) to specify a character's numeric value. Hexadecimal references are specified similarly to decimal references, except that an x immediately precedes the number:

```
&#xNum;
```

Using this form, the copyright character with the decimal value of 169 is referenced in hexadecimal as the following:

```
&#xA9;
```

Since decimal and hexadecimal references represent two equivalent solutions to the same problem (referencing characters), there is no technical reason to choose one over the other. However, most of us are much more comfortable working with decimal numbers since it's the number system used in everyday life. It ultimately has to do with your degree of comfort with each number system; the decimal system is probably much more familiar to you.

> If you aren't naturally a binary thinker (few of us are), then you might find hexadecimal numbers to be somewhat confusing. Hexadecimal numbers are strange-looking because they use the letters A–F to represent the numbers 10–15. As an example, the decimal number 60 is 3C in hexadecimal; the C represents decimal 12, whereas the 3 represents decimal 48 (3 × 16); 12 plus 48 is 60. Most programming languages denote hexadecimal numbers by preceding them with an x, which was no doubt an influence on the XML representation of hexadecimal character references.

The Wonderful World of Entities

Just as bricks serve as the building blocks of many houses, *entities* are special units of storage that serve as the building blocks of XML documents. Entities are typically identified with a unique name and are used to contain content within a document. To help understand the role of entities, it helps to think of elements as describing the logical structure of a document, whereas entities describe the physical structure. Entities often correspond with files that are stored on a file system, such as the file that holds an XML document. However, entities don't have to be associated with files in any way; an entity can be associated with a database record or even a piece of memory. The significance is that entities represent a unit of storage in an XML document.

Although most entities have names, a few notable ones do not. The *document entity,* which is the top-level entity for a document, does not have a name. The document entity is important because it usually contains the entire document. This entity is then broken down into subentities, which are often broken down further. The breakdown of entities ends when you arrive at nothing but content. The other entity that goes unnamed is the external DTD, if one exists. As an example, the `TallTales.dtd` external DTD you saw in previous hours is an entity, as is the root document element `talltales`. Following is an excerpt from the Tall Tales document that illustrates the relationship between the external DTD and the root document element:

```
<?xml version="1.0"?>
<!DOCTYPE talltales SYSTEM "TallTales.dtd">

<talltales>
  <!-- Document markup -->
</talltales>
```

In this code the `talltales` root element and the `TallTales.dtd` external DTD are referenced in the document type declaration. To clarify how entities are storage constructs, consider the fact that the contents of the external DTD could be directly inserted in the document type declaration, in which case it would no longer be considered an entity. What makes the DTD an entity is the fact that its storage is external.

The document entity is a unique entity in that it is declared in the document type declaration. Most other entities are declared in an *entity declaration,* which must appear before the entities can be used in the document. An entity declaration consists of a unique entity name and a piece of data that is associated with the name. Following are some examples of data that you might reference as entities:

- A string of text
- A section of the DTD

6

- An external file containing text data
- An external file containing binary data

This list reveals that entities are extremely flexible when it comes to the types of data that can be stored in them. Although the specific data within an entity can certainly vary widely, there are two basic types of entities that are used in XML documents: parsed entities and unparsed entities. *Parsed entities* store data that is parsed (processed) by an XML application, which means that parsed entities can contain only text. *Unparsed entities* aren't parsed and therefore can be either text or binary data.

Parsed entities end up being merged with the contents of a document when they are processed. In other words, parsed entities are directly inserted into documents as if they were directly part of the document to begin with. Unparsed entities cannot be handled in this manner because XML applications are unable to parse them. As an example, consider the difficulty of combining a binary JPEG image with the text content of an XML document. Since binary data and text data don't mix well, unparsed entities are never merged directly with a document.

If an XML application can't process and merge an unparsed entity with the rest of a document, how does it use the entity as document data? The answer to this question lies in *notations,* which are XML constructs used to identify the entity type to an XML processor. In addition to identifying the type of an unparsed entity, a notation also specifies a helper application that can be used to process the entity. A good example of a helper application for an unparsed entity is an image viewer, which would be associated with a GIF or JPEG image entity, or maybe a less-used image format such as TIFF. The point is that a notation tells an XML application how to handle an unparsed entity using a helper application.

If you've ever had your Web browser prompt you for a plug-in to view a special content type such as an Adobe Acrobat file (.PDF document), then you understand how important helper applications can be.

Parsed Entities

You know that parsed entities are entities containing XML data that is processed by an XML application. There are two fundamental types of parsed entities:

- General entities
- Parameter entities

The next couple of sections explore these types of entities in more detail.

General Entities

General entities are parsed entities that are designed for use in document content. If you have a string of text that you'd like to isolate as a piece of reusable document data, then a general entity is exactly what you need. A good example of such a reusable piece of text is the copyright notice for a Web site, which appears the same across all pages. Before you can reference a general entity in a document, you must declare it using a general entity declaration, which takes the following form:

```
<!ENTITY EntityName EntityDef>
```

The unique name of the entity is specified in `EntityName`, whereas its associated text is specified in `EntityDef`. All entity declarations must be placed in the DTD. If an entity is used only in a single document, then you can place the declaration in the internal DTD; otherwise you'll want to place it in the external DTD so it can be shared. Following is an example of a general entity declaration:

```
<!ENTITY copyright "Copyright &#169;2001 Michael Morrison.">
```

Just in case you've already forgotten from earlier in the hour, the © character reference in the code is the copyright symbol.

You are now free to use the entity anywhere in the content of a document. General entities are referenced in document content using the entity name sandwiched between an ampersand (&) and a semicolon (;), as the following form shows:

```
&EntityName;
```

Following is an example of referencing the `copyright` entity:

```
My Life Story.
&copyright;
My name is Michael and this is my story.
```

In this example, the contents of the `copyright` entity are replaced in the text where the reference occurs, in between the title and the sentence. The `copyright` entity is an example of a general entity that you must declare yourself. This is how most entities are used in XML. However, there are a handful of predefined entities in XML that you can use without declaring. I'm referring to the five predefined entities that correspond to special characters, which you learned about back in Hour 2. Following is a list of the entities just in case you don't quite remember them:

6

- Less-than symbol (<) — <
- Greater-than symbol (>) — >
- Quote symbol (") — "
- Apostrophe symbol (') — '
- Ampersand symbol (&) — &

These predefined entities serve as an exception to the rule of having to declare all entities before using them; beyond these five entities, all entities must be declared before being used in a document.

Parameter Entities

The other type of parsed entity supported in XML is the *parameter entity,* which is a general entity that is used only within a DTD. Parameter entities are used to help modularize the structure of DTDs by allowing you to store commonly used pieces of declarations. For example, you might use a parameter entity to store a list of commonly used attributes that are shared among multiple elements. As with general entities, you must declare a parameter entity before using it in a DTD. Parameter entity declarations have the following form:

```
<!ENTITY % EntityName EntityDef>
```

Parameter entity declarations are very similar to general entity declarations, with the only difference being the presence of the percent sign (%) and the space on either side of it. The unique name of the parameter entity is specified in `EntityName`, whereas the entity content is specified in `EntityDef`. Following is an example of a parameter entity declaration:

```
<!ENTITY % autoelems "year, make, model">
```

This parameter entity describes a portion of a content model that can be referenced within elements in a DTD. Keep in mind that parameter entities apply only to DTDs. Parameter entities are referenced using the entity name sandwiched between a percent sign (%) and a semicolon (;), as the following form shows:

```
%EntityName;
```

Following is an example of referencing the `autoelems` parameter entity in a hypothetical automotive DTD:

```
<!ELEMENT car (%autoelems;)>
<!ELEMENT truck (%autoelems;)>
<!ELEMENT suv (%autoelems;)>
```

This code is equivalent to the following:

```
<!ELEMENT car (year, make, model)>
<!ELEMENT truck (year, make, model)>
<!ELEMENT suv (year, make, model)>
```

It's important to note that parameter entities really come into play only when you have a large DTD with repeating declarations. Even then you should be careful how you modularize a DTD with parameter entities because it's possible to create unnecessary complexity if you layer too many parameter entities within each other.

Unparsed Entities

Unparsed entities aren't processed by XML applications and are capable of storing text or binary data. Since it isn't possible to embed the content of binary entities directly in a document as text, binary entities are always referenced from an external location, such as a file. Unlike parsed entities, which can be referenced from just about anywhere in the content of a document, unparsed entities must be referenced using an attribute of type ENTITY or ENTITIES. Following is an example of an unparsed entity declaration using the ENTITY attribute:

```
<!ELEMENT player EMPTY>
<!ATTLIST player
  name CDATA #REQUIRED
  position CDATA #REQUIRED
  photo ENTITY #IMPLIED>
```

In this code, photo is specified as an attribute of type ENTITY, which means that you can assign an unparsed entity to the attribute. Following is an example of how this is carried out in document content:

```
<player name="Rolly Fingers" position="pitcher" photo="rfpic"/>
```

In this code, the binary entity rfpic is assigned to the photo attribute. Even though the binary entity has been properly declared and assigned, an XML application won't know how to handle it without a notation declaration, which you find out about a little later in the hour.

Internal Versus External Entities

The physical location of entities is very important in determining how entities are referenced in XML documents. Thus far I've made the distinction between parsed and unparsed entities. Another important way to look at entities is to consider how they are stored. *Internal entities* are stored within the document that references them and are parsed entities out of necessity. *External entities* are stored outside of the document that references them and can be either parsed or unparsed.

6

By definition, any entity that is not internal must be external. This means
that an external entity is stored outside of the document where the entity is
declared. A good example of an external entity is a binary image; images
are always stored in separate files from the documents that reference them.

Unparsed external entities are often binary files such as images, which obviously cannot
be parsed by an XML processor. Unparsed external entities are identified using the
NDATA keyword in their entity declaration; NDATA (Not DATA) simply indicates that the
entity's content is not XML data.

External entity declarations are different than internal entity declarations because they
must reference an external storage location. Files associated with external entities can be
specified in one of two ways, depending on whether the file is located on the local file
system or is publicly available on a network:

- SYSTEM—the file is located on the local file system or on a network
- PUBLIC—the file is a public-domain file located in a publicly accessible place

When specifying the location of external entities, you must always use the
SYSTEM keyword to identify a file on a local system or network; the PUBLIC
keyword is optional and is used in addition to the SYSTEM keyword.

The file for an external entity is specified as a URI, which is very similar to the more
familiar URL. You can specify files using a relative URI, which makes it a little easier
than listing a full path to a file. XML expects relative URIs to be specified relative to the
document within which an entity is declared. Following is an example of declaring a
JPEG image entity using a relative URI:

```
<!ENTITY skate SYSTEM "skate.jpg" NDATA JPEG>
```

In this example, the skate.jpg file would need to be located on the local file system in
the same directory as the file (document) containing the entity declaration. The NDATA
keyword is used to indicate that the entity does not contain XML data. Also, the type of
the external entity is specified as JPEG. Unfortunately, XML doesn't support any built-in
binary entity types such as JPEG, even though JPEG is a widely known image format.
You must use notations to establish entity types for unparsed entities. Fortunately, you
learn about notations in the next section.

The Significance of Notations

Unparsed entities are unable to be processed by XML applications, which means that applications have no way of knowing what to do with them unless you specify helper information that allows an application to rely on a helper application to process the entity. The helper application could be a browser plug-in or a standalone application that has been installed on a user's computer. Either way, the idea is that a notation directs an XML application to a helper application so that unparsed entities can be handled in a meaningful manner. The most obvious example of this type of handling is an external binary image entity, which could be processed and displayed by an image viewer (the helper application).

Notations are used to specify helper information for an unparsed entity and are required of all unparsed entities. Following is an example of a notation that describes the JPEG image type:

```
<!NOTATION JPEG SYSTEM "image/jpeg">
```

In this example, the name of the notation is JPEG, and the helper information is image/jpeg, which is a universal type that identifies the JPEG image format. It is expected that an XML application could somehow use this helper information to query the system for the JPEG type in order to figure out how to view JPEG images. So, this information would come into play when an XML application encounters the following image entity:

```
<!ENTITY skate SYSTEM "skate.jpg" NDATA JPEG>
```

If you didn't want to trust the XML application to figure out how to view the image on its own, you can get more specific with notations and specify an application, as follows:

```
<!NOTATION JPEG SYSTEM "Photoed.exe">
```

This code associates the Microsoft Photo Editor application (Photoed.exe) with JPEG images so that an XML application can use it to view JPEG images. Following is an example of what a complete XML document looks like that contains a single image as an unparsed entity:

```
<?xml version="1.0" standalone="no"?>

<!DOCTYPE image [
<!NOTATION JPEG SYSTEM "PhotoEd.exe">
<!ENTITY skate SYSTEM "skate.jpg" NDATA JPEG>

<!ELEMENT image EMPTY>
<!ATTLIST image source ENTITY #REQUIRED>
]>

<image source="skate"/>
```

6

While this code does all the right things in terms of providing the information necessary to process and display a JPEG image, it still doesn't work in major Web browsers because none of them support unparsed entities at the moment. In truth, Web browsers know that the entities are unparsed; they just don't know what to do with them. Hopefully this will be remedied soon.

Working with CDATA

Just as an XML processor doesn't process unparsed entities, you can mark content within an XML document so that it isn't processed. This type of content is known as unparsed character data, or CDATA. CDATA in a document must be marked specially so that it is treated differently than the rest of an XML document. For this reason, the part of a document containing CDATA is known as a CDATA section. You define a section of CDATA code by enclosing it within the symbols <![CDATA[and]]>. Following is an example of a CDATA section, which should make the usage of these symbols a little clearer:

```
This is my self-portrait:
<![CDATA[
   *****
  * @ @ *
  *  )  *
  * ~~~ *
   *****
]]>
```

In this example, the crude drawing of a face is kept intact because it isn't processed as XML data. If it wasn't enclosed in a CDATA section, the white space within it would be processed down to a few spaces, and the drawing would be ruined. CDATA sections are very useful any time you want to preserve the exact appearance of text. You can also place legitimate XML code in a CDATA section to temporarily disable it and keep it from being processed.

Summary

Although the code for many XML documents is somewhat self-explanatory, there are situations where it can be beneficial to provide additional information about XML code using comments. This hour showed you how to use comments, which allows you to make your code easier to understand. In addition to comments, you also learned how characters of text are encoded in XML document. Although you may not ever change the character encoding scheme of your documents from the default setting, it is nonetheless important to understand why there are different encoding options.

After learning about comments and character encoding schemes, you spent the bulk of this hour getting acquainted with entities. You found out about parsed entities and unparsed entities, not to mention the difference between internal and external entities. From there you learned the significance of notations and how they impact unparsed entities. Finally, the hour concluded with a quick discussion of CDATA sections.

Q&A

Q How exactly are parsed entities merged with document content?

A You can think of the merger of parsed entities with document content as a search-and-replace operation. For example, if you had a certain word in a word processor document that you wanted to replace with a phrase, you would perform a search-and-replace, which replaces each occurrence of the word with the phrase. Parsed entities work in a very similar manner, except that the word is the entity reference and the phrase is the entity data; an XML processor carries out the search-and-replace process.

Q Why is it necessary to use notations for familiar binary data types such as GIF and JPEG images?

A GIF and JPEG images are "familiar" only within the context of a Web browser, which is inherently associated with HTML. XML is a much broader technology that doesn't necessarily have a direct tie with a Web browser. Therefore, no partiality is given to Web data types over any other data types. XML's approach is to require notations for all binary entities.

Q Why would I ever want to place text in an external entity?

A Although any text could be included directly in an XML document as an internal entity, any large pieces of text that are shared among several documents would benefit greatly from being placed in external files. The storage of these entities would then be isolated in one place, and they could simply be referenced by each document.

Workshop

The Workshop is designed to help you anticipate possible questions, review what you've learned, and begin learning how to put your knowledge into practice.

Quiz

1. How do you identify a comment in an XML document?
2. What is the significance of the document entity?

3. If you needed to reference a binary image file in an XML document, what kind of entity would you use?

4. What is the difference between internal and external entities?

Quiz Answers

1. Comments are specified in a document between the `<!--` and `-->` symbols.

2. The document entity is the top-level entity for a document and contains all other entities in the document.

3. In order to reference binary data in an external file, you must use an unparsed entity.

4. Internal entities are stored within the document that references them and are always parsed entities. External entities are stored outside of the document that references them and can be either parsed or unparsed entities.

Exercises

1. Add comments to the TrainLog.xml example document that include additional information about each of the training sessions.

2. Modify the TrainLog.xml example document so that it uses general entities for each of the training locations: Warner Park and Natchez Trace Parkway. These entities eliminate the need to repeatedly enter the locations as additional training sessions are entered.

HOUR 7

Putting Namespaces to Use

> For every complex problem, there is a solution that is simple, neat, and wrong.
>
> —H. L. Mencken (journalist and social critic)

Although Mr. Mencken may be correct in his statement about oversimplifying the solution to complex problems, namespaces represent a relatively simple XML solution that works quite well. As you know, XML allows you to create custom markup languages, which are languages that contain elements and attributes of your own creation. XML is incredibly flexible in this regard, but there is nothing stopping two people from creating markup languages with very similar, if not identical, elements and attributes. What happens if you need to use both of these markup languages in a single document? There would obviously be a clash between identically named elements and attributes in the languages. Fortunately, as you learn in this hour, namespaces allow you to solve this problem with very little effort.

In this hour, you'll learn

- Why namespaces are important to XML
- How namespace names are guaranteed to be unique
- How to declare and reference namespaces in XML documents
- How to use namespaces to merge schemas

Understanding Namespaces

As a young kid I was often confused by the fact that two people could have the same name yet not be related. It just didn't register with me that it's possible for two families to exist independently of one another with the same last name. Of course, now I understand why it's possible, but I'm still kind of bummed by the fact that I'm not the only Michael Morrison walking around. In fact, I'm not even close to being the most famous Michael Morrison—the real name of John Wayne, the famous actor, was actually Marion Michael Morrison. But I digress.

The reason I bring up the issue of people having the same names yet not being related is because it parallels the problem in XML when different markup languages have elements and attributes that are named the same. The XML problem is much more severe, however, because XML applications aren't smart enough to judge the difference between the context of elements from different markup languages that share the same name. It's up to the XML developer to ensure that uniqueness abounds when it comes to the elements and attributes used in documents. Fortunately, namespaces make it possible to enforce such uniqueness without too much of a hassle.

A *namespace* is a collection of names that can be used as element or attribute names in an XML document. To draw a comparison between an XML namespace and the real world, if you considered the first names of all the people in your immediate family, they would belong to a namespace equivalent to your last name. XML namespaces are similar because they represent groups of names for related elements and attributes. Most of the time an individual namespace corresponds directly to a custom markup language, but that doesn't necessarily have to be the case. You also know that namespaces aren't a requirement of XML documents, as you haven't really used them throughout the book thus far.

The purpose of namespaces is to eliminate name conflicts between elements and attributes. To better understand how this type of name clash might occur in your own XML documents, consider an XML document that contains information about a video and music collection. You might use a custom markup language unique to each type of information (video and music), which means that each language would have its own elements and attributes. However, you are using both languages within the context of a single XML document, which is where the potential for problems arises. If both markup languages include an element named title that represents the title of a video or music compilation, there is no way for an XML application to know which language you intended to use for the element. The solution to this problem is to assign a namespace to each of the markup languages, which will then provide a clear distinction between the elements and attributes of each language when they are used.

In order to fully understand namespaces, you need a solid grasp on the concept of scope in XML documents. The scope of an element or attribute in a document refers to the relative location of the element or attribute within the document. If you visualize the elements in a document as an upside-down tree that begins at the top with the root element, then child elements of the root element appear just below the root element as branches (Figure 7.1). Each element in a "document tree" is known as a *node*. Nodes are very important when it comes to processing XML documents because they determine the relationship between parent and child elements. The *scope* of an element refers to its location within this hierarchical tree of elements. So, when I refer to the scope of an element or attribute, I'm talking about the node in which the element or attribute is stored.

FIGURE 7.1

An XML document coded in ETML can be visualized as a hierarchical tree of elements, where each leaf in the tree is known as a node.

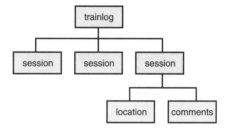

Scope is important to namespaces because it's possible to use a namespace within a given scope, which means it impacts only elements and attributes beneath a particular node. Contrast this with a namespace that has global scope, which means the namespace applies to the entire document. Any guess as to how you might establish a global namespace? It's easy—you just associate it with the root element, which houses the remainder of the document. You learn much more about scope as it applies to namespaces throughout the remainder of this hour. Before you get to that, however, it's time to learn where namespace names come from.

7

Naming Namespaces

The whole point of namespaces is that they provide a means of establishing unique identifiers for elements and attributes. It is therefore imperative that each and every namespace have a unique name. Obviously, there would be no way to enforce this rule if everyone was allowed to make up their own domain names out of thin air, so a clever naming scheme was established that tied namespaces to URIs (Uniform Resource Identifiers). URIs usually reference physical resources on the Internet and are guaranteed to be unique. So, a namespace is essentially the name of a URI. For example, my Web site is located at `http://www.michaelmorrison.com`. To help guarantee name uniqueness in any XML documents that I create, I could associate the documents with my namespace:

```
<movies xmlns:movie="http://www.michaelmorrison.com/ns/movies">
```

The `ns` in the namespace name `http://www.michaelmorrison.com/ns/movies` stands for namespace and is often used in URL namespace names. It isn't a necessity but it's not a bad idea in terms of being able to quickly identify namespaces. If you don't want to use a URI as the basis for a namespace name, you could also use the URN (Universal Resource Name) of a Web resource to guarantee uniqueness. URNs are slightly different from URLs and define a unique location-independent name for a resource that maps to one or more URLs. Following is an example of using a URN to specify a namespace for my Web site:

```
<movies xmlns:movie="urn:michaelmorrison.com:ns:movies">
```

 There is often confusion among XML developers regarding the relationship between URLs, URNs, and URIs. Perhaps the most important distinction to make is that URIs encompass both URLs and URNs. URNs differ from URLs in that URLs describe the physical location of a particular resource, whereas URNs define a unique location-independent name for a resource that maps to one or more URLs. An easy way to distinguish between URLs and URNs is to examine their names: URLs all begin with an Internet service prefix such as `ftp:`, `http:`, and so on, whereas URNs typically begin with the `urn:` prefix.

Keep in mind that a namespace doesn't actually point to a physical resource, even if its URI does. In other words, the only reason namespaces are named after URIs is because URIs are guaranteed to be unique—they could just as easily be named after social security numbers. This means that within a domain name you can create URIs that don't actually reference physical resources. So, although there may not be a directory named `pets` on my Web server, I can still use a URI named `http://www.michaelmorrison.com/ns/pets` to name a namespace. The significance is that the `michaelmorrison.com` domain name is mine and is therefore guaranteed to be unique. This is important because it allows you to organize XML documents based upon their respective namespaces while guaranteeing uniqueness among the namespace names.

Declaring and Using Namespaces

Namespaces are associated with documents by way of elements, which means that you declare a namespace for a particular element with the scope you want for the namespace. More specifically, you use a *namespace declaration,* which looks a lot like an attribute of the element. In many cases you want a namespace to apply to an entire document, which means you'll use the namespace declaration with the root element. A namespace declaration takes the following form:

```
xmlns:Prefix="NameSpace"
```

The xmlns attribute is what notifies an XML processor that a namespace is being declared. The NameSpace portion of the namespace declaration is where the namespace itself is identified. This portion of the declaration identifies a URI that guarantees uniqueness for elements and attributes used within the scope of the namespace declaration.

The *Prefix* part of the namespace declaration allows you to set a prefix that will serve as a shorthand reference for the namespace throughout the scope of the element in which the namespace is declared. The *Prefix* of a namespace is optional and ultimately depends on whether you want to use qualified or unqualified element and attribute names throughout a document. A qualified name includes the *Prefix* portion of the namespace declaration and consists of two parts: the prefix and the local portion of the name. Examples of qualified names include movie:title, movie:director, and movie:rating. To use qualified names, you must provide *Prefix* in the namespace declaration. Following is a simple example of a qualified name:

```
<mov:title>Raising Arizona</mov:title>
```

In this example the prefix is mov and the local portion of the name is title. Unqualified names don't include a prefix and are either associated with a default namespace or no namespace at all. The *Prefix* of the namespace declaration isn't required when declaring a default namespace. Examples of unqualified names are title, director, and rating. Unqualified names in a document look no different than if you weren't using namespaces at all. The following code shows how the movie example would be coded using unqualified names:

```
<title>Raising Arizona</title>
```

7

Notice that in this example the `<title>` and `</title>` tags are used so that you would never know a namespace was involved. In this case, you are either assuming a default namespace is in use or that there is no namespace at all.

It's important to clarify why you would use qualified or unqualified names because the decision to use one or the other determines the manner in which you declare a namespace. There are two different approaches to declaring namespaces:

- Default declaration—the namespace is declared without a prefix; all element and attribute names within its scope are referenced using unqualified names and are assumed to be in the namespace.

- Explicit declaration—the namespace is declared with a prefix; all element and attribute names associated with the namespace must use the prefix as part of their qualified names or else they are not considered part of the namespace.

The next sections dig a little deeper into these namespace declarations.

Default Namespaces

Default namespaces represent the simpler of the two approaches to namespace declaration. A *default namespace declaration* is useful when you want to apply a namespace to an entire document or section of a document. When declaring a default namespace, you don't use a prefix with the `xmlns` attribute. Instead, elements are specified with unqualified names and are therefore assumed to be part of the default namespace. In other words, a default namespace declaration applies to all unqualified elements within the scope in which the namespace is declared. Following is an example of a default namespace declaration for a movie collection document:

```
<movies xmlns="http://www.michaelmorrison.com/ns/movies">
  <movie type="comedy" rating="PG-13" review="5" year="1987">
    <title>Raising Arizona</title>
    <comments>A classic one-of-a-kind screwball love story.</comments>
  </movie>

  <movie type="comedy" rating="R" review="5" year="1988">
    <title>Midnight Run</title>
    <comments>The quintessential road comedy.</comments>
  </movie>
</movies>
```

In this example, the `http://www.michaelmorrison.com/ns/movies` namespace is declared as the default namespace for the movie document. This means that all of the unqualified elements in the document (`movies`, `movie`, `title`, and so on) are assumed to be part of the namespace. A default namespace can also be set for any other element in a document, in which case it applies only to that element and its children. For example, you could set a namespace for one of the title elements, which would override the default namespace set in the movies element. Following is an example of how this is done:

```
<movies xmlns="http://www.michaelmorrison.com/ns/movies">
  <movie type="comedy" rating="PG-13" review="5" year="1987">
    <title>Raising Arizona</title>
    <comments>A classic one-of-a-kind screwball love story.</comments>
  </movie>

  <movie type="comedy" rating="R" review="5" year="1988">
    <title xmlns="http://www.michaelmorrison.com/ns/title">Midnight
Run</title>
    <comments>The quintessential road comedy.</comments>
  </movie>
</movies>
```

Notice in the title element for the second movie element that a different namespace is specified. This namespace applies only to the title element and overrides the namespace declared in the movies element. While this example doesn't necessarily make a good argument for why you would override a namespace, it can be a bigger issue in documents where you mix different XML languages.

Explicit Namespaces

An explicit namespace is useful whenever you want exacting control over the elements and attributes that are associated with a namespace. This is often necessary in documents that rely on multiple schemas because there is a chance of having a name clash between elements and attributes defined in the two schemas. *Explicit namespace declarations* require a prefix that is used to distinguish elements and attributes that belong to the namespace being declared. The prefix in an explicit declaration is used as a shorthand notation for the namespace throughout the scope in which the namespace is declared. More specifically, the prefix is paired with the local element or attribute name to form a qualified name of the form *Prefix:Local*. Following is how the movie example looks with qualified element and attribute names:

```
<mov:movies xmlns:mov="http://www.michaelmorrison.com/ns/movies">
  <mov:movie mov:type="comedy" mov:rating="PG-13" mov:review="5"
  mov:year="1987">
    <mov:title>Raising Arizona</mov:title>
    <mov:comments>A classic one-of-a-kind screwball love story.</mov:comments>
  </mov:movie>

  <mov:movie mov:type="comedy" mov:rating="R" mov:review="5" mov:year="1988">
    <mov:title>Midnight Run</mov:title>
    <mov:comments>The quintessential road comedy.</mov:comments>
  </mov:movie>
</mov:movies>
```

7

The namespace in this code is explicitly declared by the name mov in the namespace declaration; this is evident in the fact that the name mov is specified after the xmlns keyword. Once the namespace is declared, you can use it with any element and attribute names that belong in the namespace, which in this case is all of them.

I mentioned earlier that one of the primary reasons for using explicit namespaces is when multiple schemas are being used in a document. In this situation, you will likely declare both namespaces explicitly and then use them appropriately to identify elements and attributes throughout the document. Listing 7.1 is an example of a media collection document that combines both movies and music information into a single format:

LISTING 7.1 The Media Collection Example Document

```
 1: <?xml version="1.0"?>
 2:
 3: <mediacollection xmlns:mov="http://www.michaelmorrison.com/ns/movies"
 4:    xmlns:mus="http://www.michaelmorrison.com/ns/music">
 5:    <mov:movie mov:type="comedy" mov:rating="PG-13" mov:review="5"
 6:      mov:year="1987">
 7:      <mov:title>Raising Arizona</mov:title>
 8:      <mov:comments>A classic one-of-a-kind screwball love story.
 9:      </mov:comments>
10:    </mov:movie>
11:
12:    <mov:movie mov:type="comedy" mov:rating="R" mov:review="5"
       mov:year="1988">
13:      <mov:title>Midnight Run</mov:title>
14:      <mov:comments>The quintessential road comedy.</mov:comments>
15:    </mov:movie>
16:
17:    <mus:music type="indy" review="5" year="1990">
18:      <mus:title>Cake</mus:title>
19:      <mus:artist>The Trash Can Sinatras</mus:artist>
20:      <mus:label>Polygram Records</mus:label>
21:      <mus:comments>Excellent acoustical instruments and extremely witty
22:        lyrics.</mus:comments>
23:    </mus:music>
24:
25:    <mus:music type="rock" review="5" year="1991">
26:      <mus:title>Travelers and Thieves</mus:title>
27:      <mus:artist>Blues Traveler</mus:artist>
28:      <mus:label>A&amp;M Records</mus:label>
29:      <mus:comments>The best Blues Traveler recording, period.</mus:comments>
30:    </mus:music>
31: </mediacollection>
```

In this code the mov and mus namespaces (lines 3 and 4) are explicitly declared in order to correctly identify the elements and attributes for each type of media. Notice that without these explicit namespaces it would be difficult for an XML processor to tell the difference between the title and comments elements because they are used in both movie and music entries.

Just to help hammer home the distinction between default and explicit namespace declarations, let's take a look at one more example. This time the media collection declares the movie namespace as the default namespace and then explicitly declares the music namespace using the mus prefix. The end result is that the movie elements and attributes don't require a prefix when referenced, whereas the music elements and attributes do. Check out the code in Listing 7.2 to see what I mean:

LISTING 7.2 A Different Version of the Media Collection Example Document That Declares the Movie Namespace as a Default Namespace

```
 1: <?xml version="1.0"?>
 2:
 3: <mediacollection xmlns="http://www.michaelmorrison.com/ns/movies"
 4:    xmlns:mus="http://www.michaelmorrison.com/ns/music">
 5:   <movie type="comedy" rating="PG-13" review="5" year="1987">
 6:     <title>Raising Arizona</title>
 7:     <comments>A classic one-of-a-kind screwball love story.</comments>
 8:   </movie>
 9:
10:   <movie type="comedy" rating="R" review="5" year="1988">
11:     <title>Midnight Run</title>
12:     <comments>The quintessential road comedy.</comments>
13:   </movie>
14:
15:   <mus:music type="indy" review="5" year="1990">
16:     <mus:title>Cake</mus:title>
17:     <mus:artist>The Trash Can Sinatras</mus:artist>
18:     <mus:label>Polygram Records</mus:label>
19:     <mus:comments>Excellent acoustical instruments and extremely witty
20:        lyrics.</mus:comments>
21:   </mus:music>
22:
23:   <mus:music type="rock" review="5" year="1991">
24:     <mus:title>Travelers and Thieves</mus:title>
25:     <mus:artist>Blues Traveler</mus:artist>
26:     <mus:label>A&amp;M Records</mus:label>
27:     <mus:comments>The best Blues Traveler recording, period.</mus:comments>
28:   </mus:music>
29: </mediacollection>
```

7

The key to this code is the default namespace declaration, which is identified by the lone xmlns attribute (line 3); the xmlns:mus attribute explicitly declares the music namespace (line 4). When the xmlns attribute is used by itself with no associated prefix, it is declaring a default namespace, which in this case is the music namespace.

Namespaces and XSD Schemas

If you recall, I hedged a little back in Hour 5 when discussing namespaces as they relate to XSD schemas. Namespaces actually play an extremely important role in XSD schemas, but I didn't want to digress too much in that hour and sidetrack you with namespaces. For this reason, I want to revisit the topic of namespaces and XSD schemas to clarify exactly how namespaces impact schemas.

The xsd Prefix

The first thing to understand about namespaces and schemas is that there is nothing magical about the prefix xsd. If you recall from Hour 5, the prefix xsd is used with the XSD schema as a means of referencing elements and attributes that are used to construct schemas for your own custom markup languages. For example, following is the namespace declaration for the ETML.xsd schema document:

```
<xsd:schema xmlns:xsd="http://www.w3.org/2000/10/XMLSchema">
```

This code shows how the prefix xsd is used to declare the XSD schema explicitly. Now that you understand how prefixes work with explicit namespace declarations, you know that this prefix could be named anything you want. Of course, there is no reason to deviate from xsd since it has become somewhat of a standard among XML developers, but I wanted to point out that there is nothing hardwired into XML when it comes to namespace prefixes.

Referencing Schema Documents

In addition to providing a means of referencing the schema of schemas in your schema documents, namespaces also play an important role in documents that rely on an XSD schema for validation. The following code shows how the trainlog.xml document from Hour 5 uses the xmlns:xsi attribute to declare the namespace containing the noNamespaceSchemaLocation attribute. If this sounds confusing, I think a quick explanation will clear things up. In order to identify the physical schema document for a document, you must use a special attribute and assign the location of the schema document to it. There are two attributes you can use to accomplish this task:

- schemaLocation—locates a schema and its associated namespace
- noNamespaceSchemaLocation—locates a schema with no namespace

These attributes are standard attributes that are located in a namespace named
`http://www.w3.org/2000/10/XMLSchema-instance`. In order to properly reference
either of these attributes, you must first explicitly declare the namespace in which they
are located. It is standard to use the `xsi` prefix for this namespace, as the following
attribute assignment shows:

```
xmlns:xsi="http://www.w3.org/2000/10/XMLSchema-instance"
```

With this namespace declared, you can now use one of the schema location attributes to
reference the physical schema document. Following is an example of how this task was
carried out for the training log document back in Hour 5:

```
<trainlog
  xmlns:xsi="http://www.w3.org/2000/10/XMLSchema-instance"
  xsi:noNamespaceSchemaLocation="etml.xsd">
```

In this example the `noNamespaceSchemaLocation` attribute is used because you don't
care about associating the ETML schema with a namespace. If, however, you wanted to
associate it with a namespace, you would use the `schemaLocation` attribute instead:

```
<trainlog
  xmlns:xsi="http://www.w3.org/2000/10/XMLSchema-instance"
  xsi:schemaLocation="http://www.michaelmorrison.com/ns/etml etml.xsd">
```

Notice in the `schemaLocation` attribute that two pieces of information are provided: the
namespace for the schema and the location of the schema document. The
`schemaLocation` attribute is useful whenever you are working with a schema and you
want to associate it with a namespace.

Summary

If you're familiar with the old sitcom "Newhart," you no doubt remember the two brothers who were both named Darrel. Although brothers with the same first name make for
good comedy, similar names in XML documents can be problematic. I'm referring to
name clashes that can occur when elements and attributes are named the same across
multiple custom markup languages. This problem can be easily avoided by using namespaces, which allow you to associate elements and attributes with a unique name.
Namespaces are an important part of XML because they solve the problem of name
clashing among XML documents.

This hour introduced you to namespaces and also gave you some practical insight regarding how they are used in XML documents. You began the hour by learning the basics of
namespaces and their significance to XML. From there you learned how namespaces are

7

named. You then found out how to declare and use namespaces in documents. And finally, the hour concluded by revisiting XSD schemas and uncovering a few interesting tricks involving schemas and namespaces.

Q&A

Q **When a name clash occurs in an XML document, why can't an XML proces-sor resolve it by looking at the scope of the elements and attributes, as opposed to requiring namespaces?**

A Although it is technically possible for an XML processor to resolve an element or attribute based solely on its scope, it isn't a good idea to put that much faith in the processor. Besides, there are some situations where this simply isn't possible. For example, what if the element causing the name clash is the root element in a docu-ment? Because it has a global scope, there is no way to determine the schema to which it belongs.

Q **Do I have to use a namespace to uniquely identify the elements and attributes in my custom markup language?**

A No. In fact, if you never plan on sharing your schema with others or using it in conjunction with other schemas, then there really is no pressing need to declare a unique namespace.

Q **Why would I ever want to create a modular schema?**

A Modular schemas enter the picture only when a schema gets large and complex. When this happens, it can often be difficult to maintain a grasp on the schema because the schema document is so huge. By breaking the document down into modular components, the overall structure of the schema becomes easier to under-stand. Modular schemas also are very useful when there is information that is repeated throughout a schema because you can simply reference the information in multiple places rather than duplicating the code.

Workshop

The Workshop is designed to help you anticipate possible questions, review what you've learned, and begin learning how to put your knowledge into practice.

Quiz

1. Why are namespaces named after URIs?

2. What is the general form of a namespace declaration?

3. What is the difference between default and explicit namespace declaration?

Quiz Answers

1. Namespaces are named after URIs because URIs are guaranteed to be unique.

2. The general form of a namespace declaration is `xmlns:Prefix="NameSpace"`.

3. A default namespace declaration is useful when you want to apply a namespace to an entire document or section of a document, whereas an explicit namespace is useful whenever you want exacting control over the elements and attributes that are associated with a namespace

Exercises

1. Using a domain name that you or your company owns, determine a unique namespace name that you could use with the Tall Tales document from Hour 4.

2. Modify the Tall Tales document from Hour 4 so that the elements and attributes defined in its schema are associated with the namespace you just created.

7

Hour 8

Validating XML Documents

In the future, airplanes will be flown by a dog and a pilot. And the dog's job will be to make sure that if the pilot tries to touch any of the buttons, the dog bites him.

—Scott Adams

In the quote, the job of Scott Adams's dog is to prevent human error in piloting an airplane. The idea is that computers will have things enough under control that human pilots will only get in the way. Although the complete removal of human pilots is not too probable in the near future, the prospect of computer-flown airplanes highlights the need for rock solid software systems that are 100% error free. Whether or not you look forward to flying on an airplane piloted by computers, as an XML developer you should make it a huge priority to develop XML documents that are 100% error free.

Fortunately, schemas (DTDs and XSDs) make it possible to assess the validity of XML documents. This hour shows you how to use various tools to validate documents against a DTD or XSD.

In this hour, you'll learn

- The ins and outs of document validation
- The basics of validation tools and how to use them
- How to assess and repair invalid XML documents

Document Validation Revisited

As you know by now, the goal of most XML documents is to be a valid document. Document validity is extremely important because it guarantees that the data within a document conforms to a standard set of guidelines as laid out in a schema (DTD or XSD). Not all documents have to be valid, which is why I used the word "most" a moment ago. For example, some XML applications might use XML to code small chunks of data that really don't require the thorough validation options made possible by a schema. Even in this case, however, all XML documents must be well formed. A well-formed document, as you may recall, is a document that adheres to the fundamental structure of the XML language. Rules for well-formed documents include matching start tags with end tags and setting values for all attributes used.

An XML application can certainly determine if a document is well formed without any other information, but it requires a schema in order to assess document validity. This schema typically comes in the form of a DTD (Document Type Definition) or XSD (XML Schema Definition), which you learned about in Hours 4 and 5. To recap, schemas allow you to establish the following ground rules that XML documents must adhere to in order to be considered valid:

- Establish the elements that can appear in an XML document, along with the attributes that can be used with each
- Determine whether an element is empty or contains content (text and/or child elements)
- Determine the number and sequence of child elements within an element
- Set the default value for attributes

It's probably safe to say that you have a good grasp on the usefulness of schemas, but you might be wondering about the details of how an XML document is actually validated with a schema. This task begins with the *XML processor,* which is typically a part of an

XML application. The job of an XML processor is to process XML documents and somehow make the results available for further processing or display within an application. A modern Web browser, such as Internet Explorer 5.5, includes an XML processor that is capable of processing an XML document and displaying it using a style sheet. The XML processor knows nothing about the style sheet—it just hands over the processed XML content for the browser to render.

The actual processing of an XML document is carried out by a special piece of software known as an *XML parser*. An XML parser is responsible for the nitty-gritty details of reading the characters in an XML document and resolving them into meaningful tags and relevant data. There are two types of parsers capable of being used during the processing of an XML document:

- Standard (nonvalidating) parser
- Validating parser

A standard XML parser, or nonvalid parser, reads and analyzes a document to ensure that it is well formed. A standard parser basically checks to make sure that you've followed the basic language and syntax rules of XML. Standard XML parsers do not check to see if a document is valid—that's the job of a validating parser. A validating parser picks up where a standard parser leaves off by comparing a document with its schema and making sure it adheres to the rules laid out in the schema. Because a document must be well formed as part of being valid, a standard parser is still used when a document is being validated. In other words, a standard parser first checks to see if a document is well formed, and then a validating parser checks to see if it is valid.

 In actuality, a validating parser includes a standard parser so that there is technically only one parser that can operate in two different modes.

When you begin looking for a means to validate your documents, make sure you find an XML application that includes a validating parser. Without a validating parser, there is no way to validate your documents. You can still see if they are well formed by using a standard parser only, which is certainly important, but it's generally a good idea to go ahead and carry out a full validation.

Validation Tools

It's good to develop an eye for clean XML code, which makes it possible to develop XML documents with a minimal amount of errors. However, it's difficult for any human to perform such a technical task flawlessly, which is where XML validation tools come into play. XML validation tools are used to analyze the contents of XML documents to make sure they conform to a schema. There are two main types of validation tools available:

- Web-based tools
- Standalone tools

Web-based tools are Web pages that allow you to enter the path (URI) of an XML document to have it validated. The upside to Web-based tools is that they can be used without installing special software—just open the Web page in a Web browser and go for it! The downside to Web-based validation tools is that they sometimes don't work well when you don't have files available on the Internet. For example, if you're working on an XML document on your local hard drive, it can be tough getting a Web-based validation tool to work properly. Typically it's a matter of getting the tool to recognize the schema; if the schema is located on the Internet there usually isn't a problem, but if it's located on your local hard drive as well, then it can be tough getting things to work properly.

If you're planning to do a lot of XML development work on your local hard drive, then you might want to consider using a standalone validation tool. Standalone validation tools are tools that you must install on your computer in order to use. These kinds of tools range from full-blown XML editors such as XML Spy to command-line XML validators such as the W3C's XSV validator. Standalone validation tools have the benefit of allowing you to validate local files with ease. The drawback to these tools is that some of them aren't cheap, and they must be installed on your computer. However, if you don't mind spending a little money, a standalone tool can come in extremely handy.

For the record, not all stand-alone tools cost money. For example, the W3C's XSV validator is available for free download at http://www.w3.org/XML/Schema.

Regardless of what type of validation tool you decide to use, it's important to point out that there is a big distinction between validating documents against DTDs and validating them against XSDs. Although some tools support both types of schemas, many tools do not. You should therefore consider what type of schema you plan on using when assessing the different tools out there.

DTD Validation

DTDs have been around much longer than XSDs, so you'll find that there are many more validation tools available for DTDs. One of the best tools I've found is made available by Brown University's Scholarly Technology Group, or STG. STG's tool comes in the form of a Web page known as the XML Validation Web page, which is accessible online at `http://www.stg.brown.edu/service/xmlvalid/`. Of course, this validation tool falls into the category of Web-based tools. Figure 8.1 shows the STG XML Validation Web page.

FIGURE 8.1

Brown University's Scholarly Technology Group has an XML Validation Web page that can be used to validate DTDs.

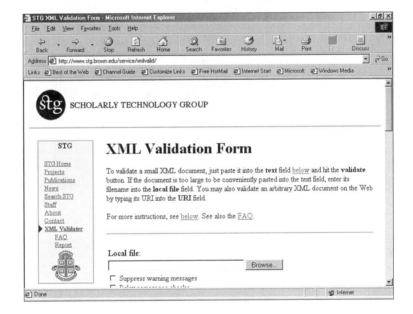

Similar to most Web-based validation tools, there are two approaches available for validating documents with the XML Validation Web page:

- Access the document on the Internet
- Access the document locally

Depending on your circumstances, the latter option is probably the simplest since you will likely be developing XML documents locally. As I mentioned earlier, sometimes validators have problems with local schemas, so the easier route in terms of having the validator run smoothly is to stick your document(s) and schema on a computer that is accessible on the Internet via a URI. That way you are guaranteeing that the validator can find the document and its schema, both of which are required for validation.

After specifying the document to the XML Validation Web page and hitting the Validate button, any errors found during validation will be displayed in your Web browser (Figure 8.2).

FIGURE 8.2

The STG XML Validation Web page reveals errors in an XML document during validation.

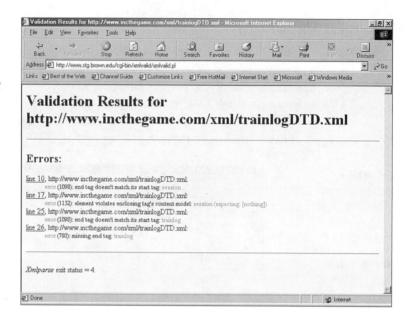

In the figure I deliberately removed a closing `</comments>` tag, which invalidates the document. Fortunately, the XML Validation Web page caught the problem and alerted me. After repairing the problem and initiating the validation process again, everything turns out fine (Figure 8.3).

FIGURE 8.3

The STG XML Validation Web page reports that a document is indeed valid.

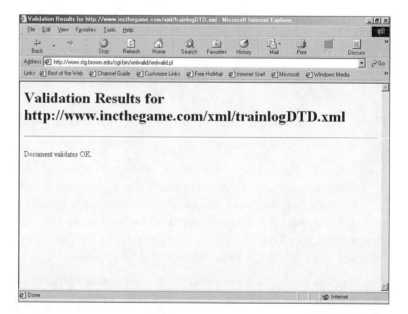

If you want a quick (and affordable) way to validate local documents against a DTD, then I highly recommend Microsoft's XML Notepad, which you first learned about in Hour 2. You can download XML Notepad for free from Microsoft's Developer Network Web site at `http://msdn.microsoft.com/library/en-us/dnxml/html/xmlpadintro.asp`. The version of XML Notepad currently available is actually a beta release, but it still works quite well for validating XML documents against DTDs. Figure 8.4 shows XML Notepad reporting an error in a document during validation.

FIGURE 8.4

Microsoft's XML Notepad is a good tool for performing DTD document validation on local XML documents.

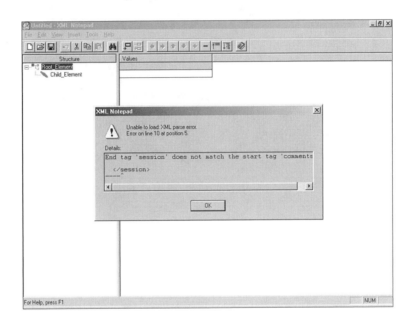

A significant step up from XML Notepad is XML Spy, by Altova, which includes extensive support for XML document viewing, editing, and validation using both DTDs and XSDs. XML Spy isn't free, but you can download a 30-day evaluation version from the XML Spy Web site at `http://www.xmlspy.com/`. When you initially open a document in XML Spy, it will automatically attempt to validate the document against a DTD or XSD if one exists. If no schema exists, XML Spy will still check to make sure the document is well formed. Figure 8.5 shows a document with an error after validation has failed in XML Spy.

FIGURE 8.5

XML Spy is quite adept at catching errors in XML documents during validation.

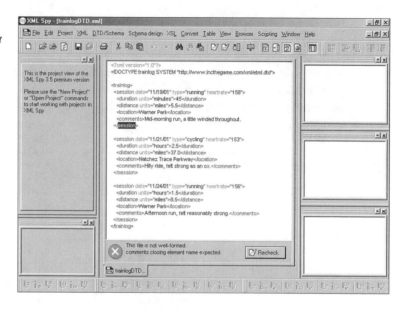

You can tell in the figure that XML Spy is extremely informative when it comes to detecting errors and alerting you to them. In fact, in this example the line of code immediately following the missing `</comments>` tag is highlighted to indicate where the problem lies. This kind of detailed error analysis is what makes tools such as XML Spy earn their keep. Figure 8.6 shows a successfully validated document in XML Spy.

FIGURE 8.6

Once a file has been successfully validated, you can use XML Spy's graphical user interface to view and edit the document visually.

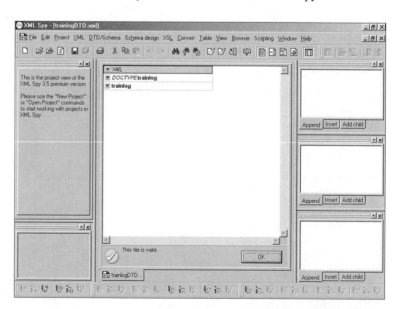

In addition to DTD and XSD validation, XML Spy includes loads of other features that make it a reasonable investment if you plan on doing much XML document development. In case you're wondering, this isn't an endorsement for XML Spy; I just happened to find it a useful XML tool with an evaluation version that was freely available for download. There are other XML tools on the market with similar features, and I encourage you to investigate several of them before making a purchase. Visit XML.com at `http://www.xml.com/` to learn more about available tools.

XSD Validation

You'll be glad to know that validating XML documents against an XSD is not much different than validating them against DTDs. It's still important to have the XSD properly associated with the documents, as you learned how to do back in Hour 5. Once that's done, it's basically a matter of feeding the document to a validation tool that is capable of handling XSD schemas. Unfortunately, XSD is a new enough technology that there aren't as many tools that support it, at least compared to those that support DTDs. Even so, it's not as if you need an army of validation tools to validate your documents—one is enough to do the job in most cases!

The best Web-based XSD validation tool is made available by the W3C. Not surprisingly, this tool is called the W3C Validator for XML Schema and is located at `http://www.w3.org/2001/03/webdata/xsv/`. This Web-based validator works similarly to the Web-based DTD validator you learned about in the previous section. You specify the URI of a document and the validator does all the work. Figure 8.7 shows the main page for the W3C Validator.

The underlying XML processor used in the W3C Validator for XML Schema Web page is called XSV and is also available from the W3C as a standalone validator. You can download this standalone command-line validator for free from the W3C at `http://www.w3.org/XML/Schema`.

FIGURE 8.7

The W3C Validator for XML Schema is a Web-based tool for validating XML documents against XSD schemas.

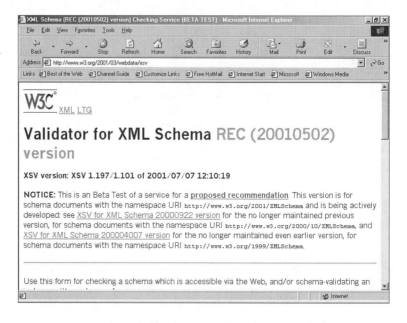

If you are planning on working with a lot of documents locally or maybe are looking for additional features in a validation tool, then I'd return to the familiar XML Spy tool I mentioned in the previous section. In addition to DTD validation, XML Spy also supports XSD validation. Figure 8.8 shows a document that fails validation against an XSD in XML Spy.

FIGURE 8.8

A document fails validation in XML Spy due to the misusage of an enumerated data type.

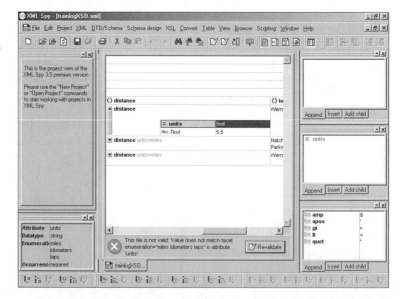

As you may notice in the figure, the specific error in the document is the misusage of an enumerated data type. Following is the line of code causing the error:

```
<distance units="feet">5.5</distance>
```

If you recall, the `units` attribute of the `distance` element expects a value of `miles`, `kilometers`, or `laps`. Since the attribute is set to `feet`, which doesn't conform to the XSD, the document is ruled invalid by XML Spy. That's exactly the kind of error-reporting information you want out of a validation tool.

Repairing Invalid Documents

If you have any programming experience, then the term "debugging" is no doubt familiar to you. If not, get ready because debugging is often the most difficult part of any software development project. Debugging refers to the process of finding and fixing errors in a software application. Depending on the complexity of the code in an application, debugging can get quite messy. The process of repairing invalid XML documents is in many ways similar to debugging software. However, XML isn't a programming language and XML documents aren't programs, which makes things considerably easier for XML developers. That's the good news.

The other good news is that validation tools give you a huge boost when it comes to making your XML documents free of errors. Not only do most validation tools alert you to the existence of errors in a document, but also most of them will give you a pretty good idea about where the errors are in the document. This is no small benefit. Even an experienced XML developer can overlook the most obvious errors after staring at code for long periods of time. Not only that, but XML is an extremely picky language, which leaves the door wide open for you to make mistakes. Errors are, unfortunately, a natural part of the development process, be it software, XML documents, or typing skills that you are developing.

So, knowing that your XML documents are bound to have a few mistakes, how do you go about finding and eliminating the errors? The first step is to run the document through a standard XML parser to check that the document is well formed. Remember that any validation tool will check if a document is well formed if you don't associate the document with a schema. So, the first time you create a document take it for a spin through a validation tool without associating it with a schema. At this stage the tool will report only errors in the document that have to do with it being well formed. In other words, no validity checks will be made, which is fine for now.

Errors occurring during the well-formed check include typos in element and attribute names, unmatched tag pairs, and unquoted attribute values, to name a few. These errors should be relatively easy to find, and at some point you should get pretty good at creating documents that are close to being well-formed the first try. In other words, it isn't too terribly difficult to avoid the errors that keep a document from being well formed.

Once you've determined that your document is well formed, you can wire it back to a schema and take a shot at checking it for validity. Don't be too disappointed if several errors are reported the first time around. Keep in mind that you are working with a very demanding technology in XML that insists on things being absolutely 100% accurate. You must use elements and attributes in the exact manner as they are mentioned in a schema; anything else will lead to validity errors.

Perhaps the trickiest validity error is that of invalid nesting. If you accidentally close an element in the wrong place with a misplaced end tag, it can really confuse a validation tool and give you some strange results. Following is a simple example of what I'm talking about:

```
<session date="2001-11-19" type="running" heartrate="158">
  <duration>PT45M</duration>
  <distance units="miles">5.5</distance>
  <location>Warner Park</location>
  <comments>Mid-morning run, a little winded throughout.
</session>
</comments>
```

In this code the closing `</comments>` tag appears after the closing `</session>` tag, which is an overlap error because the entire `comments` element should be inside of the `session` element. The problem with this kind of error is that it often confuses the validation tool. There is no doubting that you'll get an error report, but it may not isolate the error as you had hoped. It's even possible for the validation tool to get confused to the extent that a domino effect results, where the single misplaced tag causes many other errors. So, if you get a slew of errors that don't seem to make much sense, study your document carefully and make sure all of your start and end tags match up properly.

Beyond the misplaced end tag problem, most validity errors are relatively easy to track down with the help of a good validation tool. Just pay close attention to the output of the tool, and tackle each error one at a time. With a little diligence, you can have valid documents without much work.

Summary

In previous hours you learned how to create XML documents and schemas that could be used to validate those documents for technical accuracy. What you didn't learn how to do, however, was actually carry out the validation of XML documents. Document validation isn't something you can carry out yourself with a pencil and piece of paper, or even a calculator—validation is an automated process carried out by a special software application known as a validation tool, or validator. Validation tools are a critical part of the XML development process because they allow you to determine the correctness of your documents.

In this hour you learned how document validation is carried out by XML applications. More specifically, you learned about standard and validating parsers and how they fit into the validation equation. You then learned how to use some of the different validation tools available for use in validating XML documents. And finally, you found out how to track down and repair errors in XML documents.

Q&A

Q Is it possible to validate HTML Web pages?

A Strictly speaking, it isn't possible to validate HTML-based documents because HTML isn't actually an XML language and therefore doesn't conform to the rules of XML. However, you can code Web pages in XHTML, which is a markup language that can be validated. XHTML is an XML-based language that is very similar to HTML but with the improved structure of XML. You learn all about XHTML in Hour 18, "Getting to Know XHTML."

Q Do I have to check a document for well-formedness before moving on to checking it for validity?

A No. I recommend only the two-stage check on a document because it helps to clarify the different types of errors commonly found in XML documents. Your goal should be to develop enough XML coding skills to avoid most well-formedness errors, which frees you up to spend most of your time tackling the peskier validity errors. Knowing this, at some point you may decide to jump straight into the validity check for documents as you gain experience.

Workshop

The Workshop is designed to help you anticipate possible questions, review what you've learned, and begin learning how to put your knowledge into practice.

Quiz

1. What is an XML processor?
2. What's the difference between a standard parser and a validating parser?
3. What is the main limitation of Web-based XML validation tools?

Quiz Answers

1. An XML processor is usually part of a larger XML application, and its job is to process XML documents and somehow make the results available for further processing or display within the application.

2. A standard parser first checks to see if a document is well formed, whereas a validating parser further checks to see if it is valid.

3. Web-based XML validation tools can be difficult to use when the documents to be validated (and their associated schemas) are stored on a local hard drive.

Exercises

1. Modify one of the training log example documents so that the code intentionally violates the ETML schema. Run the file through a validation tool and take note of the error(s) reported.

2. Repair the error code in the training log document and make sure that it validates properly in a validation tool.

PART III

Formatting and Displaying XML Documents

Hour

HOUR 9

XML Formatting Strategies

A doctor can bury his mistakes, but an architect can only advise his clients to plant vines.

—Frank Lloyd Wright

One mistake I hope you don't make is to select the wrong formatting technology for displaying your XML documents. There are two fundamentally different approaches, both of which you learn about in this hour and in the remainder of this part of the book. I'm referring to Cascading Style Sheets (CSS) and eXtensible Style Language (XSL). CSS is already in use around the Web as a means of formatting HTML Web pages above and beyond the limited formatting capabilities of HTML. XSL, on the other hand, is purely designed for use with XML and is ultimately much more powerful and flexible than CSS. Even so, these technologies aren't really in competition with each other. As you learn in this hour, they offer unique solutions to different problems, so you will likely find a use for each of them in different scenarios.

In this hour, you'll learn

- The basics of style sheets and XML formatting
- When and why to use CSS and XSL on the Web
- The practical differences between CSS and XSL style sheets

Style Sheets and XML Formatting

Very few XML-based markup languages are designed to accommodate the formatting of content described with them. This makes sense considering that the whole premise of XML is to provide a way of associating meaning to information. The appearance of information is very much a secondary issue in XML. Of course, there are situations where it can be very important to view XML content in a more understandable context than raw XML code (elements and attributes), in which case it becomes necessary to format the content for display. Formatting XML content for display primarily involves determining the layout and positioning of the content, along with the fonts and colors used to render the content and any related graphics that accompany the content. XML content is typically formatted for specific display purposes, such as within a Web browser.

XML documents are formatted using special formatting instructions known as *styles*. A style can be something as simple as a font size or as powerful as a transformation of an XML element to an HTML element. The general mechanism used to apply formatting to XML documents is known as a *style sheet*. I say "general" because there are two different approaches to styling XML documents with style sheets: CSS (Cascading Style Sheets) and XSL (eXtensible Style Language). Although I'd love to jump into a detailed discussion of CSS and XSL, I think a quick history lesson is in order so that you understand the relevance of style sheets. The next couple of sections provide you with some background on style sheets as they relate to HTML, along with how they enter the picture with XML.

The Need for Style Sheets

If it wasn't for the success of HTML, it's unlikely that XML would have ever been created. The concept of using a markup language to code information is nothing new, but the idea of doing it with a simple, compact language is entirely new. HTML is the first markup language that made it possible to code information in a relatively compact format that could be displayed without too much complexity. However, HTML was never designed as a presentation language. Generally speaking, markup languages are designed to add structure and context to information, which usually has nothing to do with how the information is displayed. The idea is that you use markup to describe the content of documents and then apply styles to the content to render it for display purposes. The problem with this approach is that it hasn't been used much with HTML. This has to do with the fact that HTML evolved so rapidly that presentation elements were added to the language without any concern over how it might complicate things.

In its original form, HTML stuck to the notion of being a purely content-based markup language. More specifically, HTML was designed as a markup language that allowed physicists to share technical notes. Early Web browsers allowed you to view HTML documents, but the browsers, not the HTML markup, determined the layout of the documents. For example, paragraphs marked up with the <p> tag might have been displayed in a 12-point Arial font in a certain browser. A different browser might have used a 14-point Helvetica font. The point is that the browsers made the presentation decisions, not the documents themselves, which is in keeping with the general concept of a markup language.

As you probably know, things changed quickly for HTML when the popularity of the Web necessitated improvements in the appearance of Web pages. In fact, HTML quickly turned into something it was never meant to be—a jumbled mess of content and presentation markup. At the time it made sense to hack on presentation elements to HTML because it allowed for better-looking Web pages. Another factor that complicated HTML was the "browser wars," which pitted Web browser vendors against one another in a game of feature one-upmanship that resulted in all kinds of new HTML presentation tags. These tags proved extremely problematic for Web developers because they were usually supported on only one browser or another.

To summarize my HTML soapbox speech, we all got a little carried away and tried to turn HTML into something it was never intended to be. No one really thought about what would happen after a few years of tacking on tag after presentation tag to HTML. Now the Web development community has taken some time to assess the future of the Web and is going back to the ideal of separating content from presentation. Style sheets provide the mechanism that makes it possible to separate content from presentation and bring some order to HTML. Whereas style sheets are a good idea for HTML documents, they are a necessity for displaying XML documents—more on this in a moment. A style sheet addresses the presentation needs of HTML documents by defining layout and formatting rules that tell a browser how to display the different parts of a document.

Unlike HTML, XML doesn't include any standard elements that can be used to describe the appearance of XML documents. For example, there is no standard <b> tag in XML for adding bold formatting to text in XML. For this reason, style sheets are an absolute necessity when it comes to displaying XML documents.

Technically, you could create your own XML-based markup language and include any presentation-specific tags you wanted, such as <bold>, <big>, <small>, <blurry>, and so on. However, Web browsers are designed specifically to understand HTML and HTML only and therefore wouldn't inherently understand your presentation tags. This is why style sheets are so important to XML.

Getting to Know CSS and XSL

Style sheets aren't really anything new to Web developers, but they've been very slow to take off primarily due to the fact that browser support for them has been sketchy up until recent versions. *Cascading Style Sheets,* or *CSS,* represent the HTML approach to style sheets because they were designed specifically to solve the presentation problems inherent in HTML. Since CSS originally targeted HTML, it has been around the longest and has garnered the most support among Web developers. Even so, CSS has been plagued by inconsistent support in Web browsers; only the latest releases of Internet Explorer and Netscape Navigator fully support CSS without glaring inconsistencies.

eXtensible Style Language, XSL, is a much newer technology than CSS and represents the pure XML approach to styling XML documents. XSL has had somewhat of a hurdle to clear in terms of browser acceptance but the latest releases of both Internet Explorer and Netscape Navigator provide solid support for a subset of XSL known as XSLT (XSL Transformation), which allows you to translate XML documents into HTML. XSLT doesn't tackle the same layout and formatting issues as CSS and therefore isn't really a competing technology. The layout and formatting portion of XSL is known as XSL Formatting Objects, or XSL-FO, and is rapidly approaching the status of formal recommendation, which is essentially the W3C's stamp of approval for new technologies. Unfortunately, Web browsers typically trail the W3C in terms of embracing and supporting new technologies, so we aren't likely to see XSL-FO support in Web browsers for a little while.

Since XSL-FO is a relatively complex technology that is currently unsupported in Web browsers, I opted not to cover it in any significant detail in this book. However, you learn a great deal about XSLT in Hour 12, "eXtensible Style Language (XSL) Fundamentals," and Hour 13, "Transforming XML with XSLT." XSLT provides plenty of flexibility in terms of translating XML documents for display in Web browsers.

Generally speaking, you can think of XSL's relationship to XML as being similar to CSS's relationship to HTML. This comparison isn't entirely accurate since XSL effectively defines a superset of the styling functionality in CSS thanks to XSL-FO. The next couple of sections explain CSS and XSL in more detail.

Cascading Style Sheets (CSS)

As you've learned, CSS is a style sheet language designed to style HTML documents, thereby allowing Web developers to separate content from presentation. Prior to CSS, the only options for styling HTML documents were scripting languages and hybrid solutions such as Dynamic HTML (DHTML). CSS is much simpler to learn and use than these approaches, which makes it ideal for styling HTML documents. Although CSS was designed for use with HTML, there is nothing stopping you from using it with XML. In fact, it is quite useful for styling XML documents.

When a CSS style sheet is applied to an XML document, it uses the structure of the document as the basis for applying style rules. More specifically, the hierarchical "tree" of document data is used to apply style rules. Although this works in some scenarios, it's sometimes necessary to alter the structure of an XML document before applying style rules. For example, you might want to sort the contents of a document alphabetically before displaying it. CSS is very useful for styling XML data, but it has no way of allowing you to collate, sort, or otherwise rearrange document data. This type of task is best suited to a transformation technology such as XSLT. The bottom line is that CSS is better suited to the simple styling of XML documents. Of course, you can always transform a document using XSLT and then style it with CSS, which is in many ways the best of both worlds, at least in terms of XML and style sheets.

On behalf of die-hard CSS advocates, I'd like to point out that you can transform an XML document using a scripting language and the Document Object Model (DOM) prior to applying CSS style sheets, which achieves roughly the same effect as using XSLT to transform the document. Although the DOM certainly presents an option for transforming XML documents, there are those of us who would rather use a structured transformation language instead of having to rely on custom scripts. You learn how to use scripts and the DOM with XML in Part IV, "Processing and Managing XML Data."

Extensible Style Language (XSL)

Earlier in the hour I mentioned that XSL consists of two primary components that address the styling of XML documents: XSLT and XSL-FO. XSLT stands for XSL Transformation and is the component of XSL that allows you to transform an XML document from one language to another. For example, with XSLT you could translate one of your custom ETML documents into HTML that is capable of being displayed in a Web browser. The other part of XSL is XSL-FO, which stands for XSL Formatting Objects. XSL-FO is somewhat of a supercharged CSS designed specifically for XML. Both XSLT and XSL-FO are implemented as XML-based markup languages. Using these two languages, Web developers have control over both the transformation of XML document content and its subsequent display.

Since both components of XSL are implemented as XML languages, style sheets created from them are XML documents. This allows you to create XSL style sheets using familiar XML syntax, not to mention being able to use XML development tools. You might see a familiar connection between XSL and another fairly new XML technology, XML Schema. As you may recall from the previous hour, XML Schema is implemented as an XML language (XSD) that replaces a pre-XML approach (DTD) for describing the structure of XML documents. XSL is similar in that it, too, employs XML languages to eventually replace a pre-XML approach (CSS) to styling XML documents.

Rendering XML with Style Sheets

Although the general premise of style sheets is to provide a means of displaying XML content, it's important to understand that style sheets still don't have complete control over how XML content appears. For example, text that is styled with emphasis in a style sheet might be displayed in italics in a traditional browser, but it could be spoken with emphasis in a browser for the visually impaired. This distinction doesn't necessarily impact the creation of style sheets, but it is worth keeping in mind, especially as new types of Web-enabled devices are created. Some of these new devices will render documents in different ways than we're currently accustomed to.

The concept of different devices rendering XML documents in different ways has been referred to as *cross-medium rendering* due to the fact that the devices typically represent different mediums. Historically, HTML has had to contend with *cross-browser rendering,* which was caused by different browsers supporting different presentation tags. Even though style sheets alleviate the cross-browser problem, they don't always deal with the cross-medium problem. To understand what I mean by this, consider CSS style sheets, which provide a means of applying layout rules to XML so that it can be displayed. The relatively simplistic styling approach taken by CSS isn't powerful enough to deal with the cross-medium issue because it can't transform an XML document into a different format, which is often required to successfully render a document in a different medium.

XSLT addresses the need for transforming XML documents according to a set of highly structured patterns. For display purposes, you can use XSLT to translate an XML document into an HTML document. This is the primary way XML developers are currently using XSL because it doesn't require anything more on the part of browsers than support for XSLT; they don't have to be able to render a document directly from XML. CSS doesn't involve any transformation; it simply provides a means of describing how different parts of a document should be displayed.

9

Some people incorrectly perceive XSL and CSS as competing technologies, but they really aren't. Granted, XSL-FO does everything that CSS can do, and much more, and if the W3C has its way, FSL-FO will eventually replace CSS.

Leveraging CSS and XSLT on the Web

You've already spent some time learning about the differences between CSS and XSL, but it's worth going through a more detailed comparison so that you have a solid understanding of your style sheet options. More importantly, I want to point out some of the issues for choosing one style sheet technology over the other when working with documents in a Web environment. The technologies are just similar enough that it can be difficult determining when to use which one. You may find that the best approach to styling XML documents is a hybrid approach involving both XSL and CSS.

There are two key differences between XSLT and CSS, both of which I've alluded to earlier in the hour:

- CSS allows you to style HTML documents (XSLT cannot)
- XSLT allows you to transform XML documents (CSS cannot)

You're here to learn about XML, not HTML, so the first difference between CSS and XSLT might not seem to matter much. However, when you consider the fact that many XML applications currently involve HTML documents to some degree, this may be an issue when assessing the appropriate style sheet technology for a given project. The second difference is critical in that CSS provides no direct means of transforming XML documents. You can use a scripting language with the DOM to transform XML documents, but that's another issue that requires considerable knowledge of XML scripting, which you gain in Part IV, "Processing and Managing XML Data." Unlike scripting languages, CSS was explicitly designed for use by nonprogrammers, which explains why it is so easy to learn and use. CSS simply attaches style properties to elements in an XML/HTML document. The simplicity of CSS comes with limitations, some of which follow:

- CSS cannot reuse document data
- CSS cannot conditionally select document data (other than hiding specific types of elements)
- CSS cannot calculate quantities or store values in variables
- CSS cannot generate dynamic text, such as page numbers

These limitations of CSS are important because they are noticeably missing in XSLT. In other words, XSLT is capable of carrying out these tasks and therefore doesn't suffer from the same weaknesses. If you don't mind a steeper learning curve, the XSLT capabilities for searching and rearranging document content are far superior to CSS. Of course, XSLT doesn't directly support formatting styles in the way that CSS does, so you may find that using XSLT by itself still falls short in some regards. This may lead you to consider pairing XSLT with CSS for the ultimate flexibility in styling XML documents. Following are a couple of ways that XSLT and CSS can be used together to provide a hybrid XML style sheet solution:

1. Use XSLT to transform XML documents into HTML documents that are styled with CSS style sheets.
2. Use XSLT to transform XML documents into XML documents that are styled with CSS style sheets.

The first approach represents the most straightforward combination of XSLT and CSS because its results are in HTML form, which is more easily understood by Web browsers. In fact, a Web browser doesn't even know that XML is involved when using this approach; all that the browser sees is a regular HTML document that is the result of an XSLT transformation on the server. The second approach is interesting because it involves styling XML code directly in browsers. This means that it isn't necessary to first transform XML documents into HTML documents; the only transformation that takes place in this case is the transformation from one XML document into another XML document that is better suited for presentation.

CSS and XSLT in Action

The next few hours spend plenty of time exploring the inner workings of CSS and XSLT, but I hate for you to leave this hour without seeing a practical example of each technology in action. Earlier in the book I used an XML document (talltales.xml) that contained questions and answers for a trivia game called Tall Tales as an example. I'd like to revisit that document, as it presents a perfect opportunity to demonstrate the basic usage of CSS and XSLT style sheets. Listing 9.1 is the Tall Tales trivia document:

LISTING 9.1 The Tall Tales Example XML Document

```
 1: <?xml version="1.0"?>
 2:
 3: <talltales>
 4:   <tt answer="a">
 5:     <question>
 6:       In 1994, a man had an accident while robbing a pizza restaurant in
 7:       Akron, Ohio, that resulted in his arrest. What happened to him?
 8:     </question>
 9:     <a>He slipped on a patch of grease on the floor and knocked himself out.</a>
10:     <b>He backed into a police car while attempting to drive off.</b>
11:     <c>He choked on a breadstick that he had grabbed as he was running out.</c>
12:   </tt>
13:
14:   <tt answer="c">
15:     <question>
16:       In 1993, a man was charged with burglary in Martinsville, Indiana,
17:       after the homeowners discovered his presence. How were the homeowners
18:       alerted to his presence?
19:     </question>
20:     <a>He had rung the doorbell before entering.</a>
21:     <b>He had rattled some pots and pans while making himself a waffle in
22:       their kitchen.</b>
23:     <c>He was playing their piano.</c>
24:   </tt>
25:
26:   <tt answer="a">
27:     <question>
28:       In 1994, the Nestle UK food company was fined for injuries suffered
29:       by a 36 year-old employee at a plant in York, England. What happened
30:       to the man?
31:     </question>
32:     <a>He fell in a giant mixing bowl and was whipped for over a minute.</a>
33:     <b>He developed an ulcer while working as a candy bar tester.</b>
34:     <c>He was hit in the head with a large piece of flying chocolate.</c>
35:   </tt>
36: </talltales>
```

Nothing is too tricky here; it's just XML code for questions and answers in a quirky trivia game. Notice that each question/answer set is enclosed within a tt element—this will be important in a moment when you see the XSLT style sheet used to transform the document. Before you get to that, however, you must first see the easier solution to styling the document, which involves a CSS style sheet.

The CSS Solution

The CSS solution to styling any XML document is simply to provide style rules for the different elements in the document. These style rules are applied to all of the elements in a document in order to provide a visualization of the document. In the case of the Tall Tales document, there are really only five elements of interest: tt, question, a, b, and c. Listing 9.2 is the CSS style sheet (talltales.css) that defines style rules for these elements:

LISTING 9.2   The talltales.css CSS Style Sheet for Formatting the Tall Tales XML Document

```
 1: tt {
 2:   display: block;
 3:   width: 750px;
 4:   padding: 10px;
 5:   margin-bottom: 10px;
 6:   border: 4px double black;
 7:   background-color: silver;
 8: }
 9:
10: question {
11:   display: block;
12:   color: black;
13:   font-family: Times, serif;
14:   font-size: 16pt;
15:   text-align: left;
16: }
17:
18: a, b, c {
19:   display: block;
20:   color: brown;
21:   font-family: Times, serif;
22:   font-size: 12pt;
23:   text-indent: 15px;
24:   text-align: left;
25: }
```

Before we go any further, understand that I don't expect you to understand this CSS code. You don't formally learn about CSS style rules until the next hour—right now I just wanted to throw out a practical example so you could at least see what a CSS style sheet looks like. If you already have experience with CSS by way of HTML, then this style sheet should be pretty easy to understand. If not, then you can hopefully study it and at least take in the high points. For example, it's not too hard to figure out that colors and fonts are being set for each of the elements. Figure 9.1 shows the result of using this style sheet to display the `talltales.xml` document in Internet Explorer.

FIGURE 9.1

The Tall Tales example document is displayed in Internet Explorer using a CSS style sheet.

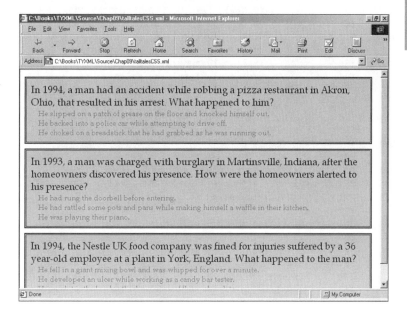

Although you can't quite make out the colors in this figure, it's apparent from the style sheet code that colors are being used to display the elements. Now it's time to take a look at how XSLT can be used to arrive at the same visual result.

The XSLT Solution

The XSLT approach to the Tall Tales document involves translating the document into HTML. Although it's possible to simply translate the document into HTML and let HTML do the job of determining how the data is displayed, a better idea is to use inline CSS styles to format the data directly within the HTML code. Keep in mind that when you translate an XML document into HTML using XSLT, you can include anything that you would otherwise include in an HTML document, including inline CSS styles. Listing 9.3 is the XSLT style sheet (`talltales.xsl`) for use with the Tall Tales document:

LISTING 9.3   The `talltales.xsl` XSLT Style Sheet for Transforming the Tall Tales XML Document into HTML

```
 1: <?xml version="1.0"?>
 2: <xsl:stylesheet xmlns:xsl="http://www.w3.org/TR/WD-xsl">
 3:   <xsl:template match="/">
 4:     <html>
 5:       <head>
 6:       </head>
 7:       <body>
 8:         <xsl:for-each select="talltales/tt">
 9:           <div style="width:750px; padding:10px; margin-bottom: 10px;
10:             border:4px double black; background-color:silver">
11:             <xsl:apply-templates select="question"/>
12:             <xsl:apply-templates select="a"/>
13:             <xsl:apply-templates select="b"/>
14:             <xsl:apply-templates select="c"/>
15:           </div>
16:         </xsl:for-each>
17:       </body>
18:     </html>
19:   </xsl:template>
20:
21:   <xsl:template match="question">
22:     <div style="color:black; font-family:Times,serif; font-size:16pt">
23:       <xsl:value-of/>
24:     </div>
25:   </xsl:template>
26:
27:   <xsl:template match="a|b|c">
28:     <div style="color:brown; font-family:Times,serif; font-size:12pt;
29:     text-indent:15px">
30:       <xsl:value-of/>
31:     </div>
32:   </xsl:template>
33: </xsl:stylesheet>
```

Notice that this style sheet is considerably more complex than its CSS counterpart. This has to do with the fact that this style sheet is actually constructing an HTML document on the fly. In other words, the XSLT code is describing how to build an HTML document out of XML data, complete with inline CSS styles. Again, you could accomplish a similar feat without the CSS styles, but you wouldn't be able to make the resulting page look exactly like the result of the CSS style sheet. This is because XSLT isn't in the business of controlling font sizes and colors; XSLT is all about transforming data. Figure 9.2 shows the result of viewing the `talltales.xml` document in Internet Explorer using the XSLT style sheet.

FIGURE 9.2

The Tall Tales example document is displayed in Internet Explorer using an XSLT style sheet.

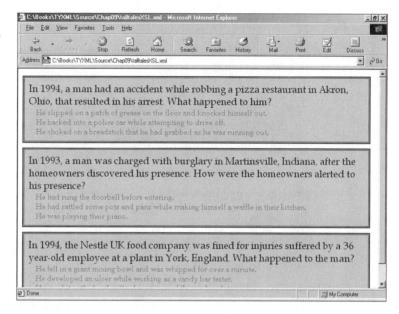

If you look back to Figure 9.1, you'll be hard pressed to tell the difference between it and this figure. In fact, the only noticeable difference is the file name of the document in the title bar of the Web browser. This reveals how it is often possible to accomplish similar tasks using either CSS or XSLT. Obviously, CSS is superior for styling simple XML documents due to the simplicity of CSS style sheets. However, any time you need to massage the data in an XML document before displaying it, you'll have to go with XSLT.

Summary

Style sheets represent an important technological innovation with respect to the Web because they make it possible to exert exacting control over the appearance of content in both HTML and XML documents. Style sheets allow markup languages such as HTML and other custom XML-based languages to focus on their primary job—structuring data according to its meaning. With a clean separation between content and presentation, documents coded in HTML and XML are better organized and more easily managed.

This hour introduced you to the basics of style sheets, including the two main style sheet technologies that are applicable to XML: CSS and XSL. Although XSL and CSS solve similar problems, they are very different technologies. Although you learned the fundamentals of how and when to use each type of style sheet, the remaining hours in this part of the book paint a much clearer picture of what can be done in both CSS and XSLT.

Q&A

Q **Why is it so important to separate the presentation of a document from its content?**

A It's been proven time and again that mixing data with its presentation severely hampers the structure and organization of the data because it becomes very difficult to draw a line between what is content and what is presentation. For example, it is currently difficult for search engines to extract meaningful information about Web pages because most HTML documents are concerned solely with how information is to be displayed. If those documents were coded according to meaning, as opposed to worrying so much about presentation, the Web and its search engines would be much smarter. Of course, we all care about how information looks, especially on the Web, so no one ever said to do away with presentation. The idea is to make a clean separation between content and separation so that both of them can be more easily managed.

Q **What does it mean to state that XSL-FO is a superset of CSS?**

A When I say that XSL-FO is a superset of CSS, I mean that XSL-FO is designed to encompass the functionality of CSS and also go far beyond CSS. In other words, XSL-FO is designed to support the features of CSS along with many new features of its own. The idea behind this approach is to provide a smooth migration path between CSS and XSL-FO because XSL-FO inherently supports CSS.

Workshop

The Workshop is designed to help you anticipate possible questions, review what you've learned, and begin learning how to put your knowledge into practice.

Quiz

1. What is the significance of style sheets for HTML documents?

2. What kinds of standard elements does XML include for describing the appearance of XML documents?

3. What are the two major parts of XSL?

4. In the Tall Tales trivia example, how did the `talltales.xsl` style sheet make use of CSS to format the `talltales.xml` document?

Quiz Answers

1. A style sheet addresses the presentation needs of HTML documents by defining layout and formatting rules that tell a browser how to display the different parts of a document.

2. XML doesn't include any kind of standard elements for describing the appearance of XML documents, which is why style sheets are so important for displaying XML documents.

3. The two major parts of XSL are XSLT (XSL Transformation) and XSL-FO (XSL Formatting Objects). XSLT allows you to translate XML documents into other languages, but it doesn't tackle the same layout and formatting issues as CSS. XSL-FO addresses the layout and formatting of XML documents and is considered a superset of CSS.

4. The `talltales.xsl` style sheet made use of inline CSS styles to format the `talltales.xml` document, which means that style rules were applied directly within HTML tags.

Exercises

1. Modify the `talltales.css` style sheet so that the fonts and colors are different. Open the `talltalesCSS.xml` document in a Web browser to view the results.

2. Try to match the changes you just made to the `talltales.css` style sheet in the `talltales.xsl` style sheet. Open the `talltalesXSL.xml` document in a Web browser to view the results.

9

HOUR 10

The Basics of Cascading Style Sheets (CSS)

There is unexpected beauty hidden everywhere in this world—one just has to be open to seeing it. Remember that the next time you sneeze on your monitor.

—Nathan Walton

Unless you think tags and attributes are beautiful, there arguably isn't a whole lot of visual beauty in XML. However, you can spend a relatively small amount of time creating a style sheet that will add significant beauty to your XML documents. One style sheet approach known as Cascading Style Sheets (CSS) allows you to attach formatting styles to individual elements within an XML document. These styles are then used to determine how the elements in the document are rendered for display within a Web browser. Even though the XML language doesn't inherently include any mechanism for defining how a document looks, CSS makes it possible to add a view to XML documents. This hour explores the basics of CSS, including how to create style sheets for XML documents with CSS.

In this hour, you'll learn

- The basic structure and syntax of CSS
- The layout and formatting of CSS style properties
- How to associate a CSS style sheet with an XML document
- How to create a basic CSS style sheet for an existing XML document

Getting to Know CSS

You learned in the previous hour that CSS allows you to format XML content so that it can be displayed in Web browsers. CSS first came about as a means of improving the presentation of HTML content, but it turns out that it also works quite well with XML content. CSS is itself a language that defines style constructs such as fonts, colors, and positioning, which are used to describe how data is displayed. CSS styles are stored in *style sheets,* which contain *style rules* that apply styles to elements of a given type. Style sheet rules are usually placed in external style sheet documents with the filename extension .css.

The "cascading" part of CSS refers to the manner in which style sheet rules are applied to elements in an XML (or HTML) document. More specifically, styles in CSS form a hierarchy where more specific styles override more general styles. It is the responsibility of CSS to determine the precedence of style rules according to this hierarchy, which gives the rules a cascading effect. In some ways, you can think of the cascading mechanism in CSS as being similar to genetic inheritance, where general traits are passed on from a parent, but more specific traits are entirely unique to an individual; base style rules are applied throughout a style sheet but can be overridden by more specific style rules.

Like many Web-related technologies, CSS has undergone revisions since its original release. The original version of CSS was known as CSS1 and included basic support for formatting Web page content. CSS2 built on the feature set of CSS1 by adding powerful new features, such as the absolute positioning of content. There is a CSS3 in the works, but popular Web browsers only support CSS1 and CSS2. All of the CSS example code in this book is compliant with CSS1 and CSS2, which means you should have no problem using it with popular Web browsers, such as Internet Explorer and Netscape Navigator.

If you've never used CSS with HTML, you'll be glad to know that it is very simple in structure and quite easy to use with XML. The application of style rules is determined by *selectors,* which are CSS constructs that identify portions of an XML document. A selector establishes the link between a document and a style or set of styles. There are three kinds of selectors used in CSS:

- Element type—selects an element of a given type
- Attribute class—selects an element of a certain class that is identified by a special attribute
- Attribute ID—selects an element with an ID that is identified by a special attribute

An *element type selector* selects an element of a given type and applies a style or set of styles to it. This is the simplest approach to using CSS because there is a simple one-to-one mapping between element types and styles. As an example, you could use an element type selector to define a set of styles dictating the margins and font for an element named `message` in an XML document. Any messages marked up with this element would be displayed according to the styles defined in the style rule with the `message` element type selector. Following is an example of such a style rule:

```
message {
  display:block;
  margin-bottom:5px;
  font-family:Courier;
  font-size:14pt
}
```

This example uses an element type selector to select the `message` element and apply a series of styles to it. The end result is that all elements of type `message` appearing in a document will have a 5-pixel margin and will be rendered in a 14-point Courier font. Following is an example of how you might mark up a message in an XML document:

```
<message>
It's very lonely here - I really miss you.
</message>
```

As you know, there is no standard `message` element in XML; in fact, there are no standard elements of any kind in XML. This example simply demonstrates how you would apply a style to an element that stores a text message.

An *attribute class selector* is a little more specific than the element type selector in that it allows you to apply styles to elements based upon an attribute. In addition to applying styles based upon a type of element, CSS uses attribute selectors to look for specific elements containing a special attribute with a certain value. This attribute is named `class` and is capable of having virtually any value you desire. The premise of the `class` attribute is that you use it to define classes of styles within a given element type. Following is an example of how you might define a special class of messages that are urgent:

```
message.urgent {
  display:block;
  margin-bottom:5px;
  font-family:Courier;
  font-size:14pt;
  font-style:italic;
  color:red
}
```

The class name in this example is `urgent`, which is identified by separating it from the element type with a period (.). Following is an example of how you would mark up a paragraph corresponding to this style rule:

```
<message class="urgent">
The sky is falling!
</message>
```

As you can see, the `urgent` class name is provided as the value of the `class` attribute of the `<message>` tag. This is the standard approach to using CSS attribute class selectors in XML documents. However, there is one other option when it comes to using CSS selectors: attribute ID selectors.

For the utmost in styling flexibility, you can use an *attribute ID selector,* which establishes a style rule that can be applied to any element regardless of its type. Like attribute class selectors, attribute ID selectors rely on a special attribute. However, in this case the attribute is named `id`, and it isn't associated with any particular element type. Following is an example of creating a style rule using an attribute ID selector:

```
#groovy {
  color:green;
  font-family:Times;
  font-style:italic;
  font-weight:bold;
}
```

This example creates a style rule with an attribute ID selector named `groovy`; the pound sign (#) is used to indicate that this is an attribute ID selector. To use this style, you simply reference it as a value of the `id` attribute in any element type. Following is an example of how you might use the style with a `message` element:

```
<message id="groovy">
I'm feeling pretty groovy!
</message>
```

Unlike the urgent attribute class selector, which is specific to the message element, the groovy attribute ID selector can be used with any element, in which case the element will be displayed with the groovy styles. For example, following is an example of how the groovy selector can be used with an element named note:

```
<note id="groovy">
Pick up leisure suit from laundry.
</note>
```

Although selectors play an important role in determining how styles are applied to documents, they are only a part of the CSS equation. The other major part of style sheet syntax is the *style declaration,* which is used to specify a style property and its associated value. You've already seen style declarations in the preceding selector examples, but now it's time to learn how they work. Style declarations in CSS are similar in some ways to attributes XML in that they assign a value to a property. CSS supports a wide range of style properties that can be set to establish the style of a given style rule. Together with selectors, style declarations comprise the syntax of a CSS style rule, which follows:

```
Selector {
  Property1:Value1;
  Property2:Value2;
  ...
}
```

Following is the message style rule that you saw earlier in the hour, which helps to reveal the structure of style declarations:

```
message {
  display:block;
  margin-bottom:5px;
  font-family:Courier;
  font-size:14pt
}
```

The message example style rule includes four style properties: display, margin-bottom, font-family, and font-size. Each of these properties has a value associated with it that together comprise the style rule of the message element. Notice that each style property and value is separated by a colon (:), whereas the property/value pairs are separated by semicolons (;).

The message example showed how to create a style rule for a single element. It is also possible to create a style rule for multiple elements, in which case the style rule applies to all of the elements. To establish a style rule for multiple elements, you create the style declaration and separate the element types with commas (,) in a single style rule:

10

```
ssnum, phonenum, email {
  display:none;
}
```

In this example, the value none is set in the display style property for the ssnum, phonenum, and email elements. The idea behind this example is that these elements contain sensitive information that you wouldn't want displayed; setting the display property to none results in the elements not being displayed.

A CSS Style Primer

You now have a basic knowledge of CSS style sheets and how they are based upon style rules that describe the appearance of elements in XML documents. You've seen several examples of style properties, many of which are self-explanatory in terms of their usage. However, it's worth taking time to get you acquainted with some of the more commonly used style properties in CSS. The next hour, "Styling XML Content with CSS," digs deeper into the styling of text with CSS. The next few sections of this hour, however, provide a quick overview of some of the most important styles and allow you to get started using CSS in your own style sheets.

CSS includes a variety of style properties that are used to control fonts, colors, alignment, and margins, to name just a few facets of XML content styling. The style properties in CSS can be broadly grouped into two major categories:

- Layout properties
- Formatting properties

Layout properties consist of properties that impact the positioning of XML content. For example, layout properties allow you to control the width, height margin, padding, and alignment of content and even go so far as to allow you to place content at exact positions on a page.

Layout Properties

One of the most important layout properties is the display property, which describes how an element is displayed with respect to other elements. There are four possible values for the display property:

- block—the element is displayed on a new line, as in a new paragraph
- list-item—the element is displayed on a new line with a list-item mark (bullet) next to it
- inline—the element is displayed inline with the current paragraph
- none—the element is not displayed

It's easier to understand the `display` property if you visualize each element in an XML document occupying a rectangular area when displayed. The `display` property controls the manner in which this rectangular area is displayed. For example, the `block` value results in the element being placed on a new line by itself, whereas the `inline` value places the element next to the content immediately preceding it. The `display` property is one of the few style properties that you will define for most style rules. Following is an example of how to set the display property:

```
display:block;
```

The `display` property relies on a concept known as *relative positioning*, which means that elements are positioned relative to the location of other elements on a page. CSS also supports *absolute positioning*, which allows you to place an element at an exact location on a page, independent of other elements. You learn more about both of these types of positioning in the next hour.

10

You control the size of the rectangular area for an element with the `width` and `height` attributes. Like many size-related CSS properties, `width` and `height` property values can be specified in several different units of measurement:

- `in`—inches
- `cm`—centimeters
- `mm`—millimeters
- `px`—pixels
- `pt`—points

These unit types are used immediately after the value of a measurement in a style sheet. You can mix and match units however you choose within a style sheet, but it's generally a good idea to be consistent across a set of similar style properties. For example, you might want to stick with points for font properties or pixels for dimensions. Following is an example of setting the width of an element using pixel units:

```
width:200px;
```

Formatting Properties

CSS formatting properties are used to control the appearance of XML content, as opposed to controlling the physical position of the content. One of the most commonly used formatting properties is the `border` property, which is used to establish a visible boundary around an element with a box or partial box. The following border properties provide a means of describing the borders of an element:

- `border-width`—the width of the border edge
- `border-color`—the color of the border edge
- `border-style`—the style of the border edge
- `border-left`—the left side of the border
- `border-right`—the right side of the border
- `border-top`—the top of the border
- `border-bottom`—the bottom of the border
- `border`—all of the border sides

The border-width property is used to establish the width of the border edge and is often expressed in pixels, as the following code demonstrates:

```
border-width:5px;
```

The `border-color` and `border-style` properties are used to set the border color and style, respectively. Following is an example of how these two properties are set:

```
border-color:blue;
border-style:dotted;
```

The `border-style` property can be set to any of the following values:

- `solid`—a single-line border
- `double`—a double-line border
- `dashed`—a dashed border
- `dotted`—a dotted border
- `groove`—a border with a groove appearance
- `ridge`—a border with a ridge appearance
- `inset`—a border with an inset appearance
- `outset`—a border with an outset appearance
- `none`—no border

The `border-style` property values are fairly self-explanatory; the `solid` and `double` styles are the most common. The default value of the `border-style` property is `none`, which is why elements don't have a border unless you set the border property to a different style.

The `border-left`, `border-right`, `border-top`, and `border-bottom` properties allow you to set the border for each side of an element individually. If you want a border to appear the same on all four sides, you can use the single `border` property and express the border styles more concisely. Following is an example of using the `border` property to set a border that consists of two red lines that are a total of ten pixels in width:

```
border:10px double red;
```

The color of an element's border can be set with the `border-color` property, and the color of the inner region of an element can be set using the `color` and `background-color` properties. The `color` property sets the color of text in an element, and the `background-color` property sets the color of the background behind the text. Following is an example of setting both color properties to predefined colors:

```
color:black;
background-color:orange;
```

You can also assign custom colors to these properties by specifying the colors as hexadecimal RGB (Red Green Blue) values. Following is an example of such assignments:

```
background-color:#999999;
color:rgb(0,0,255);
```

> You learn more about CSS colors and RGB values in the next hour, "Styling XML Content with CSS."

In addition to setting the color of XML content and its associated background, you can also control the alignment and indentation associated with the content. This is accomplished with the `text-align` and `text-indent` properties, as the following code demonstrates:

```
text-align:center;
text-indent:12px;
```

Once you have an element properly aligned and indented, you might be interested in setting its font. The following CSS font properties are used to set the various parameters associated with fonts:

- `font-family`—the family of the font
- `font-size`—the size of the font
- `font-style`—the style of the font (`normal` or `italic`)
- `font-weight`—the weight of the font (`light`, `medium`, `bold`, and so on)

The font-family property specifies a prioritized list of font family names. A prioritized list is used instead of a single value to provide alternatives in case a font isn't available on a given system. The font-size property specifies the size of the font using a unit of measurement, usually points. Finally, the font-style property sets the style of the font, whereas the font-weight property sets the weight of the font. Following is an example of setting these font properties:

```
font-family: Arial, sans-serif;
font-size: 36pt;
font-style: italic;
font-weight: medium;
```

 Content alignment, indentation, and fonts are covered in more detail in the next hour. The purpose of covering them here is to give you a brief introduction to CSS formatting so that you can begin creating style sheets without being overwhelmed with style property details.

Wiring a Style Sheet to an XML Document

Style rules wouldn't be of much use if you didn't have a means of wiring them to an XML document in order to style the document's content. CSS style sheets used with XML documents are usually referred to as *external style sheets* because are stored in separate text files with a .css extension. The file is then referenced by XML documents that use the style sheet to determine how their content is displayed. The xml-stylesheet processing instruction is used to associate an external style sheet with an XML document. This processing instruction includes a couple of attributes that determine the type and location of the style sheet:

- type—the type of the style sheet (text/css, for example)
- href—the location of the style sheet

These two attributes are both required in order to wire a style sheet to an XML document. Following is an example of how to use the xml-stylesheet processing instruction with the type and href attributes:

```
<?xml-stylesheet type="text/css" href="talltales.css"?>
```

In this example, the type attribute is used to specify that the type of the style sheet is text/css, which means that the style sheet is a CSS style sheet. The style sheet file is then referenced in the href attribute, which in this case points to the file talltales.css.

It is necessary to specify the type of a style sheet in the `xml-stylesheet` processing instruction because there are other types of style sheets, such as XSLT style sheets. You learn all about XSLT style sheets in Hour 12, "eXtensible Style Language (XSL) Fundamentals," and Hour 13, "Transforming XML with XSLT."

It's important to note that external style sheets represent the only way to use CSS directly with XML documents without the assistance of any other technology. I say this because it is possible to incorporate style sheets into the formatting of XML documents a little differently when you are also using XSLT. More specifically, with XSLT you are actually translating an XML document into an HTML document for display purposes. Knowing this, it is possible to use inline styles directly with HTML elements in order to apply styles to XML content indirectly. You can also use external style sheets with HTML documents that are translated from XML. You learn how to carry out both of these style approaches in Hour 12.

10

Your First CSS Style Sheet

None of this style sheet stuff would make much sense if you didn't get to see it in the context of a complete example. In fact, you really haven't gotten a chance to glimpse the end result of style properties throughout this hour, even though you've seen lots of small code examples. Listing 10.1 contains the code for an XML document that stores a couple of contacts. This document is an example of how you might use XML to store a contact list for personal or business contacts.

LISTING 10.1 The Contacts Example XML Document

```
 1: <?xml version="1.0"?>
 2: <?xml-stylesheet type="text/css" href="contacts.css"?>
 3: <!DOCTYPE contacts SYSTEM "contacts.dtd">
 4:
 5: <contacts>
 6:   <!-- This is my good friend Frank. -->
 7:   <contact>
 8:     <name>Frank Rizzo</name>
 9:     <address>1212 W 304th Street</address>
10:     <city>New York</city>
11:     <state>New York</state>
12:     <zip>10011</zip>
13:     <phone>
14:       <voice>212-555-1212</voice>
15:       <fax>212-555-1213</fax>
16:     </phone>
```

continues

LISTING 10.1 Continued

```
17:     <company>Frank&apos;s Ratchet Service</company>
18:   </contact>
19:
20:   <!-- This is my old college roommate Sol. -->
21:   <contact>
22:     <name>Sol Rosenberg</name>
23:     <address>1162 E 412th Street</address>
24:     <city>New York</city>
25:     <state>New York</state>
26:     <zip>10011</zip>
27:     <phone>
28:       <voice>212-555-1818</voice>
29:       <fax>212-555-1819</fax>
30:     </phone>
31:     <company>Rosenberg&apos;s Shoes &amp; Glasses</company>
32:   </contact>
33: </contacts>
```

Notice in the code for the Contacts document that an external style sheet (contacts.css) is associated with the document through the xml-stylesheet processing instruction (line 2). Beyond that, there is nothing specific to style sheets in the XML code. However, it's important to understand the role of a style sheet in this example, which is to display the mailing address for each contact. Knowing this, it is necessary to hide the phone number and company name when formatting the content for display. This is accomplished in the contacts.css style sheet, which is shown in Listing 10.2.

LISTING 10.2 The contacts.css Style Sheet Used to Format the Contacts XML Document

```
 1: contact {
 2:   display:block;
 3:   width:275px;
 4:   margin-bottom:10px;
 5:   border:5px double black;
 6:   color:black;
 7:   background-color:yellow;
 8:   text-align:center;
 9: }
10:
11: name {
12:   display:block;
13:   font-family:Times, serif;
14:   font-size:15pt;
15:   font-weight:bold;
16: }
```

continues

LISTING 10.2   Continued

```
17:
18: address {
19:    display:block;
20:    font-family:Times, serif;
21:    font-size:13pt;
22: }
23:
24: city, state, zip {
25:    display:inline;
26:    font-family:Times, serif;
27:    font-size:13pt;
28: }
29:
30: phone, company {
31:    display:none;
32: }
```

10

This style sheet relies on familiar style properties that you learned about in this hour. Each relevant element in the Contacts document (`contact`, `name`, `address`, `city`, `state`, `zip`, `phone`, and `company`) is styled in the style sheet so that its display parameters are clearly stated. A border is established around the `contact` element (line 5), which contains the remaining elements. The other important code to notice is the code that hides the phone and company elements so that they aren't displayed (lines 30–32). This style sheet results in the contacts being displayed as a list of mailing addresses that could easily be printed out as address labels (Figure 10.1).

FIGURE 10.1

The Contacts example document is displayed in Internet Explorer using the `contacts.css` *style sheet.*

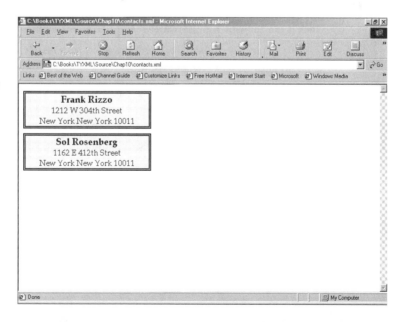

Although the `contacts.css` style sheet is relatively simple in structure, it is nonetheless a good example of how CSS can be used to format and position XML content on a page for viewing.

Summary

Cascading Style Sheets (CSS) were originally created for use with HTML, but they also work quite well with XML. CSS focuses purely on the positioning and formatting of XML content and doesn't involve itself with processing or otherwise translating XML code. Although this makes CSS limited in some respects, it also makes it quite simple to learn and use for styling XML documents. When all you need to do is simply format XML content using presentation styles, CSS is the perfect solution.

This hour introduced you to CSS and how it is used to style XML documents. You got started by learning the basics of CSS, including the fundamental layout and formatting styles that are used to style XML content. You then learned how to associate an external style sheet with an XML document, which is a necessity if you plan on seeing the fruits of your CSS labors. Finally, you put together a complete style sheet for an XML document containing contact information. Admittedly, you didn't exactly become a CSS expert in this hour, but you certainly learned enough to begin formatting XML documents for display on the Web. The next hour digs a little deeper into CSS and focuses on the details of positioning XML content and formatting text.

Q&A

Q Does it matter which unit of measure I use when sizing XML content with CSS?

A No. The rendering engine in a Web browser is responsible for interpreting all of the standard units of measure and handling the necessary conversions.

Q Is there a way to place XML content exactly where I want it to be displayed?

A Yes. This approach to positioning XML content is known as absolute positioning and is covered in the next hour, "Styling XML Content with CSS." The approach you learned about in this hour is the default approach, which is known as relative positioning.

Q Why can't I just place style rules directly in XML code?

A XML code must adhere to XML syntax, which consists of elements and attributes. CSS is not an XML-based markup language, which immediately excludes its usage within XML documents using familiar XML elements and attributes. Technically, it could be possible to use inline CSS styles with XML content by way of a special attribute, such as `style`, which is supported in HTML. However, even this special attribute would need to be supported by the particular XML-based markup language being used in the document. Since there is no such standard XML language, the `style` attribute isn't recognized in XML documents for viewing in Web browsers. In other words, you must use external style sheets if you plan on using CSS alone to style your XML documents.

Workshop

The Workshop is designed to help you anticipate possible questions, review what you've learned, and begin learning how to put your knowledge into practice.

Quiz

1. What is the purpose of an element type selector?

2. What two pieces of information does a style declaration involve?

3. How does the `block` value differ from the `inline` value in the `display` property?

4. How do you associate an external CSS style sheet with an XML document?

Quiz Answers

1. An element type selector selects an element of a given type and applies a style or set of styles to it. This represents the simplest approach to using CSS because there is a one-to-one mapping between element types and styles.

2. A style declaration is used to pair a style property with its associated value.

3. When used with the `display` property, the `block` value results in an element being placed on a new line by itself, whereas the `inline` value places the element next to the content immediately preceding it.

4. The `xml-stylesheet` processing instruction is used to associate an external CSS style sheet with an XML document.

Exercises

1. Add a new element named `email` to the Contacts XML document and its associated DTD. This element should contain the e-mail address of each contact.

2. Modify the `contacts.css` style sheet so that the new `email` element is hidden from display.

Hour 11

Styling XML Content with CSS

It's not an optical illusion; it just looks like one.
—Phil White

Fortunately, due to its relative simplicity there are no optical illusions associated with CSS; all of the visual "trickery" in CSS is made possible with clear and concise style properties. CSS style properties, although simple to use, actually provide a considerable degree of flexibility over the positioning and formatting of XML content. This hour picks up where the previous hour left off by revealing more details of CSS. More specifically, CSS positioning and the specifics of formatting text are examined more closely. You learn how to control the flow of text on a page, not to mention how to use fonts, colors, background images, and letter spacing.

In this hour, you'll learn

- The two different approaches used to position XML content using CSS
- How to control the layering of elements with CSS
- How to use margins and padding to control the spacing around and within elements
- How to format text using several different CSS style properties

Inside CSS Positioning

In the previous hour you learned how to position XML content using the default approach to CSS positioning, which is known as relative positioning. In *relative positioning,* content is displayed according to the flow of a page, where each element physically appears after the element preceding it in an XML document. The content for an XML element still appears within a rectangular area, but the area itself is positioned relative to other elements that are being displayed. You can think of relative positioning as being akin to laying out checkers on a checkerboard; the checkers are arranged from left to right, and when you get to the edge of the board you move on to the next row. Elements that are styled with the block value for the display property are automatically placed on a new row, whereas inline elements are placed on the same row immediately next to the element preceding them.

Although relative positioning might sound somewhat limiting, you have to keep in mind that child elements are always positioned relative to their parents. So, the hierarchy of elements in an XML document can dramatically affect how the elements appear when styled with CSS. As an example, the following code is an excerpt from the contacts.css style sheet that you saw in the previous hour:

```
contact {
  display:block;
  width:275px;
  margin-bottom:10px;
  border:5px double black;
  color:black;
  background-color:yellow;
  text-align:center;
}

name {
  display:block;
  font-family:Times, serif;
  font-size:15pt;
  font-weight:bold;
}
```

Although these elements appear to be completely independent from a CSS perspective, the name element is in fact a child of the contact element. Therefore, when using relative positioning, the name element is displayed with respect to the contact element. In other words, the name element appears within the rectangular area set aside for the contact element, which in this case is 275 pixels wide.

Relative positioning is the default positioning approach used by CSS, so if you don't specify the positioning of a style rule, it will default to relative positioning.

The other type of positioning supported by CSS is known as *absolute positioning* because it allows you to set the exact position of XML content on a page. Although absolute positioning gives you the freedom to spell out exactly where an element is to appear, this position is still relative to any parent elements that appear on the page. In this regard, absolute positioning is still somewhat similar to relative positioning. However, absolute positioning allows you to specify the exact location of an element's rectangular area with respect to its parent's area, which is very different from relative positioning.

If you think about the ramifications of absolute positioning, you'll realize that there is a potential problem associated with the freedom of placing elements anywhere you want on a page. I'm referring to *overlap,* which is when an element takes up space used by another element. There is nothing stopping you from specifying the absolute locations of elements so that they overlap. In this case, CSS relies on the z-index of each element to determine which element is on the top and which is on the bottom. You learn more about the z-index of elements in the next section. For now, let's take a look at exactly how you control whether or not a style rule uses relative or absolute positioning.

The type of positioning (relative or absolute) used by a particular style rule is determined by the position property, which is capable of having one of the following two values: relative or absolute. After specifying the type of positioning, you then specify the specific position of a style rule using the following properties:

- left—the left position offset
- right—the right position offset
- top—the top position offset
- bottom—the bottom position offset

11

You might think that these position properties make sense only for absolute positioning, but they actually apply to both types of positioning. However, the position properties are interpreted differently depending on the type of positioning used. Under relative positioning, the position of an element is specified as an offset relative to the original position of the element. So, if you set the left property of an element to 25px, the left side of the element will be shifted over 25 pixels from its original (relative) position. Since the original position of the element is relative to other elements, the final position is still considered a relative position. An absolute position, on the other hand, is specified relative to the parent of the element to which the style is applied. So, if you set the left property of an element to 25px under absolute positioning, the left side of the element will appear 25 pixels to the right of the parent element's left edge.

To better understand the difference between absolute and relative positioning, check out the following XML code:

```
<squares>
  <square class="one">
  Square One
  </square>
  <square class="two">
  Square Two
  </square>
  <square class="three">
  Square Three
  </square>
  <square class="four">
  Square Four
  </square>
</squares>
```

Admittedly, this XML code doesn't mean much, but it's a good way to demonstrate the difference between relative and absolute positioning. Notice in the code that there are several square elements, each with a different class and therefore a different style rule. Listing 11.1 contains a style sheet for this code that uses relative positioning to arrange the squares.

LISTING 11.1 The squares_rel.css Style Sheet That Uses Relative Positioning to Style the Squares XML Document

```
1: square {
2:    display:block;
3:    position:relative;
4:    width:100px;
5:    height:75px;
6:    border:10px single black;
7:    color:black;
```

continues

LISTING 11.1 Continued

```
 8:    text-align:center;
 9: }
10:
11: square.one {
12:   background-color:red;
13: }
14:
15: square.two {
16:   background-color:green;
17: }
18:
19: square.three {
20:   background-color:blue;
21: }
22:
23: square.four {
24:   background-color:yellow;
25: }
```

This code sets the position style property to relative (line 3), which explicitly causes the square style rule to use relative positioning. Since the remaining style rules are inherited from the square style rule, they also inherit its relative positioning. In fact, the only difference between the other style rules is that they have different background colors. Figure 11.1 shows the Squares document as it is displayed in Internet Explorer using the style sheet with relative positioning.

FIGURE 11.1

The Squares example document is displayed in Internet Explorer using a style sheet with relative positioning.

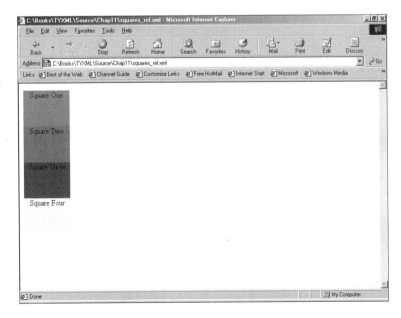

11

Notice in the figure that the `square` elements are displayed one after the next, which is what you would expect from relative positioning. To make things more interesting, you can change the positioning to absolute and explicitly specify the placement of the squares. Listing 11.2 contains a modified style sheet for the Squares document that uses absolute positioning to arrange the squares.

LISTING 11.2 The `squares_abs.css` Style Sheet That Uses Absolute Positioning to Style the Squares XML Document

```
 1: square {
 2:    display:block;
 3:    position:absolute;
 4:    width:100px;
 5:    height:75px;
 6:    border:10px single black;
 7:    color:black;
 8:    text-align:center;
 9: }
10:
11: square.one {
12:    background-color:red;
13:    left:0px;
14:    top:0px;
15: }
16:
17: square.two {
18:    background-color:green;
19:    left:75px;
20:    top:25px;
21: }
22:
23: square.three {
24:    background-color:blue;
25:    left:150px;
26:    top:50px;
27: }
28:
29: square.four {
30:    background-color:yellow;
31:    left:225px;
32:    top:75px;
33: }
```

This style sheet sets the `position` property to `absolute`, which is necessary in order for the style sheet to use absolute positioning (line 3). Additionally, the `left` and `top` properties are set for each of the inherited square style rules. However, the position of each of these rules is set so that the elements will be displayed overlapping each other, as shown in Figure 11.2.

FIGURE 11.2

*The Squares example
document is displayed
in Internet Explorer
using a style sheet with
absolute positioning.*

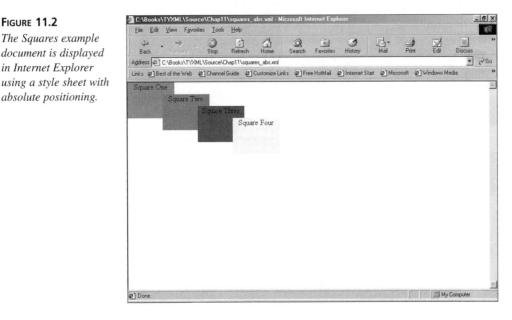

This figure shows how absolute positioning allows you to place elements exactly where you want them. It also reveals how easy it is to arrange elements so that they overlap each other. You might be curious as to how a Web browser knows which elements to draw on top when they overlap. Fortunately, CSS includes a style property that gives you complete control over the appearance of overlapped elements.

Tinkering with the z-Index

You just saw how it doesn't take much trouble to position elements on a page so that they overlap each other. There are no doubt situations where you'd like to be able to carefully control the manner in which elements overlap each other. For this reason, CSS includes the z-index property, which allows you to set the order of elements with respect to how they stack on top of each other. Although the name *z-index* might sound a little strange, it refers to the notion of a third dimension (Z) that projects into the computer screen, in addition to the two dimensions (X and Y) that go across and down the screen. Another way to think of the z-index is the relative position of a magazine within a stack of magazines. A magazine nearer the top of the stack has a higher z-index than a magazine lower in the stack. Similarly, an overlapped element with a higher z-index is displayed on top of an element with a lower z-index.

The z-index of a style rule is specified using the z-index property, which is set to a numeric value that indicates the relative z-index of the rule. The number assigned to a z-index has meaning only with respect to other style rules in a style sheet, which means that setting the z-index for a single rule doesn't really mean much. On the other hand, if you set the z-index for several style rules that apply to overlapped elements, then the elements with the higher z-index values will appear on top of elements with lower z-index values.

 Regardless of the z-index value you set for a style rule, an element displayed with the rule will always appear on top of its parent.

Listing 11.3 contains another version of a style sheet for the Squares XML document that has z-index settings to alter the natural overlap of elements.

LISTING 11.3 The `squares_z.css` Style Sheet Alters the z-order of Elements in the Squares XML Document

```
 1: square {
 2:    display:block;
 3:    position:absolute;
 4:    width:100px;
 5:    height:75px;
 6:    border:10px single black;
 7:    color:black;
 8:    text-align:center;
 9: }
10:
11: square.one {
12:    background-color:red;
13:    z-index:0;
14:    left:0px;
15:    top:0px;
16: }
17:
18: square.two {
19:    background-color:green;
20:    z-index:3;
21:    left:75px;
22:    top:25px;
23: }
24:
25: square.three {
26:    background-color:blue;
27:    z-index:2;
28:    left:150px;
```

continues

LISTING 11.3 Continued

```
29:    top:50px;
30: }
31:
32: square.four {
33:    background-color:yellow;
34:    z-index:1;
35:    left:225px;
36:    top:75px;
37: }
```

The only change in this code from what you saw in Listing 11.2 is the addition of the z-index settings in each of the derived square style rules. Notice that the first square has a setting of 0 (line 13), which should make it the lowest element in terms of the z-index, whereas the second square has the highest z-index (line 20). Figure 11.3 shows the Squares document as displayed with this style sheet, which clearly shows how the z-index impacts the displayed content.

FIGURE 11.3

The Squares example document is displayed in Internet Explorer using a style sheet that alters the z-order of the squares.

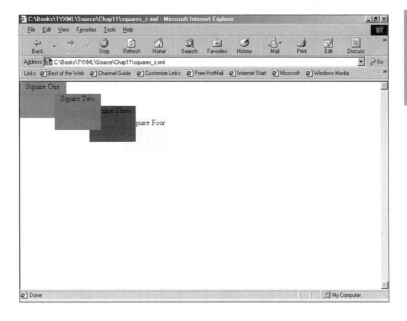

The figure reveals how the z-index style property makes it possible to carefully control the overlap of elements.

Creating Margins

CSS supports margins that allow you to add empty space around the outside of the rectangular area for an element. Following are the style properties that you use to set the margins for style rules:

- margin-top—sets the top margin
- margin-right—sets the right margin
- margin-bottom—sets the bottom margin
- margin-left—sets the left margin
- margin—sets the top, right, bottom, and left margins as a single property

You can specify margins using any of the individual margin properties or with the single margin property. Regardless of how you set the margins for a style rule, it's important to note that you can specify the size of a margin using either units or a percentage. If you decide to set a margin as a percentage, keep in mind that the percentage is calculated based upon the size of the entire page, not the size of the element. So, if you set the margin-left property to 25%, the left margin of the element will end up being 25% of the width of the entire page. The following code shows how to set the top and bottom margins for one of the squares in the Squares XML document that you've been working with throughout this hour:

```
square.two {
  background-color:green;
  margin-top:5px;
  margin-bottom:20px;
}
```

In this example, the top margin is set to 5 pixels, and the bottom margin is set to 20 pixels. The results of this code are shown in Figure 11.4.

FIGURE 11.4

The Squares example document is displayed in Internet Explorer using a style sheet that sets top and bottom margins for one of the squares.

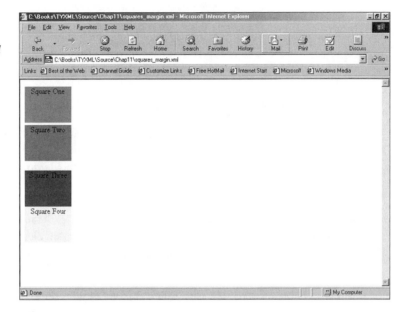

This figure shows how the top and bottom margins appear above and below the second square. Keep in mind that these margins don't encroach on the content area of any of the squares—they all maintain their original size. In other words, the margins appear around the elements.

If you want to set all of the margins for a style rule, then you'll probably want to simplify the code and use the `margin` property. This property is somewhat flexible in that it offers three different approaches to specifying the margins for a style rule. These different approaches vary based upon how many values you use when setting the `margin` property:

- One value—the size of all the margins
- Two values—the size of the top/bottom margins and the left/right margins (in that order)
- Four values—the size of the top, right, bottom, and left margins (in that order)

As you can see, the `margin` property allows you to provide one, two, or four values when you set it. Following is an example of how you would set the vertical margins (top/bottom) to 5 pixels and the horizontal margins (left/right) to 10% for a style rule:

```
margin:5px 10%;
```

In this code, the top and bottom margins are both set to 5 pixels, whereas the left and right margins are both set to 10%. Of course, if you wanted to be a little clearer you could achieve the same effect with the following setting:

```
margin:5px 10% 5px 10%;
```

A Little Padding for Safety

Similar to margins, padding is used to add extra space to elements via CSS style properties. However, padding differs from margins in that padding adds space inside the rectangular area of an element, as opposed to around it. For this reason, padding actually imposes on the amount of content area available within an element. As an example, if you create a style rule for an element that establishes a width of 50 pixels and a height of 30 pixels and then sets the padding of the rule to 5 pixels, the remaining content area will be 40 pixels by 20 pixels. Also, since the padding of an element appears within the element's content area, it will assume the same style as the content of the element, such as the background color.

You specify the padding of a style rule using one of the padding properties, which work very much like the margin properties. The following padding properties are available for use in setting the padding of style rules:

- `padding-top`—sets the top padding
- `padding-right`—sets the right padding
- `padding-bottom`—sets the bottom padding
- `padding-left`—sets the left padding
- `padding`—sets the top, right, bottom, and left padding as a single property

Similar to margins, you can set the padding of style rules using individual padding properties or the single `padding` property. Padding can also be expressed using either a unit of measurement or a percentage. Following is an example of how you might set the left and right padding for a style rule so that there are 10 pixels of padding on each side of an element's content:

```
padding-left:10px;
padding0-right:10px;
```

Also similar to margins, you can set all of the padding for a style rule with a single property, the `padding` property. You can use the same three approaches available for the `margin` property to set the `padding` property. Following is an example of how you would set the vertical padding (top/bottom) to 12 pixels and the horizontal padding (left/right) to 8 pixels for a style rule:

```
padding:12px 8px;
```

Following is more explicit code that performs the same task by specifying all of the padding values:

```
padding:12px 8px 12px 8px;
```

Keeping Things Aligned

Knowing that XML content doesn't always fill the entire width of the rectangular area in which it is displayed, it is often helpful to control the alignment of the content. Even if text within a rectangular area extends to multiple lines, alignment still enters the picture because you may want the text justified left or right or centered. There are a couple of style properties that allow you to control the alignment of XML content: text-align and vertical-align. The text-align property aligns XML content horizontally within its bounding area and can be set to left, right, or center. Following is an example of using the text-align property to center a contact in the contacts.css style sheet that you saw in the previous hour:

```
contact {
  display:block;
  width:275px;
  margin-bottom:10px;
  border:5px double black;
  color:black;
  background-color:yellow;
  text-align:center
}
```

The last style property defined in this style rule involves setting the text-align style to center, which results in the contact element being centered within its parent. In the case of the contacts.css style sheet, the parent of the contact element is the page itself, so the element is centered on the page.

The vertical-align property is similar to text-align except that it is used to align elements vertically. The vertical-align property specifies how an element is aligned with its parent or in some cases the current line of elements on the page. When I say "current line," I'm really referring to the vertical placement of elements that appear within the same parent element. In other words, I'm talking about inline elements. If several inline elements appear on the same line, you can set their vertical alignments the same to align them vertically. Following are the acceptable values for use with the vertical-align property:

- top—aligns the top of an element with the current line
- middle—aligns the middle of an element with the middle of its parent
- bottom—aligns the bottom of an element with the current line

11

- `text-top`—aligns the top of an element with the top of its parent
- `baseline`—aligns the baseline of an element with the baseline of its parent
- `text-bottom`—aligns the bottom of an element with the bottom of its parent
- `sub`—aligns an element as a subscript of its parent
- `super`—aligns an element as a superscript of its parent

These property values are self-explanatory for the most part. The only tricky issue relates to whether a value aligns an element with the current line or its parent. When aligning an element with its parent, the baseline of the parent is the bottom of text appearing in the parent, excluding any letters that reach down below others, such as the letters g and y. Following is an example of how the `vertical-align` property is used to center text vertically:

```
contact {
  display:block;
  width:275px;
  margin-bottom:10px;
  border:5px double black;
  color:black;
  background-color:yellow;
  text-align:center;
  vertical-align:middle
}
```

This code shows how simple it is to modify a style rule so that the XML content is aligned vertically. In this case the `contact` element is vertically aligned with the middle of its parent.

The Ins and Outs of Text Formatting

CSS allows you to position and format a wide range of content, including HTML content, but when it comes to XML content you are really just dealing with text. Knowing this, it's important to have a solid understanding of how CSS is used to format text content. The next few sections tackle the following aspects of text formatting with CSS:

- Fonts
- Colors and image backgrounds
- Text spacing

Working with Fonts

When it comes to text formatting, nothing really impacts the overall appearance of text more so than the font used to display the text. You learned in the previous hour that CSS includes several styles for setting the font for text content. However, I now want to take a closer look at these font properties and also show you a more concise way to specify the font for a style rule. Following are the CSS font style properties that you can use to alter the font of text content:

- font-style—sets the style of a font
- font-weight—sets the thickness of a font
- font-size—sets the size of a font
- font-family—sets the family of a font
- font—sets the style, thickness, size, and family of a font within a single property

The first four properties should be familiar to you from the previous hour. If you recall, the font-style property allows you to set the style of a font and can be set to normal or italic; the default value is normal. The font-weight property sets the weight, or thickness, of a font and can be set to any of the following values: extra-light, light, demi-light, medium, demi-bold, bold, or extra-bold. The default value of the font-weight property is medium, which is an average font weight. The font-size property sets the size of a font using a unit of measure such as points (pt). The font-family property sets the family, or face, of a font, which is the name used to describe the font. Following is an example of how you use these four style properties together to establish a font style rule:

```
title {
  display:block;
  font-style:italic;
  font-weight:bold;
  font-size:18pt;
  font-family:Courier, serif
}
```

Notice in this code that the font-family style rule actually consists of two family names: Courier and serif. The reason for this is because there is no guarantee that a particular font will be available on a given system. To solve this problem, you can list alternate font families that will be used in the event that the primary family isn't available. In the title example, the Courier font family is specified as the primary family, but the secondary serif family will be used if the Courier family isn't available. If none of the font families are available, it is the responsibility of a Web browser to find a suitable match within the font families that are available.

11

Although the previous `title` example shows a perfectly reasonable approach to setting the font styles for a style rule, there is a better approach if you plan on setting several font styles. I'm referring to the `font` style property, which combines the other four font styles into a single property. To use the `font` property, you simply list the style, weight, size, and family of the font separated by spaces. Following is an example of how the `font` property makes the `title` style rule much more concise:

```
title {
  display:block;
  font:italic bold 18pt Courier, serif;
}
```

As this code reveals, the `font` property provides a good way to simplify the code for font styles. However, the `font` property is really only a convenience property and doesn't actually add any features of its own.

Jazzing Up Text with Colors and Image Backgrounds

If changing the font of text doesn't provide you with enough flexibility, you can go a step further and spice up text by altering its color and background appearance. Using CSS, it is possible to set the color of text, the background color shown behind text, and even a background image that appears behind text. Following are the properties that make this kind of visual trickery happen:

- `color`—sets the foreground color of text
- `background-color`—sets the background color of text
- `background-image`—sets the background image of text
- `background-repeat`—determines how the background image of text appears
- `background`—sets the background color, image, and repeat of text within a single property

The `color` property sets the color of text and can be set to any of the following standard colors: `aqua`, `black`, `blue`, `fuchsia`, `gray`, `green`, `lime`, `maroon`, `navy`, `olive`, `purple`, `red`, `silver`, `teal`, `white`, and `yellow`. Following is an example of how you might set the color in a style rule using the `color` property:

```
title {
  display:block;
  font:italic bold 18pt Courier, serif;
  color:green
}
```

In this example, the text color of the `title` element is set to `green`, which results in the text content for the element being displayed in green. If you'd like to specify a color other than one of the standard colors, you can create a custom color and assign it to the `color` property. To do so, you must create the custom color as a combination of the primary colors red, green, and blue. The combination of red, green, and blue color components is known as RGB and is the color system used to specify custom colors in CSS. The red, green, and blue color components are expressed as hexadecimal numbers that are stuck together to form a complete custom color value, such as `#00FF00`, which is the color green.

> If you've never worked with hexadecimal numbers then they will no doubt look strange to you at first. This is because hexadecimal numbers use a combination of letters and numeric digits, as opposed to just numeric digits. Instead of consisting of numbers from 0 to 10, the hexadecimal system consists of numbers from 0 to F, where the letters A through F continue on from 9. In other words, A is 10, B is 11, and so on. The lowest two-digit hexadecimal number is 00, whereas the highest is FF.

A custom color consists of six digits, which are actually three two-digit pairs, preceded by a number symbol (#). Each one of the two-digit pairs represents one of the three primary color components (red, green, and blue). Perhaps the best way to understand how custom numbers are encoded in hexadecimal is to look at the hexadecimal values for several of the standard colors:

- `aqua`—`#00FFFF`
- `black`—`#000000`
- `blue`—`#0000FF`
- `fuchsia`—`#FF00FF`
- `gray`—`#808080`
- `green`—`#00FF00`

Granted, this isn't all of the standard colors, but it should give you an idea as to how custom colors are described by hexadecimal values. Following is an example of how you would set the color property to the color blue using a hexadecimal value:

`color:#0000FF;`

Now that you have a better understanding of how color works in CSS, let's return to the discussion of formatting text with color. Similar to the `color` property, the `background-color` property accepts a color, but in this case the color represents the background color of a style rule, not the text color. Following is an example of the background-color property in action:

```
title {
  display:block;
  font:italic bold 18pt Courier, serif;
  color:green;
  background-color:#808080
}
```

In this example, green text is drawn over a gray background thanks to the `color` and `background-color` properties. If a background color isn't quite fancy enough for you, then you can specify a background image that is displayed behind the text content of an element. The `background-image` property accomplishes this task, as the following example reveals:

```
title {
  display:block;
  font:italic bold 18pt Courier, serif;
  color:green;
  background-image:url(monkey.gif)
}
```

In this example, the background image named `monkey.gif` is specified for the `title` style rule. Notice that the image URL is enclosed in parentheses that follow the word `url`; this is how image URLs must be specified when using the `background-image` property.

> It is possible to specify both a background color and a background image, in which case the background color will show through any transparent areas of the image.

When you set a background image for a style rule, the image is automatically tiled to fill the entire rectangular area of the element that is displayed. If you want to control the manner in which a background image is tiled, you can do so with the `background-repeat` property, which accepts the following values: `repeat`, `repeat-x`, `repeat-y`, and `no-repeat`. The default value is `repeat`. The `no-repeat` value displays only the background image once, whereas the `repeat-x` and `repeat-y` values tile the image repeatedly in the X and Y directions, respectively. Following is an example of setting the `background-repeat` property to have a background image appear only once:

```
title {
  display:block;
  font:italic bold 18pt Courier, serif;
  color:green;
  background-image:url(monkey.gif);
  background-repeat:no-repeat
}
```

If you'd like to specify several background properties without entering as much code, you can use the `background` property, which sets the background color, image, and repeat properties in a single style. Following is an example of setting the `background` property for the `title` style rule:

```
title {
  display:block;
  font:italic bold 18pt Courier, serif;
  color:green;
  background:gray url(monkey.gif) no-repeat
}
```

In this example, the `background` property is used to set a background color, to set a background image, and also to specify that the image be displayed only once.

Tweaking the Spacing of Text

If you're interesting in taking the formatting of text one step further than fonts, colors, and backgrounds, then you need to consider text spacing. Text spacing impacts both the indentation of paragraphs and the spacing that appears between characters of text. You can arrive at some interesting text effects by playing around with the spacing between characters. There are two CSS style properties that allow you to control the indentation and character spacing of text: `text-indent` and `letter-spacing`. These two properties both can be specified in units that you are hopefully familiar with by now: points (`pt`), inches (`in`), centimeters (`cm`), or pixels (`px`). Following is an example of how to set the indentation of a paragraph of text using the `text-indent` property:

```
message {
  display:block;
  text-indent:1.5in
}
```

11

This code sets the indentation of the message element to one-and-a-half inches, which means the first line of the text in the element will be displayed an inch-and-a-half over from the left edge of the element's rectangular area.

Although the letter-spacing property impacts text much differently than the text-indent property, it is specified similarly. Following is an example of how to alter the character spacing of the message element:

```
message {
  display:block;
  text-indent:1.5in;
  letter-spacing:5pt
}
```

In this example, the letter spacing of the message style rule is set to 5 points, which means the individual characters in the message will be separated by an additional 5 points when displayed. An interesting facet of the letter-spacing property is that it can also be used to move letters closer together by specifying a negative value.

Your Second Complete Style Sheet

You've covered a lot of new territory in this hour, and hopefully you've been able to digest all of it. Just in case it hit you too fast, I'd like to take a moment to show you how everything you've learned fits into a complete CSS example. The example involves an XML document called news.xml that contains a news story marked up with XML code. Listing 11.4 contains the code for the News example document, which could feasibly be used by a newspaper or newsletter Web site to encode stories.

LISTING 11.4 The News Example XML Document

```
 1: <?xml version="1.0"?>
 2: <?xml-stylesheet type="text/css" href="news.css"?>
 3:
 4: <news>
 5:   <header>
 6:     <headline>
 7:     Local Author Breaks Ankle In Gruesome Skateboard Accident
 8:     </headline>
 9:     <byline>
10:     By Eric Martin
11:     </byline>
12:     <dateline>
13:       <location>Nashville, Tennessee</location>
14:       <date>Tuesday December 11 2001 4:52 CST</date>
```

continues

LISTING 11.4   Continued

```
15:      </dateline>
16:    </header>
17:
18:    <story>
19:      <p>Local nerd author Michael Morrison broke his ankle today while
20:      skateboarding on a ramp at an undisclosed location. This injury comes
21:      as a considerable blow to Morrison considering that he recently
22:      emerged from retirement to make another go at skateboarding. Against
23:      the wishes of friends of family, Morrison decided to return to
24:      skateboarding where risk is a fact of life. His terse response to the
25:      injury was <quote>I don't think my ankle was supposed to bend that
26:      way</quote>.</p>
27:
28:      <p>Witnesses to the accident recall the gruesome aftermath. Fellow skater
29:      and witness Darin Masters said <quote>his ankle was twisted around like
30:      one of those little balloon animals</quote>. While out of commission for
31:      a few months, Mr. Morrison has vowed to make yet another return to the
32:      sport.</p>
33:    </story>
34: </news>
```

Admittedly, the news story in this case isn't exactly front page material, but it does reveal how the XML markup is used to add context to the content in the story. The goal of this example is to create a style sheet that displays the news story in a format similar to how you are accustomed to seeing printed stories in a newspaper. In other words, the title should appear in a large font followed by a much smaller byline and dateline and then the body of the story. The elements that factor into the style sheet are `headline`, `byline`, `dateline`, `p`, and `quote`. You could easily use absolute positioning to carefully lay out each of the elements in this example document, but it is not necessary. Rather than go into the details of absolute positioning, it is simpler in this case to carefully align the elements with the `text-align` property so that they appear where you want them. Listing 11.5 contains the code for the `news.css` style sheet, which is used to style the News XML document for display.

LISTING 11.5   The `news.css` Style Sheet Used to Format the News XML Document

```
1: headline {
2:    display:block;
3:    width:400px;
4:    border-bottom:5px double black;
5:    text-align:right;
6:    color:olive;
7:    font-family:Times, serif;
```

continues

LISTING 11.5 Continued

```
 8:    font-size:32pt;
 9: }
10:
11: byline {
12:    display:inline;
13:    width:200px;
14:    text-align:left;
15:    color:black;
16:    font-family:Times, serif;
17:    font-size:14pt;
18: }
19:
20: dateline {
21:    display:inline;
22:    width:200px;
23:    text-align:right;
24:    color:black;
25:    font-family:Times, serif;
26:    font-size:11pt;
27:    font-style:italic;
28: }
29:
30: p {
31:    display:block;
32:    width:400px;
33:    margin-bottom:8px;
34:    color:black;
35:    font-family:Times, serif;
36:    font-size:12pt;
37: }
38:
39: quote {
40:    display:inline;
41:    font-style:italic;
42: }
```

Although this style sheet is certainly larger than the Contacts style sheet you saw in the previous hour, it is actually very straightforward if you study each of the style rules carefully. For example, the headline style rule has a width, bottom border, text color, and font, and it has its text aligned right (lines 1–9). The byline style rule is defined as an inline rule (line 21) and aligns text to the right (line 23). The p style rule sets a bottom margin in order to provide exact spacing between paragraphs (line 33). All of the style rules use different sized fonts except for quote, which inherits the font size of its parent style rule, which in this case is p. The resulting view of the News document using the news.css style sheet is shown in Figure 11.5.

Figure 11.5

The News example document is displayed in Internet Explorer using the `news.css` *style sheet.*

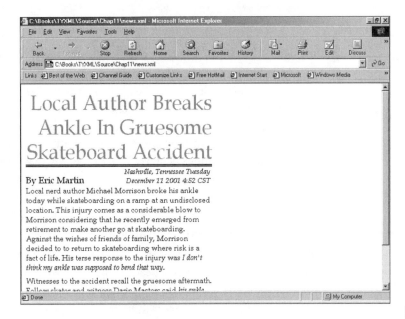

Summary

When it comes to positioning and formatting XML content for display within Web pages, CSS proves to be a powerful and easy-to-use technology. CSS gives you the ability to carefully control the positioning of XML content on a page and align it as desired. Once you've positioned XML content on a page, you have the option of formatting the text using a variety of different CSS style properties. Through these style properties, you can control the font, color, background, and spacing of text, which gives you considerable flexibility in determining the appearance of text.

This hour explored CSS styles in more detail by digging deeply into the positioning of XML content, as well as into the formatting of text. You began the hour by learning the difference between relative and absolute positioning and how each are used to position elements. You then learned about several other CSS positioning features such as z-index, margins, padding, and content alignment. You then moved on to learn some details about how to format text, which included coverage of fonts, colors, backgrounds, and text spacing. You wrapped up the hour by studying a complete CSS example that pulled together most of what you learned throughout the hour.

Q&A

Q How do you know when to use relative versus absolute positioning?

A Although there are no set guidelines regarding the usage of relative versus absolute positioning, the general idea is that absolute positioning is required only when you want to exert a fine degree of control over how content is positioned. This has to do with the fact that absolute positioning allows you to position content down to the exact pixel, whereas relative positioning is much less predictable in terms of how it positions content. This isn't to say that relative positioning can't do a good job of positioning XML content; it just means that absolute positioning is more exacting.

Q If you don't specify the z-index of two elements that overlap each other, how do you know which element will appear on top?

A If the `z-index` property isn't set for overlapping elements, the element appearing later in the XML content will appear on top. The easy way to remember this is to think of a Web browser drawing each element on a page as it reads it from the XML document; elements read later in the document are drawn on top of those read earlier.

Q Is there a way to know if a font is installed on a system when specifying it in a style sheet?

A No. Different users may have different fonts installed, and there is no way to predict what fonts will be available. The best solution to this problem is to use popular fonts or system fonts and always provide a secondary font that is ideally a system font.

Workshop

The Workshop is designed to help you anticipate possible questions, review what you've learned, and begin learning how to put your knowledge into practice.

Quiz

1. What is the difference between relative and absolute positioning?
2. What CSS style property do you use to control the manner in which elements overlap each other?
3. What is the significance of the `font` property?
4. How would you specify that a style rule is supposed to indent the first line of a paragraph by 6 centimeters?

Quiz Answers

1. In relative positioning, content is displayed according to the flow of a page, where each element physically appears after the element preceding it in an XML document. Absolute positioning, on the other hand, allows you to set the exact position of XML content on a page.

2. The `z-index` style property is used to control the manner in which elements overlap each other.

3. The `font` style property combines the other four font styles into a single property, which simply offers a more convenient approach to specifying font styles.

4. To specify that a style rule is supposed to indent the first line of a paragraph by 6 centimeters, you would use the style setting `text-indent:6cm`.

Exercises

1. Modify the `news.css` style sheet so that the story text is displayed with a gray background. Hint: This requires you to modify the style rule for the p element.

2. Modify the `news.css` style sheet so that the letter spacing of the headline is wider than normal.

11

HOUR 12

eXtensible Style Language (XSL) Fundamentals

Someone told me that each equation I included in the book would halve the sales.

—Stephen Hawking (on his book *A Brief History of Time*)

Unlike Mr. Hawking, I'm not afraid of a little extra complexity hurting the sales of this book. In reality, XSL is a more complex style sheet technology than CSS, so there is no way to thoroughly cover style sheets without things getting a little messy. Fortunately, as you learn in this hour, XSL is a technology that has considerably more to offer than CSS. In fact, XSL is designed to do a whole lot more than just format XML content for display purposes; it gives you the ability to completely transform XML documents.

You learn in this hour how to transform XML documents into HTML documents that can be viewed in Web browsers. Additionally, you hopefully will realize that the extra complexity in XSL is quite worth the learning curve because of its immense power and flexibility.

In this hour, you'll learn

- The basics of XSL and the technologies that comprise it
- The building blocks of the XSL Transformation (XSLT) language
- How to wire an XSL style sheet to an XML document
- How to develop an XSLT style sheet

Understanding XSL

As you've learned in previous hours, style sheets are special documents or pieces of code that are used to format XML content for display purposes. This definition of a style sheet is perfectly accurate for CSS, which is a style sheet technology that originated as a means of adding tighter control of HTML content formatting. XSL is also a style sheet technology, but it reaches beyond the simple formatting of content by also allowing you to completely transform content. Unlike CSS, XSL was solely designed as a style sheet technology for XML. In many ways, XSL accomplishes the same things that can be accomplished using CSS. However, XSL goes much further than CSS in its support for manipulating the structure of XML documents.

As you might expect, XSL is implemented using XML, which means that you code XSL style sheets using XML code. Even so, you may find it necessary to still use CSS in conjunction with XSL, at least in the near future. The reason for this has to do with the current state of XSL support in Web browsers. The component of XSL currently supported in Web browsers is XSLT, which allows you to transform XML documents via style sheet code. XSLT doesn't directly support the formatting of XML content for display purposes. The formatting component of XSL is XSL Formatting Objects, or XSL-FO, which consists of special style objects that can be applied to XML content to format it for display. XSL-FO is currently not supported in any major Web browsers and is therefore unavailable for commercial use for the moment. In the meantime, XSLT is quite useful when paired with CSS; XSLT allows you to transform any XML document into HTML that can be styled and displayed with CSS in a Web browser.

You learn more about XSLT, XSL-FO, and the other component of XSL, XPath, later in the hour.

It is important to understand how an XSL style sheet is processed and applied to an XML document. This task begins with an XML processor, which is responsible for reading an XML document and processing it into meaningful pieces of information known as *nodes*. More specifically, you learned earlier in the book that XML documents are processed into a hierarchical tree containing nodes for each piece of information in a document. For example, every element and attribute in a document represents a node in the tree representation of a document. Thinking in terms of an XML document as a tree is extremely important when it comes to understanding XSL. After a document has been processed into a tree, a special processor known as an *XSL processor* begins applying the rules of an XSL style sheet to the document tree.

The XSL processor starts with the root node (root element) in the tree and uses it as the basis for performing pattern matching in the style sheet. *Pattern matching* is the process of using patterns to identify nodes in the tree that are to be processed according to XSL styles. These patterns are stored within constructs known as *templates* in XSL style sheets. The XSL processor analyzes templates and the patterns associated with them to process different parts of the document tree. When a match is made, the portion of the tree matching the given pattern is processed by the appropriate style sheet template. At this point, the rules of the template are applied to the content to generate a result tree. The *result tree* is itself a tree of data, but the data in this case has somehow been transformed by the style sheet. To put it another way, the XSL processor takes a document tree as input and generates another tree, a result tree, as output. Figure 12.1 illustrates the process of using a pattern to match a portion of a document tree and then applying a pattern to it to generate a result tree.

FIGURE 12.1

A pattern is used to match a portion of a document, which is then transformed into a result tree using a template.

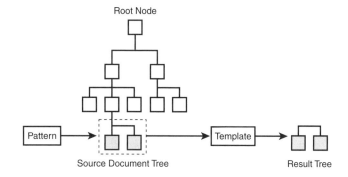

Root Node

Pattern

Source Document Tree

Template

Result Tree

12

When I refer to "tree" of data, I'm really talking about the logical structure of the data. To better understand what I mean, think in terms of your family tree, where each relationship forms a branch and each person forms a leaf, or node, on the tree. The same logical relationships apply to XML trees, except the nodes are elements and attributes as opposed to people.

The result tree may contain XML code, HTML code, or special objects known as XSL formatting objects. In the case of XML code, the result tree represents a transformation from one form of XML to another. In the case of HTML code, the result tree represents a transformation from XML code into HTML code that can be viewed in a Web browser. Technically speaking, you can't use traditional HTML code as the basis for an XSL result tree because traditional HTML isn't considered an XML-based language. However, if the HTML code adheres to XHTML standards, which is a stricter version of HTML formulated as an XML language, then everything will work fine. You learn more about XHTML in Hour 18, "Getting to Know XHTML." You also learn how to transform XML code into HTML (XHTML) later in this hour in the section titled, "Your First XSLT Style Sheet."

In order to finish creating the result tree, the XSL processor continues processing each node in the document tree, applying all of the templates defined in the style sheet. When all of the nodes have been processed and all of the style sheet templates applied, the XSL processor returns the completed result tree, which is often in a format suitable for display. I say "often" because it is possible to use XSL to transform a document from one XML language to another instead of to HTML, in which case the resulting document may or may not be used for display purposes.

The Pieces and Parts of XSL

In order to understand the relevance of XSL technologies, it's important to examine the role of the XSL processor once more. The XSL processor is responsible for performing two fundamental tasks:

- Construct a result tree from a transformation of a source document tree
- Interpret the result tree for formatting purposes

The first task addressed by the XSL processor is known as *tree transformation* and involves transforming a source tree of document content into a result tree. Tree transformation is basically the process of transforming XML content from one XML language into another and involves the use of XSLT. The second task performed by the XSL processor involves examining the result tree for formatting information and formatting the content for each node accordingly. This task requires the use of XSL-FO and is currently not supported directly in Web browsers. Even so, it is a critical part of XSL that will likely play a significant role in the future of XML.

Although it certainly seems convenient to break up XSL processing into two tasks, there is a much more important reason for doing so than mere convenience. One way to understand this significance is to consider CSS, which supports only the formatting of XML content. The limitations of CSS are obvious when you consider that a source document can't really be modified in any way for display purposes. On the other hand, with XSL you have complete freedom to massage the source document at will during the transformation part of the document processing. The one-two punch of transformation followed by formatting provides an incredible degree of flexibility for rendering XML documents for display.

The two fundamental tasks taken on by the XML processor directly correspond to two XSL technologies: XSLT and XSL-FO. Additionally, there is a third XSL technology, XPath, that factors heavily into XSLT. XSLT and XSL-FO are both implemented as XML languages, which makes their syntax familiar. This also means that style sheets created from them are XML documents. The interesting thing about these two components of XSL is that they can be used together or separately. You can use XSLT to transform documents without any concern over how the documents are formatted. Similarly, you will be able to use XSL Formatting Objects to format XML documents without necessarily performing any transformation on them.

The important thing to keep in mind regarding the structure of XSL is the fact that XSL is really three languages, not one. XSLT is the XSL transformation language that is used to transform XML documents from one vocabulary to another. XSL Formatting Objects is the XSL formatting language that is used to apply formatting styles to XML documents for display purposes. And finally, XPath is a special non-XML expression language used to address parts of an XML document.

12

Although you learn the basics of XPath in this hour and the next, you aren't formally introduced to it until Hour 19, "Addressing XML Documents with XPath." In that hour you learn the details of how to address portions of an XML document using XPath.

XSL Transformation

XSL Transformation (XSLT) is the transformation component of the XSL style sheet technology. XSLT consists of an XML-based markup language that is used to create style sheets for transforming XML documents. These style sheets operate on parsed XML data in a tree form, which is then output as a result tree consisting of the transformed data. XSLT uses a powerful pattern-matching mechanism to select portions of an XML document for transformation. When a pattern is matched for a portion of a tree, a template is used to determine how that portion of the tree is transformed. You learn more about how templates and patterns are used to transform XML documents a little later in this hour.

An integral part of XSLT is a technology known as XPath, which is used to select nodes for processing and generating text. The next section examines XPath in more detail. The remainder of this hour and the next tackles XSLT in greater detail.

XPath

XPath is a non-XML expression language that is used to address parts of an XML document. XPath is different from its other XSL counterparts (XSLT and XSL-FO) in that it isn't implemented as an XML language. This is due to the fact that XPath expressions are used in situations where XML markup isn't really applicable, such as within attribute values. As you know, attribute values are simple text and therefore can't contain additional XML markup. So, although XPath expressions are used within XML markup, they don't directly utilize tags and attributes themselves.

The central function of XPath is to provide an abstract means of addressing XML document parts—for this reason, XPath forms the basis for document addressing in XSLT. The syntax used by XPath is designed for use in URIs and XML attribute values, which requires it to be extremely concise. The name XPath is based on the notion of using a path notation to address XML documents, much as you might use a path in a file system to describe the location of a file. Similar to XSLT, XPath operates under the assumption that a document has been parsed into a tree of nodes. XPath defines different types of nodes that are used to describe the nodes that appear within a tree. There is always a single root node that serves as the root of an XPath tree, and that appears as the first node in the tree. Every element in a document has a corresponding *element node* that appears in the tree under the root node. Within an element node there are other types of nodes that correspond to the element's content. Element nodes may have a unique identifier associated with them, which is used to reference the node with XPath.

Following is an example of a simple XPath expression, which demonstrates how XPath expressions are used in attribute values:

```
<xsl:for-each select="contacts/contact">
```

This code shows how an XPath expression is used within an XSLT element (`xsl:for-each`) to reference elements named `contact` that are children of an element named `contacts`. Although it isn't important for you to understand the implications of this code in an XSLT style sheet, it is important to realize that XPath is used to address certain nodes (elements) within a document.

When an XPath expression is used in an XSLT style sheet, the evaluation of the expression results in a data object of a specific type, such as a Boolean or a number. The manner in which an XPath expression is evaluated is entirely dependent upon the context of the expression, which isn't determined by XPath. This is the abstract nature of XPath that allows it to be used as a helper technology alongside XSLT to address parts of documents. The context of an XPath expression is determined by XSLT, which in turn determines how expressions are evaluated.

> XPath's role in XSL doesn't end with XSLT—XPath is also used with XLink and XPointer, which you learn about in Hour 20, "XML Linking with XLink and XPointer."

XSL Formatting Objects

XSL Formatting Objects (XSL-FO) represents the formatting component of the XSL style sheet technology and is designed to be a functional superset of CSS. This means that XSL-FO will contain all of the functionality of CSS, even though it uses its own XML-based syntax. Similar to XSLT, XSL-FO is implemented as an XML language, which is beneficial for both minimizing the learning curve for XML developers and easing its integration into existing XML tools. Also like XSLT, XSL-FO operates on a tree of XML data, which can either be parsed directly from a document or transformed from a document using XSLT. For formatting purposes, XSL-FO treats every node in the tree as a *formatting object,* with each node supporting a wide range of presentation styles. You can apply styles by setting attributes on a given element (node) in the tree.

There are formatting objects that correspond to different aspects of document formatting such as layout, pagination, and content styling. Every formatting object has properties that are used to somehow describe the object. Some properties directly specify a formatted result, such as a color or font, whereas other properties establish constraints on a set of possible formatted results. Following is perhaps the simplest possible example of XSL-FO, which sets the font family and font size for a block of text:

```
<fo:block font-family="Arial" font-size="16pt">
  This text has been styled with XSL-FO!
</fo:block>
```

12

As you can see, this code performs a similar function to CSS in establishing the font family and font size of a block of text. XSL-FO actually goes further than CSS in allowing you to control the formatting of XML content in extreme detail. The layout model employed by XSL-FO is described in terms of rectangular areas and spaces, which isn't too surprising considering that this approach is employed by most desktop publishing applications. Rectangular areas in XSL-FO are not objects themselves, however; it is up to formatting objects to establish rectangular areas and the relationships between them. This is somewhat similar to rectangular areas in CSS, where you establish the size of an area (box) by setting the width and height of a paragraph of text.

The XSL processor is heavily involved in carrying out the functionality in XSL-FO style sheets. When the XSL processor processes a formatting object within a style sheet, the object is mapped into a rectangular area on the display surface. The properties of the object determine how it is formatted, along with the parameters of the area into which it is mapped.

The immediate downside to XSL-FO is that it isn't currently supported in any major Web browsers. For this reason, I don't cover XSL-FO in any more detail throughout the book. However, if you'd like to begin experimenting with XSL-FO on your own, you can obtain a free evaluation XSL-FO formatter called XEP on the Web at `http://www.renderx.com/FO2PDF.html`. XEP is an XSL processor that is capable of using XSL-FO to render XML documents into a viewable format, such as Adobe Acrobat (PDF). XEP is made available by RenderX, Inc. Also, if you'd like to keep up with the latest information surrounding XSL-FO, please visit the XSL section of the W3C Web site at `http://www.w3.org/TR/xsl/`.

An XSLT Primer

Seeing as how XSL-FO is currently unavailable for use in major Web browsers, the practical usage of XSL must focus on XSLT for the time being. This isn't entirely a bad thing when you consider the learning curve for XSL in general. It may be that by staggering the adoption of the two technologies, the W3C may be inadvertently giving developers time to get up to speed with XSLT before tackling XSL-FO. The remainder of this hour focuses on XSLT and how you can use it to transform XML documents.

As you now know, the purpose of an XSLT style sheet is to process the nodes of an XML document and apply a pattern-matching mechanism to determine which nodes are to be transformed. Both the pattern-matching mechanism and the details of each transformation are spelled out in an XSLT style sheet. More specifically, an XSLT style sheet consists of one or more templates that describe patterns and expressions, which are used to match XML content for transformation purposes. The three fundamental constructs in an XSL style sheet are as follows:

- Templates
- Patterns
- Expressions

Before getting into these constructs, however, you need to learn about the `xsl:stylesheet` element and learn how the XSLT namespace is used in XSLT style sheets. The `stylesheet` element is the document (root) element for XSL style sheets and is part of the XSLT namespace. You are required to declare the XSLT namespace in order to use XSLT elements and attributes. Following is an example of declaring the XSLT namespace inside of the `stylesheet` element:

```
<xsl:stylesheet version="1.0" xmlns:xsl="http://
  www.w3.org/1999/XSL/Transform">
```

This example namespace declaration sets the prefix for the XSLT namespace to `xsl`, which is the standard prefix used in XSL style sheets. You must precede all XSLT elements and attributes with this prefix. Notice in the code that the XSLT namespace is `http://www.w3.org/1999/XSL/Transform`. Another important aspect of this code is the version attribute, which sets the version of XSL used in the style sheet. Currently the only version of XSL is 1.0, so you should set the `version` attribute to `1.0` in your style sheets.

The XSLT namespace is specific to XSLT and does not apply to all of XSL. If you plan on developing style sheets that use XSL-FO, you'll also need to declare the XSL-FO namespace, which is `http://www.w3.org/1999/XSL/Format` and typically has the prefix `fo`.

12

Templates

A *template* is an XSL construct that describes output to be generated based upon certain pattern-matching criteria. The idea behind a template is to define a transformation mechanism that applies to a certain portion of an XML document, which is a node or group of nodes. Although it is possible to create style sheets consisting of a single template, you will more than likely create multiple templates to transform different portions of the XML document tree.

Templates are defined in XSL style sheets using the xsl:template element, which is primarily a container element for patterns, expressions, and transformation logic. The xsl:template element uses an optional attribute named match to match patterns and expressions in an XSLT style sheet. You can think of the match attribute as specifying a portion of the XML tree for a document. The widest possible match for a document is to set the match attribute to /, which indicates that the root of the tree is to be matched. This results in the entire tree being selected for transformation by the template, as the following code demonstrates:

```
<xsl:template match="/">
...
</xsl:template>
```

If you have any experience with databases, then you might recognize the match attribute as being somewhat similar to a query in a database language. To understand what I mean by this, consider the following example, which uses the match attribute to match only elements named state:

```
<xsl:template match="state">
...
</xsl:template>
```

This template would come in useful for XML documents that have elements named state. For example, the template would match the state element in the following XML code:

```
<contact>
  <name>Frank Rizzo</name>
  <address>1212 W 304th Street</address>
  <city>New York</city>
  <state>New York</state>
  <zip>10011</zip>
  <phone>
    <voice>212-555-1212</voice>
    <fax>212-555-1213</fax>
  </phone>
  <company>Frank&apos;s Ratchet Service</company>
</contact>
```

Matching a portion of an XML document wouldn't mean much if the template didn't carry out any kind of transformation. Transformation logic is created using several template constructs that are used to control the application of templates in XSL style sheets. These template constructs are actually elements defined in the XSLT namespace. Following are some of the more commonly used XSLT elements:

- xsl:value-of—inserts the value of an element or attribute
- xsl:if—performs a conditional selection (this or that)
- xsl:for-each—loops through the elements in a document
- xsl:apply-templates—applies a template in a style sheet

A crucial part of XSLT document transformation is the insertion of document content into the result tree, which is carried out with the xsl:value-of element. The xsl:value-of element provides the mechanism for transforming XML documents because it allows you to output XML data in virtually any context, such as within HTML markup. The xsl:value-of element requires an attribute named select that identifies the specific content to be inserted. Following is an example of a simple template that uses the xsl:value-of element and the select attribute to output the value of an element named title:

```
<xsl:template match="title">
  <xsl:value-of select="."/>
</xsl:template>
```

In this example the select attribute is set to ., which indicates that the current node is to be inserted into the result tree. The value of the select attribute works very much like the path of a file on a hard drive. For example, a file on a hard drive might be specified as \docs\letters\lovenote.txt. This path indicates the folder hierarchy of the file lovenote.txt. In a similar way, the select attribute specifies the location of the node to be inserted in the result tree. A dot (.) indicates a node in the current context, as determined by the match attribute. An element or attribute name indicates a node beneath the current node, whereas two dots (..) indicate the parent of the current node. This approach to specifying node paths using a special expression language is covered in much greater detail in Hour 19, "Addressing XML Documents with XPath."

To get an idea as to how the previous example template (matching title elements) can be used to transform XML code, take a look at the following code excerpt:

```
<book>
  <title>All The King's Men</title>
  <author>Robert Penn Warren</author>
</book>
<book>
  <title>Atlas Shrugged</title>
  <author>Ayn Rand</author>
</book>
<book>
  <title>Ain't Nobody's Business If You Do</title>
  <author>Peter McWilliams</author>
</book>
```

Applying the previous template to this code would result in the following results:

```
All The King's Men
Atlas Shrugged
Ain't Nobody's Business If You Do
```

As you can see, the titles of the books are plucked out of the code because the template matched title elements and then inserted their contents into the resulting document.

12

In addition to inserting XML content using the xsl:value-of element in a style sheet, it is also possible to conditionally carry out portions of the logic in a style sheet. More specifically, the xsl:if element is used to perform conditional matches in templates. This element uses the same match attribute as the xsl:template element to establish conditional branching in templates. Following is an example of how the xsl:if element is used to test if the name of a state attribute is equal to NY:

```
<xsl:if match="@state=NY">
  <xsl:apply-templates select="location"/>
</xsl:if>
```

Notice in this code that the state attribute is preceded by an "at" symbol (@); this symbol is used in XPath to identify an attribute, as opposed to an element. Another important aspect of this code is the manner in which the location template is applied only if the state attribute is equal to NY. The end result is that only the location elements whose state attribute is set to NY are processed for transformation.

If you have any programming experience, then you are no doubt familiar with loops, which allow you to repeatedly perform an operation on a number of items. If you don't have programming experience, a loop is a way of performing an action over and over. In the case of XSLT, loops are created with the xsl:for-each element, which is used to loop through elements in a document. The xsl:for-each element requires a select attribute that determines which elements are selected as part of the loop's iteration. Following is an example of using the xsl:for-each element to iterate through a list of locations:

```
<xsl:for-each select="locations/location">
  <h1><xsl:value-of select="@city"/>,
  <xsl:value-of select="@state"/></h1>
  <h2><xsl:value-of select="description"/></h2>
</xsl:for-each>
```

In this example the xsl:for-each element is used to loop through location elements that are stored within the parent locations element. Within the loop, the city and state attributes are inserted into the result tree, along with the description element. This template is interesting in that it uses carefully placed HTML elements to transform the XML code into HTML code that can be viewed in a Web browser. Following is some example code to which you might apply this template:

```
</locations>
  <location city="Washington" state="DC">
    <description>The United States Capital</description>
  </location>
  <location city="Nashville" state="TN">
    <description>Music City USA</description>
  </location>
```

```
  <location city="Chicago" state="IL">
    <description>The Windy City</description>
  </location>
</locations>
```

Applying the previous template to this code yields the following results:

```
<h1>Washington, DC</h1>
<h2>The United States Capital</h2>
<h1>Nashville, TN</h1>
<h2>Music City USA</h2>
<h1>Chicago, IL</h1>
<h2>The Windy City</h2>
```

As you can see, the template successfully transforms the XML code into HTML code that is capable of being viewed in a Web browser. Notice that the cities and states are combined within large heading elements (h1), followed by the descriptions, which are coded in smaller heading elements (h2).

In order for a template to be applied to XML content, you must explicitly apply the template with the xsl:apply-templates element. The xsl:apply-templates element supports the familiar select attribute, which performs a similar role to the one it does in the xsl:for-each element. When the XSL processor encounters an xsl:apply-templates element in a style sheet, the template corresponding to the pattern or expression in the select attribute is applied, which means that relevant document data is fed into the template and transformed. Following is an example of applying a template using the xsl:apply-templates element:

```
<xsl:apply-templates select="location"/>
```

12

 The exception to the rule of having to use the xsl:apply-templates element to apply templates in an XSLT style sheet is the root element, whose template is automatically applied if one exists.

This code results in the template for the location element being invoked in the current context.

Patterns and Expressions

Patterns and expressions are used in XSLT templates to perform matches and are ultimately responsible for determining what portions of an XML document are passed through a particular template for transformation. A *pattern* describes a branch of an XML tree, which in turn consists of a set of hierarchical nodes. Patterns are used throughout XSL to describe portions of a document tree for applying templates. Patterns can be constructed to perform relatively complex pattern-matching tasks. When you think of patterns in this light, they form somewhat of a mini-query language that can be used to provide exacting controls over the portions of an XML document that are selected for transformation in templates.

As you learned earlier, the syntax used by XSL patterns is somewhat similar to that used when specifying paths to files on a disk drive. For example, the `contacts/contact/phone` pattern selects `phone` elements that are children of a `contact` element, which itself is a child of a `contacts` element. It is possible, and often useful, to select the entire document tree in a pattern, which is carried out with a single forward slash (`/`). This pattern is also known as the *root pattern* and is assumed in other patterns if you leave it off. For example, the `contacts/contact/phone` pattern is assumed to begin at the root of the document, which means that `contacts` is the root element for the document.

Expressions are similar to patterns in that they also impact which nodes are selected for transformation. However, expressions are capable of carrying out processing of their own, such as mathematical calculations, text processing, and conditional tests. XSL includes numerous built-in functions that are used to construct expressions within style sheets. Following is a simple example of an expression:

```
<xsl:value-of select="sum(@price)"/>
```

This code demonstrates how to use the standard `sum()` function to calculate the sum of the `price` attributes within a particular set of elements. This could be useful in a shopping cart application that needs to calculate a subtotal of the items located in the cart.

Admittedly, this discussion isn't the last word on XSL patterns and expressions. Fortunately, you learn a great deal more about patterns and expressions in Hour 19, "Addressing XML Documents with XPath." In the meantime, this introduction will get you started creating XSL style sheets.

Wiring an XSL Style Sheet to an XML Document

In the previous two hours you learned how to create and connect CSS style sheets to XML documents. These types of style sheets are known as external style sheets because they are stored in separate, external files. XSL style sheets are also typically stored in external files, in which case you must wire them to XML documents in order for them to be applied. XSL style sheets are stored in files with an `.xsl` filename extension and are wired to XML documents using the `xml-stylesheet` processing instruction. The `xml-stylesheet` processing instruction includes a couple of attributes that determine the type and location of the style sheet:

- `type`—the type of the style sheet (`text/xsl`, for example)
- `href`—the location of the style sheet

> You may notice that this discussion focuses on XSL style sheets, as opposed to XSLT style sheets. That's because XSLT style sheets are really just a specific kind of XSL style sheet, and from the perspective of an XML document there is no difference between the two. So, when it comes to associating an XSLT style sheet with an XML document, you simply reference it as an XSL style sheet.

These two attributes should be somewhat familiar to you from the discussion of CSS because they are also used to wire CSS to XML documents. The difference in their usage with XSL is revealed in their values—the `type` attribute must be set to `text/xsl` for XSL style sheets, whereas the `href` attribute must be set to the name of the XSL style sheet. These two attributes are both required in order to wire an XSL style sheet to an XML document. Following is an example of how to use the `xml-stylesheet` processing instruction with an XSL style sheet:

```
<?xml-stylesheet type="text/xsl" href="contacts.xsl"?>
```

In this example, the `type` attribute is used to specify that the type of the style sheet is `text/xsl`, which means that the style sheet is an XSL style sheet. The style sheet file is then referenced in the `href` attribute, which in this case points to the file `contacts.xsl`.

Your First XSLT Style Sheet

With just enough XSLT knowledge to get you in trouble, why not go ahead and tackle a complete example style sheet? Don't worry, this example shouldn't be too hard to grasp because it is focused on familiar territory. I'm referring to the Contacts example XML document from Hour 10. If you recall, in that hour you created a CSS to display the content from an XML document containing a list of contacts. Now it's time to take a look at how the exact same functionality is carried out using an XSLT style sheet. To refresh your memory, the Contacts XML document is shown in Listing 12.1.

12

LISTING 12.1   The Familiar Contacts Example XML Document

```
 1: <?xml version="1.0"?>
 2: <?xml-stylesheet type="text/xsl" href="contacts.xsl"?>
 3: <!DOCTYPE contacts SYSTEM "contacts.dtd">
 4:
 5: <contacts>
 6:   <!-- This is my good friend Frank. -->
 7:   <contact>
 8:     <name>Frank Rizzo</name>
 9:     <address>1212 W 304th Street</address>
10:     <city>New York</city>
11:     <state>New York</state>
12:     <zip>10011</zip>
13:     <phone>
14:       <voice>212-555-1212</voice>
15:       <fax>212-555-1213</fax>
16:     </phone>
17:     <company>Frank&apos;s Ratchet Service</company>
18:   </contact>
19:
20:   <!-- This is my old college roommate Sol. -->
21:   <contact>
22:     <name>Sol Rosenberg</name>
23:     <address>1162 E 412th Street</address>
24:     <city>New York</city>
25:     <state>New York</state>
26:     <zip>10011</zip>
27:     <phone>
28:       <voice>212-555-1818</voice>
29:       <fax>212-555-1819</fax>
30:     </phone>
31:     <company>Rosenberg&apos;s Shoes &amp; Glasses</company>
32:   </contact>
33: </contacts>
```

The only noticeable change in this version of the Contacts document is the xml-stylesheet declaration (line 2), which now references the style sheet file contacts.xsl. Beyond this change, the document is exactly as it appeared in Hour 10. Keep in mind that the role of the XSLT style sheet is to display the contacts in a format somewhat like a mailing list, where the phone number and company name are hidden. Perhaps of more significance is the fact that XSLT isn't directly capable of formatting the document content for display; don't forget that XSLT is used only to transform XML code. Knowing this, it becomes apparent that CSS must still enter the picture with this example. However, in this case CSS is used purely for display formatting, whereas XSLT takes care of determining which portions of the document are displayed.

In order to use CSS with XSLT, it is necessary to transform an XML document into HTML, or more specifically, XHTML. If you recall, XHTML is the more structured version of HTML that conforms to the rules of XML. The idea is to transform relevant XML content into an XHTML Web page that uses CSS styles for specific display formatting. The resulting XHTML document can then be displayed in a Web browser. Listing 12.2 contains the XSLT style sheet (`contacts.xsl`) that carries out this functionality.

LISTING 12.2   The `contacts.xsl` Style Sheet Used to Transform and Format the Contacts XML Document

```
 1: <?xml version="1.0"?>
 2: <xsl:stylesheet version="1.0"
 3:   xmlns:xsl="http://www.w3.org/1999/XSL/Transform">
 4:   <xsl:template match="/">
 5:     <html><head><title>Contact List</title></head>
 6:       <body>
 7:         <xsl:for-each select="contacts/contact">
 8:           <div style="width:275px; margin-bottom:10px;
 9:             border:5px double black; color:black; background-color:yellow;
10:             text-align:center">
11:             <xsl:apply-templates select="name"/>
12:             <xsl:apply-templates select="address"/>
13:             <xsl:apply-templates select="city"/>
14:             <xsl:apply-templates select="state"/>
15:             <xsl:apply-templates select="zip"/>
16:           </div>
17:         </xsl:for-each>
18:       </body>
19:     </html>
20:   </xsl:template>
21:
22:   <xsl:template match="name">
23:     <div style="font-family:Times, serif; font-size:15pt; font-weight:bold">
24:       <xsl:value-of select="."/>
25:     </div>
26:   </xsl:template>
27:
28:   <xsl:template match="address">
29:     <div style="font-family:Times, serif; font-size:13pt">
30:       <xsl:value-of select="."/>
31:     </div>
32:   </xsl:template>
33:
34:   <xsl:template match="city">
35:     <span style="font-family:Times, serif; font-size:13pt">
36:       <xsl:value-of select="."/>,
37:     </span>
38:   </xsl:template>
```

12

continues

LISTING **12.2**   Continued

```
39:
40:   <xsl:template match="state">
41:     <span style="font-family:Times, serif; font-size:13pt">
42:       <xsl:value-of select="."/>
43:     </span>
44:   </xsl:template>
45:
46:   <xsl:template match="zip">
47:     <span style="font-family:Times, serif; font-size:13pt">
48:       <xsl:value-of select="."/>
49:     </span>
50:   </xsl:template>
51: </xsl:stylesheet>
```

Although there is a fair amount of code in this style sheet, the functionality of the code is relatively straightforward. The style sheet begins by declaring the XSLT namespace (lines 2–3). With that bit of standard overhead out of the way, the style sheet creates a template used to match the root element of the document (line 4); this is indicated by the match attribute being set to /. Notice that within this template there is XHTML code that is used to construct an XHTML Web page. Inside the body of the newly constructed Web page is where the interesting things take place with the style sheet (lines 7–18).

An xsl:for-each element is used to loop through the contact elements in the document (line 7); each of the contacts is displayed inside of a div element. The specific content associated with a contact is inserted into the div element using the xsl:apply-templates element to apply a template to each piece of information. More specifically, templates are applied to the name, address, city, state, and zip child elements of the contact element (lines 11–15). Of course, in order to apply these templates, the templates themselves must exist.

The first child template matches the name element (lines 22–26) and uses CSS to format the content in the name element for display. Notice that the xsl:value-of element is used to insert the content of the name element into the transformed XHTML code. The dot (.) specified in the select attribute indicates that the value applies to the current node, which is the name element. Similar templates are defined for the remaining child elements, which are transformed and formatted in a similar fashion.

The end result of this style sheet is a transformed XHTML document that can be viewed as a Web page in a Web browser. Figure 12.2 shows the resulting Web page generated by this XSLT style sheet.

FIGURE 12.2

The Contacts example document is displayed in Internet Explorer using the contacts.xsl *style sheet.*

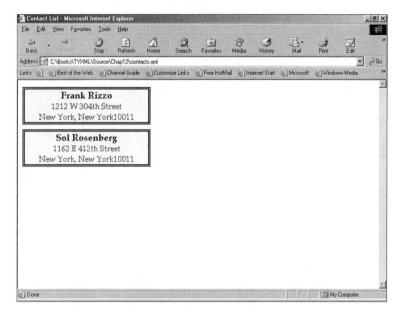

The figure reveals how the contacts.xsl style sheet carries out similar functionality as its CSS counterpart from Hour 10. However, in this case the style sheet is literally transforming XML content into XHTML content, which is then capable of being displayed in a Web browser. Although this style sheet certainly demonstrates the basic functionality of XSLT, it doesn't touch the powerful transformation features at your disposal with XSLT. I'll leave that for the next hour.

Summary

XSL (Extensible Style Language) is an extremely powerful style sheet technology that is aimed at providing a purely XML-based solution for the transformation and formatting of XML documents. XSL consists of three fundamental technologies: XSL Transformation (XSLT), XPath, and XSL Formatting Objects (XSL-FO). XSLT tackles the transformation aspect of XSL and is capable of transforming an XML document in a particular language into a completely different XML-based language. XPath is used within XSLT to identify portions of an XML document for transformation. XSL-FO is the newest component of XSL that addresses the need for a high-powered XML-based formatting language. XSL-FO is currently not supported in Web browsers, but XSLT and XPath are more than ready to deliver.

12

This hour introduced you to the different technologies that comprise XSL. In doing so, it gave you an understanding of how an XSL processor is used to process XSL style sheets. Perhaps more important is the practical knowledge you gained of XSLT, which culminated in a complete XSLT style sheet example. Just in case you're worried that this hour hit only the high points of XSLT, the next hour digs deeper into the technology and uncovers topics such as sorting nodes and using expressions.

Q&A

Q If I can't format XML documents using XSLT, why wouldn't I just use CSS to create style sheets for XML documents?

A If all you need to do is simply display the content in an XML document, then CSS may in fact be your best option. However, XSLT allows you to process XML content and gives you a fine degree of control over what content is displayed and the order in which it appears. So, even though XSLT doesn't directly play a role in formatting documents for display, it provides a considerable amount of indirect control when it comes to isolating data, sorting data (numerically or alphabetically, for example), and performing calculations on data within XML documents.

Q How can there be separate namespaces for XSLT and XSL-FO if they are both part of XSL?

A XSLT and XSL-FO have different namespaces because they are different languages. Keep in mind that each of these technologies is implemented as an XML-based markup language. Since it is possible to use the two technologies independently of one another, they occupy separate namespaces. You can certainly use both XSLT and XSL-FO in the same XSL style sheet, in which case you would declare both namespaces with their own prefixes. For the time being, however, you will likely create XSL style sheets using only XSLT, in which case you can refer to the style sheet as an XSLT style sheet.

Workshop

The Workshop is designed to help you anticipate possible questions, review what you've learned, and begin learning how to put your knowledge into practice.

Quiz

1. In regard to the XSL processor, what is pattern matching?
2. Which two XSL technologies would you rely on if you only needed to transform an XML document?

3. How do you define templates in XSLT style sheets?

4. What is the difference between patterns and expressions?

Quiz Answers

1. Pattern matching is the process of using patterns to identify nodes in the source document tree that are to be processed according to XSL styles and transformed into a result tree.

2. XSLT and XPath are the two XSL technologies that you would rely on if you only needed to transform an XML document. XSL-FO enters the picture only if you planned on formatting a document using XSL.

3. Templates are defined in XSL style sheets using the `xsl:template` element, which is primarily a container element for patterns, expressions, and transformation logic.

4. A pattern identifies a branch of an XML tree for transformation purposes. Expressions are similar to patterns in that they also impact which nodes are selected for transformation. However, unlike patterns, expressions are capable of carrying out processing of their own, such as mathematical calculations, text processing, and conditional tests.

Exercises

1. If you recall, you added a new element named `email` to the Contacts XML document in Exercise 1 of Hour 10. Modify the `contacts.xsl` style sheet to create a template for transforming the new `email` element.

2. The new `email` template doesn't impact the style sheet until you apply it. Modify the `contacts.xsl` style sheet so that the `email` template is applied along with the other contact templates.

12

Hour 13

Transforming XML with XSLT

I don't have any solution but I certainly admire the problem.

—Ashleigh Brilliant, creator of "Pot-Shots" and "Brilliant Thoughts"

When it comes to transforming XML, you have a wonderful solution in XSLT. In the previous hour you learned the basics of XSLT and were quickly introduced to the XSLT language and the way to use it to create basic XSLT style sheets. This hour picks up where the previous one left off by examining the XSLT language in more detail and showing you some interesting ways in which XSLT can be used to transform XML content. More specifically, you learn how to sort and process nodes, as well as how to perform conditional tests and computational operations with expressions. This hour arms you with the XSLT knowledge necessary to create practical XSLT style sheets that you can use in your own XML projects.

In this hour, you'll learn

- More details about the XSLT style sheet language
- How to process and sort nodes in an XSLT style sheet
- How to use patterns and expressions in XSLT
- How to apply XSLT style sheets to more challenging document transformation tasks

A Closer Look at XSLT

As you know, XSLT is an XML-based markup language that includes its own set of elements and attributes that are used to create XSLT style sheets. These style sheets are used with XML documents to transform XML content in some manner. This transformation can be something as simple as sorting the content according to a certain piece of information, such as sorting products by price, or it can be as powerful as transforming content into a completely different XML language. Regardless of how you use XSLT, it's important to have a solid understanding of the XSLT language and what it has to offer.

An XSLT style sheet is broken down into two types of information: instructions and literals. *Instructions* are the XSLT elements and attributes that describe exactly how XML content is to be transformed. *Literals,* on the other hand, are static pieces of information that are placed directly in the resulting document and therefore aren't processed in any way. You can think of the relationship between instructions and literals as the relationship between text and blanks in a traditional paper form that you might fill out; the text on the form is static and doesn't change, whereas the blanks are subject to being filled in by whomever is using the form. In the case of XSLT, the blanks are "filled in" by XSLT instructions that determine the XML content to be placed in the blanks. The resulting output document is the combination of transformed XML content and the literals located throughout a style sheet.

 Literals play a significant role in XSLT whenever you transform an XML document into an XHTML document for display in a Web browser. In order to successfully generate an XHTML document using XSLT, you must place XHTML code throughout the style sheet as literals. XSL instructions are then used to transform XML content and place it within the XHTML code.

XML content is merged with literals in a style sheet by way of the xsl:value-of element, which inserts the value of an element or attribute in the output document. To get a better understanding of how this works, consider the following example:

```
<p>Hello, my name is <xsl:value-of select="name"/></p>
```

This code shows how the xsl:value-of element is used to insert the value of a name element into an XHTML paragraph. In this example, the xsl:value-of element is the instruction, and the remaining XHTML code is the literal. Now that you understand the difference between instructions and literals, let's move on to more important business.

Creating and Applying Templates

You learned in the previous hour that templates are used in XSLT style sheets to transform a particular portion of an XML document for output to a result tree. Templates are created using the xsl:template element, which requires an attribute named match that determines which nodes of the source document tree are processed by the template. The value assigned to the match attribute is a pattern or expression that resolves to a set of nodes. An example of a commonly used value for the match attribute is a forward slash (/), which identifies the root node of a document:

```
<xsl:template match="/">
...
</xsl:template>
```

This root template is significant because it serves as the first template applied to a document. Technically, it isn't necessary to include a root template in your style sheets because the XSL processor will automatically start applying other templates with the root element if no root template exists. However, if you want to control the manner in which other templates are applied, then you'll want to create a root template. Keep in mind that you can also refer to a root element directly by name, as the following example shows:

```
<xsl:template match="news">
...
</xsl:template>
```

Since the news value assigned to the match attribute in this example is the root element of the News document from Hour 11, it has the same effect as using the forward slash to identify the root element. Although the root element gets things started in an XSLT style sheet, most of the action takes place in other templates. Templates in an XSLT style sheet are used to transform specific portions of an XML document, which are identified using the match attribute, as the following example demonstrates:

```
<xsl:template match="headline">
...
</xsl:template>
```

13

In this example, the `headline` element is matched by the template, which means the template is used to transform all content in the News document that is contained within a `headline` element. This template is usually applied from the parent template of the `headline` element, which in this case is the `news` element. In other words, the `headline` template would be applied from within the `news` template. Following is a portion of XML code for a news document to which this template could be applied:

```
<header>
  <headline>
  Local Author Breaks Ankle In Gruesome Skateboard Accident
  </headline>
  <byline>
  By Eric Martin
  </byline>
  <dateline>
    <location>Nashville, Tennessee</location>
    <date>Tuesday December 11 2001 4:52 CST</date>
  </dateline>
</header>
```

There are trickier approaches to specifying nodes using the `match` attribute. These approaches require knowledge of XPath, which you learn about in Hour 19, "Addressing XML Documents with XPath."

In this example code, the previous example template matches the `headline` element. It then becomes important to apply the template and somehow transform the `headline` element. What do I mean by "applying" a template? Applying a template means that you are invoking the template so that it actually carries out the transformation logic defined in it. It isn't always necessary to explicitly apply every template that you create because the XSL processor will automatically attempt to figure out which templates to apply to certain parts of a document using the `match` attributes of the templates. However, you will usually apply at least one template to get the ball rolling; templates are applied using the `xsl:apply-templates` element. The `xsl:apply-templates` element supports an attribute named `select` that identifies the nodes to which the template is applied. If you don't specify a value for the `select` attribute, the template will be applied to all of the child nodes of the current node. So, the `select` attribute serves to limit the nodes to which a template is applied.

Similar to the `match` attribute of the `xsl:template` element, the `select` attribute of the `xsl:apply-templates` element allows you to use XPath to carry out more advanced node selections. You learn a little more about how this is accomplished later in this hour in the section titled "Pattern Essentials." You get the whole scoop on XPath in Hour 19, "Addressing XML Documents with XPath."

If you want to apply the root template to a document, you can simply place an empty `xsl:apply-templates` element directly in the root template:

```
<xsl:template match="/">
  <xsl:apply-templates/>
</xsl:template>
```

In this example, the default template is automatically applied to the root node of the document, after which the `xsl:apply-templates` element makes sure the remaining templates are applied to children of the root element. This may sound a little confusing, so let's take a second to understand exactly what is happening. This code defines a template that handles the default node of the document, as indicated by the forward slash (`/`) value of the `match` attribute. When the XSL processor encounters the root node of the document, it automatically matches it up with this template and invokes the template to process the node. The `xsl:apply-templates` element within the template doesn't include a `select` attribute, which means that templates matching any children of the root node should be applied (illustrated in Figure 13.1).

FIGURE 13.1

The `xsl:apply-templates` *element is applied to the child elements of an XML document.*

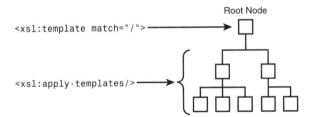

13

If you wanted to target a specific set of nodes, you could set the `select` attribute of the `xsl:apply-templates` element:

```
<xsl:template match="/">
  <xsl:apply-templates select="//headline"/>
</xsl:template>
```

In this example, the `headline` child node is identified in the `select` attribute, which means only templates matching `headline` nodes are applied. This demonstrates how the `select` attribute limits the set of nodes to which templates are applied. Incidentally, the two forward slashes (`//`) before the `headline` element name indicate that the selected `headline` elements are children of the current node (`news`).

Processing Nodes

There are several elements defined in XSLT that are used to process nodes. These node-processing elements perform a range of operations and ultimately provide you with somewhat of a programming approach to creating templates. The first of these elements is `xsl:for-each`, which allows you to process a set of nodes individually according to a certain transformation. The `xsl:for-each` element is particularly useful for database transformations where you have a set of data that must be formatted into a list or table. The `xsl:for-each` element accepts a `select` attribute that works similarly to the `select` attribute in the `xsl:apply-templates` element. Following is an excerpt of code from the `contacts.xsl` style sheet that you saw in the previous hour, which demonstrates the usefulness of the `xsl:for-each` element:

```
<xsl:for-each select="contacts/contact">
  <div style="width:275px; margin-bottom:10px; border:5px double black;
    color:black; background-color:yellow; text-align:center">
    <xsl:apply-templates select="name"/>
    <xsl:apply-templates select="address"/>
    <xsl:apply-templates select="city"/>
    <xsl:apply-templates select="state"/>
    <xsl:apply-templates select="zip"/>
  </div>
</xsl:for-each>
```

In this example, the `xsl:for-each` element is used to loop through the `contact` elements in a document. For each `contact` element in the document, the transformation code within the loop is applied. More specifically, an XHTML `div` element is created with the appropriate styles, and several templates are applied for every `contact` element. This usage of the `xsl:for-each` element allows you to effectively display a formatted list of contacts.

Another interesting XSLT node-processing element is the xsl:if element, which allows you to include conditional processing within a template. Transformation code within an xsl:if element is conditionally carried out based upon the result of the conditional expression for the element. This expression is specified in the test attribute of the xsl:if element. You learn a great deal more about expressions in Hour 19, but a quick example might help to reveal how easy they are to use with the xsl:if element:

```
<xsl:template match="name">
  <div style="font-family:Times, serif; font-size:15pt; font-weight:bold">
    <xsl:value-of select="."/>
    <xsl:if test=". = 'Michael Morrison'">
      <span> (that's me!)</span>
    </xsl:if>
  </div>
</xsl:template>
```

This code shows how you can conditionally add a literal to the output document based upon the value of the name element. The test attribute of the xsl:if element checks to see if the content of the name element is equal to 'Michael Morrison'. If the conditional expression is true, the literal text (that's me!) is inserted into the output document just after the value of the name element. If not, the value of the name element is inserted like normal.

If you find that you need to conditionally choose between more than one possible value, then you can use the xsl:choose element in conjunction with the xsl:when and xsl:otherwise elements. The xsl:choose element works a lot like the xsl:if element except that it supports multiple conditional sections, which are identified by xsl:when elements. Following is the general form of the xsl:choose element:

```
<xsl:choose>
<xsl:when test="">
</xsl:when>

<xsl:when test="">
</xsl:when>

<xsl:otherwise>
</xsl:otherwise>
</xsl:choose>
```

This code shows two different conditional sections of transformation code, which is evident by the two xsl:when elements. The final xsl:otherwise element identifies transformation code that is carried out if none of the previous xsl:when conditionals apply. Following is an example that should help show how to use these elements to create multiple conditionals:

13

```
<xsl:template match="name">
  <div style="font-family:Times, serif; font-size:15pt; font-weight:bold">
    <xsl:value-of select="."/>
    <xsl:choose>
      <xsl:when test=". = 'Michael Morrison'">
        <span> (that's me!)</span>
      </xsl:when>

      <xsl:when test=". = 'Josh Timm'">
        <span> (friend)</span>
      </xsl:when>

      <xsl:when test=". = 'Randy Hood'">
        <span> (relative)</span>
      </xsl:when>

      <xsl:otherwise">
        <span> (don't know this guy!)</span>
      </xsl:otherwise>
    </xsl:choose>
  </div>
</xsl:template>
```

This example uses an xsl:choose element and three xsl:when elements to provide three conditional transformations that add unique text next to name elements whose content matches the conditionals. An xsl:choose element is also specified to handle any name elements that don't match the conditionals.

Sorting Nodes

I've mentioned several times that one of the enormous benefits of using XSLT to transform XML documents is that you can carefully organize document content before formatting it for display with CSS or XSL-FO. One of the most common operations performed on databases is sorting, in which items are organized according to the value of a particular type of information such as date, quantity, or price. XSLT supports sorting through the xsl:sort element. This element allows you to sort the nodes in a node set according to specified criteria. The criteria for an XSLT sort operation are determined by the select, order, and data-type attributes of the xsl:sort element.

A set of nodes is sorted based upon a key, which is a pattern or expression that identifies a piece of information in the set. For example, if you wanted to sort a set of nodes on an attribute named price, then the sorting key would be set to @price. This value is assigned to the select attribute of the xsl:sort element. Another important attribute in the xsl:sort element is order, which is set to either ascending (the default) or descending. The final attribute of interest with the xsl:sort element is data-type, which allows you to specify the type of data being sorted; this attribute is important because it impacts the manner in which the sorting is carried out. The `data-type` attribute can be set to one of the following values: `text` or `number`. Following is an example of an `xsl:sort` element that is used to sort a list of names alphabetically in descending order:

```
<xsl:sort select="name" order="descending" data-type="text"/>
```

This example uses the `name` element as the key and then sorts nodes within the node set in descending order. The data type is set to `text` to indicate that the sorting routine is text-based. Following is an example of how you might use this code in the context of a real style sheet:

```
<xsl:for-each select="contacts/contact">
  <xsl:sort select="name" order="descending"/>
  <div style="width:275px; margin-bottom:10px; border:5px double black;
    color:black; background-color:yellow; text-align:center">
    <xsl:apply-templates select="name"/>
    <xsl:apply-templates select="address"/>
    <xsl:apply-templates select="city"/>
    <xsl:apply-templates select="state"/>
    <xsl:apply-templates select="zip"/>
  </div>
</xsl:for-each>
```

You probably recognize this XSLT code from the `contacts.xsl` style sheet. In this example the `xsl:sort` element is used to sort the contacts prior to displaying each of them.

Pattern Essentials

Patterns have crept into the XSLT discussion several times throughout this hour and the previous hour. I'd like to mention one more time that you get a thorough introduction to patterns in Hour 19, "Addressing XML Documents with XPath." However, XSLT uses patterns enough that I think it would be helpful to cheat a little and give you a quick primer on how to use them. This section isn't intended to make you a pattern expert, but it will hopefully give you some insight as to how patterns fit into XSLT.

As you know by now, patterns are used to address parts of XML documents much as paths in file systems are used to address folders and files. Patterns can be used to isolate specific nodes or groups of nodes and can be specified as absolute or relative. An *absolute pattern* spells out the exact location of a node or node set, whereas a *relative pattern* identifies a node or node set relative to a certain context. In the previous `contacts.xsl` example, the pattern `contacts/contact` is an absolute pattern, whereas the pattern `name` is a relative pattern. The `name` pattern is relative because it makes an assumption about the current context.

13

Patterns are used in several situations throughout XSLT, but the majority of the time you'll use them to set the `select` and `match` attributes of standard XSLT elements. The simplest pattern is the pattern that references the current node, which is a simple period (.). Following is an example of how to use this pattern:

```
<xsl:value-of select="."/>
```

The current node pattern is obviously highly dependent upon the context of the document. A pattern that isn't dependent upon context is the root pattern, which is identified with a single forward slash (/). The root pattern identifies the location of a document's root element no matter where it appears. To create an absolute pattern, you must begin with the root element and specify the exact hierarchy of nodes leading to a node or node set.

Other patterns are used to reference nodes that are above or below the current node. For example, a child node pattern is created by simply specifying the name of the node. A parent node, on the other hand, is created using two periods (..). Following is an example of using a pattern to access a parent node:

```
<xsl:value-of select=".."/>
```

You can put patterns together to get more interesting results. For example, to address a sibling node, you must first go to the parent and then reference the sibling as a child. In other words, you use the parent pattern (..) followed by a forward slash (/) followed by the sibling node name, as in the following example:

```
<xsl:value-of select="../brother"/>
```

If you want to select all of the child nodes of a given node, you can use the double slash (//) pattern, as in the following example:

```
<xsl:value-of select="//"/>
```

Lest you think patterns are limited to elements, you can easily address attributes by specifying the attribute name preceded by an at symbol (@), as in the following example:

```
<xsl:value-of select="info/@ssnum"/>
```

This code assumes that the current node contains a child element named `info` that has an attribute named `ssnum`.

Putting Expressions to Work

Similar to patterns, expressions play an important role in determining how XSLT style sheets transform XML content. However, expressions differ from patterns in that expressions are capable of carrying out programmatic operations such as comparisons and calculations. Expressions are created using patterns and additional XSLT constructs such as comparison operators and functions. The next couple of sections explain how to use these constructs to create XSLT expressions.

Working with Operators

Earlier in the hour you learned how to use the `xsl:if` and `xsl:when` elements to add conditional logic to XSLT style sheets. What you didn't learn, however, was how powerful the actual conditional parts of these elements can be. Both of these elements rely on an attribute named `test` to specify a conditional expression that essentially results in a value of true or false; if the resulting value is true, the associated XSLT code is carried out. The specific expression used by the test attribute is quite flexible and can involve several different comparison operators. Following are some of the most commonly used comparison operators that can appear within the `test` attribute:

- `=`—checks to see if two pieces of data are equal
- `!=`—checks to see if two pieces of data are unequal
- `&lt;`—checks to see if one piece of data is less than another
- `&lt;=`—checks to see if one piece of data is less than or equal to another
- `&gt;`—checks to see if one piece of data is greater than another
- `&gt;=`—checks to see if one piece of data is greater than or equal to another
- `and`—checks to see if two conditional expressions are both true
- `or`—checks to see if at least one of two conditional expressions is true

> Although the less-than and greater-than operators look strange at first, upon closer inspection you can see that they are actually just entities. If you recall, an entity is identified by sandwiching its name between an ampersand (&) and a semicolon (;). So, the greater-than-or-equal-to operator, which is specified as `&gt;=`, is ultimately resolved into >=.

13

To use these operators, you simply combine them with patterns and literal values to create expressions. For example, the following code shows how to create an `xsl:if` element that invokes a section of code only if the content of the child element named `countdown` is less than or equal to zero:

```
<xsl:if test="countdown &lt;= 0">
  Lift off!
</xsl:if>
```

The and and or operators carry out a logical comparison between two other expressions that must evaluate to a true or false value. As an example, if you wanted to expand the countdown example so that you could count in either direction, the following code would do the trick:

```
<xsl:if test="countdown &lt;= 0 or countdown &gt; 10">
  Lift off!
</xsl:if>
```

The or operator used in this example causes lift-off to occur if the value of countdown is either less than or equal to zero, or greater than 10. This example demonstrates how multiple comparison operators can be used together to create more powerful conditional expressions.

In addition to comparison operators, there are also a few familiar math operators that you may find useful:

- * — multiplies two numeric values
- div — divides two numeric values and returns the integer result
- mod — divides two numeric values and returns the integer remainder
- + — adds two numeric values
- - — subtracts two numeric values

These operators can be used in expressions to perform math operations on XML data. Following is an example of how you might multiply the contents of two child elements (quantity and unitprice) in order to calculate a total that is displayed in an XHTML document:

```
<div>
  Total price = <xsl:value-of select="quantity * unitprice"/>
</div>
```

This code reveals the flexibility of the select attribute and how a math operator can be used within it to carry out simple calculations. The values stored in the quantity and unitprice child elements are multiplied using the multiplication operator (*). The result of the multiplication is inserted into the output document as the content of an XHTML div element.

Using Standard Functions

If you thought operators were neat, you will be really impressed with the standard functions built into XSLT. These functions are much more interesting than operators because they carry out calculations that would otherwise be quite tedious using math operators alone. Following are some of the more commonly used standard functions supported in XSLT:

- `ceiling()` — round up a decimal value to the nearest integer
- `floor()` — round down a decimal value to the nearest integer
- `round()` — round a decimal value to the nearest integer
- `sum()` — add a set of numeric values
- `count()` — determine the quantity of values in a set

Although these functions are somewhat self-explanatory in terms of what kinds of calculations they carry out, it doesn't hurt to see a few of them at work in the context of a style sheet. Following is an example of how you can add up the values of a set of nodes to calculate a total with the `sum()` function:

```
<div>
  Total amount = $<xsl:value-of select="sum(cart/item/@price)"/>
</div>
```

This example would work well for a shopping cart XML document that includes a `cart` element that holds several `item` elements representing each item in the shopping cart. Notice that the `price` attribute of each `item` element is used as the basis for the sum calculation. Following is an example of the kind of XML code that could be transformed using this XSLT example:

```
<cart>
  <item price="199.99">
  DVD Player
  </item>
  <item price="699.99">
  32-Inch Television
  </item>
  <item price="249.99">
  Surround-Sound Speaker System
  </item>
</cart>
```

When applied to this code, the previous XSLT example adds together the prices of the three items to arrive at a total of 1149.97. This shopping cart example could also benefit from knowing how many items are in the shopping cart, which is accomplished with the following code:

```
<div>
  Number of items = <xsl:value-of select="count(cart/item)"/>
</div>
```

The `count()` function is used in this example to count the number of `item` elements contained within the `cart` element. As this example demonstrates, the standard functions built into XSLT allow you to perform very useful computations with little effort.

13

A Complete XSLT Example

As you've seen in the past few hours, I like to reinforce style sheet knowledge with complete example style sheets. At this point I'd like to revisit the News XML document that you saw back in Hour 11. If you recall, this document contained content for a news story complete with XML code to identify the relevant portions of the story such as the headline, byline, and body text. Listing 13.1 shows the code for the News XML document, just in case your memory is a little fuzzy.

LISTING 13.1   The News Example XML Document

```
 1: <?xml version="1.0"?>
 2: <?xml-stylesheet type="text/xsl" href="news.xsl"?>
 3:
 4: <news>
 5:   <header>
 6:     <headline>
 7:     Local Author Breaks Ankle In Gruesome Skateboard Accident
 8:     </headline>
 9:     <byline>
10:     By Eric Martin
11:     </byline>
12:     <dateline>
13:       <location>Nashville, Tennessee</location>
14:       <date>Tuesday December 11 2001 4:52 CST</date>
15:     </dateline>
16:   </header>
17:
18:   <story>
19:     <p>Local nerd author Michael Morrison broke his ankle today while
20:     skateboarding on a ramp at an undisclosed location. This injury comes
21:     as a considerable blow to Morrison considering that he recently
22:     emerged from retirement to make another go at skateboarding. Against
23:     the wishes of friends of family, Morrison decided to return to
24:     skateboarding where risk is a fact of life. His terse response to the
25:     injury was <quote>I don't think my ankle was supposed to bend that
26:     way</quote>.</p>
27:
28:     <p>Witnesses to the accident recall the gruesome aftermath. Fellow
        skater
29:     and witness Darin Masters said <quote>his ankle was twisted around like
30:     one of those little balloon animals</quote>. While out of commission for
31:     a few months, Mr. Morrison has vowed to make yet another return to the
32:     sport.</p>
33:   </story>
34: </news>
```

If you're very observant, you might notice that this News XML code is actually a little different than the code you saw in Hour 11. The only change in this code occurs in line 2 where an XSL style sheet is referenced, as opposed to a CSS. Otherwise, the document is identical to the original. In Hour 11 you created a CSS to format the document so that it could be viewed in a Web browser. Given your newfound knowledge of XSLT, can you think about how an XSLT style sheet might be structured to transform this document so that it can be viewed in a Web browser?

Obviously, XSLT alone won't be enough to prep the document for display because XSLT isn't capable of carrying out content formatting directly. The approach you saw in the previous hour involves transforming the XML code into XHTML code that is understood by Web browsers. You're going to use the same approach here in the XSLT style sheet for the News document. In order to transform each portion of the document, it is necessary to create a template that matches each major element found in the document. With those templates in place, you simply create a root template that establishes the XHTML document structure and invokes the other templates. Listing 13.2 contains the complete source code for the news.xsl style sheet, which uses this exact strategy to transform the News XML document for display within a Web browser.

LISTING 13.2 The news.xsl Style Sheet Used to Transform and Format the News XML Document

```
 1: <?xml version="1.0"?>
 2: <xsl:stylesheet version="1.0"
    xmlns:xsl="http://www.w3.org/1999/XSL/Transform">
 3:   <xsl:template match="/">
 4:     <html><head><title>Contact List</title></head>
 5:       <body>
 6:         <xsl:apply-templates/>
 7:       </body>
 8:     </html>
 9:   </xsl:template>
10:
11:   <xsl:template match="headline">
12:     <div style="width:400px; border-bottom:5px double black; text-
        align:right;
13:       color:olive; font-family:Times, serif; font-size:32pt">
14:       <xsl:value-of select="."/>
15:     </div>
16:   </xsl:template>
17:
18:   <xsl:template match="byline">
```

13

continues

LISTING 13.2 Continued

```
19:        <span style="width:200px; text-align:left; color:black;
20:          font-family:Times, serif; font-size:14pt">
21:          <xsl:value-of select="."/>
22:        </span>
23:      </xsl:template>
24:
25:      <xsl:template match="dateline">
26:        <span style="width:200px; text-align:right; color:black;
27:          font-family:Times, serif; font-size:11pt; font-style:italic">
28:          <xsl:value-of select="."/>
29:        </span>
30:      </xsl:template>
31:
32:      <xsl:template match="p">
33:        <div style="width:400px; margin-bottom:8px; color:black;
34:          font-family:Times, serif; font-size:12pt">
35:          <xsl:value-of select="."/>
36:        </div>
37:      </xsl:template>
38:
39:      <xsl:template match="quote">
40:        <span style="font-style:italic">
41:          <xsl:value-of select="."/>
42:        </span>
43:      </xsl:template>
44: </xsl:stylesheet>
```

The general structure of this style sheet should be somewhat familiar to you from the Contacts example in the previous hour. Similar to the contacts.xsl style sheet, this style sheet uses an empty apply-templates element within its root template to indirectly invoke all of the other templates in the style sheet (line 6). Notice that the root template includes XHTML code that establishes the resulting Web page (lines 4-8). From there, the headline template formats the headline of the News document using a div element and CSS styles (lines 11-16). The remaining templates continue with a similar process of placing XML content into the framework of an XHTML document and carefully applying CSS styles to get the desired formatting. Figure 13.2 shows the resulting XHTML document as viewed in Internet Explorer.

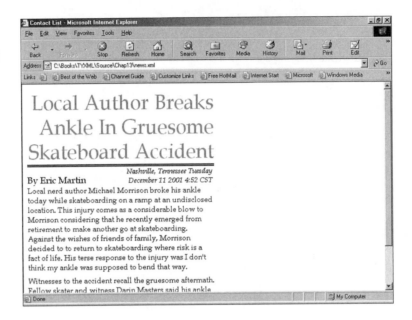

FIGURE 13.2

The News example document is displayed in Internet Explorer using the news.xsl *style sheet.*

This figure shows how an XSLT style sheet is used to transform XML content so that it appears highly formatted in a Web browser. Of course, the formatting aspect of the style sheet is actually carried out with CSS, but XSLT is still at the heart of the transformation.

Yet Another XSLT Example

I'm a little concerned about the fact that you've only seen how to create an XSLT style sheet that mimics the functionality of an existing CSS. The reason for the concern is because you might be wondering why you wouldn't just create the style sheet in CSS since the CSS version is obviously simpler to code. The answer is that you probably would be smarter to use CSS for the example style sheets that you've seen thus far because they really do nothing more than format XML content for display. The real power of XSLT is revealed when you must go a step further and actually manipulate and extract information from XML content. In this section you create an XSLT style sheet that conditionally displays content according to its value and that also performs an interesting calculation on a specific piece of information in a document.

The example document for this style sheet is a document that stores a list of vehicles for sale. If you've ever shopped for cars on the Internet, then you are probably familiar with the process of searching through lists of cars according to certain criteria. In this example you learn how to use an XSLT style sheet to format vehicle information intelligently. The

13

Vehicles example document is coded in a custom XML language that would be suitable for an online car shopping Web site. Listing 13.3 contains the code for the vehicles.xml document.

LISTING 13.3   The Vehicles Example XML Document

```
 1: <?xml version="1.0"?>
 2: <?xml-stylesheet href="Vehicles.xsl" type="text/xsl"?>
 3:
 4: <vehicles>
 5:   <vehicle year="1996" make="Land Rover" model="Discovery">
 6:     <mileage>36500</mileage>
 7:     <color>black</color>
 8:     <price>22100</price>
 9:   </vehicle>
10:
11:   <vehicle year="1998" make="Land Rover" model="Discovery">
12:     <mileage>15900</mileage>
13:     <color>teal</color>
14:     <price>32000</price>
15:   </vehicle>
16:
17:   <vehicle year="1997" make="Land Rover" model="Discovery">
18:     <mileage>46000</mileage>
19:     <color>silver</color>
20:     <price>27900</price>
21:   </vehicle>
22:
23:   <vehicle year="1997" make="Land Rover" model="Defender 90">
24:     <mileage>21050</mileage>
25:     <color>white</color>
26:     <price>41900</price>
27:   </vehicle>
28:
29:   <vehicle year="1994" make="Land Rover" model="Defender 90">
30:     <mileage>42450</mileage>
31:     <color>green</color>
32:     <price>31250</price>
33:   </vehicle>
34:
35:   <vehicle year="1996" make="Toyota" model="Land Cruiser">
36:     <mileage>34800</mileage>
37:     <color>black</color>
38:     <price>35995</price>
39:   </vehicle>
40:
41:   <vehicle year="1997" make="Toyota" model="Land Cruiser">
42:     <mileage>47150</mileage>
43:     <color>green</color>
```

continues

LISTING 13.3   Continued

```
44:       <price>37000</price>
45:    </vehicle>
46:
47:    <vehicle year="1999" make="Chevrolet" model="Suburban 2500">
48:      <mileage>3550</mileage>
49:      <color>pewter</color>
50:      <price>31995</price>
51:    </vehicle>
52:
53:    <vehicle year="1996" make="Chevrolet" model="Suburban 2500">
54:      <mileage>49300</mileage>
55:      <color>green</color>
56:      <price>25995</price>
57:    </vehicle>
58: </vehicles>
```

This code shows how the Vehicles document relies on a relatively simple markup language consisting of only a few elements: vehicles, vehicle, mileage, color, and price. Each vehicle in the document is coded as a vehicle element within the parent vehicles element. In addition to the mileage, color, and price of each vehicle, which are coded as child elements, the year, make, and model of each vehicle are coded as attributes of the vehicle element.

So what exactly should an XSLT style sheet do with this document? For the purposes of this example, I'd first like to see the style sheet sort the vehicles according to a certain criterion, such as price. Following is a template that carries out this kind of sorting process using the xsl:sort element and its order attribute:

```
<xsl:template match="vehicles">
  <xsl:apply-templates select="vehicle">
    <xsl:sort select="@price" order="descending"/>
  </xsl:apply-templates>
</xsl:template>
```

Sorting isn't the only kind of interesting transformation applicable to the Vehicles document. Consider the fact that buyers are often looking for a specific model year, especially when it comes to used vehicles. Knowing this, it might be neat to highlight vehicles from a certain model year. This can be carried out using xsl:when and xsl:otherwise elements, which allow you to conditionally transform XML content.

One final piece of information that would be interesting to know is the average price of the vehicles in the document; lucky for us, XSLT is quite capable of performing this calculation without much work. Following is an example of how this calculation could be carried out in a template:

13

```
<xsl:value-of select="round(sum(vehicles/vehicle/price) div
  count(vehicles/vehicle))"/>
```

This code makes use of the round(), sum(), and count() functions to carry out the average price calculation.

The complete XSLT style sheet for the Vehicles document is similar to the other XSLT style sheets you've seen—it must transform the XML content into XHTML so that it can be viewed in a Web browser. Unlike those style sheets, however, this one must be structured a little differently. First off, the root template has much more responsibility because there is a fair amount of formatting involved in listing the vehicles, since they need to be listed in a tabular format. Additionally, the template for the main vehicles element is kind of interesting because it must sort its child vehicle elements according to the price of each vehicle.

I think you know enough about the required functionality of the Vehicles style sheet to take a look at the complete code for it, which is shown in Listing 13.4.

LISTING 13.4   The vehicles.xsl Style Sheet Used to Transform and Format the Vehicles XML Document

```
 1: <?xml version="1.0"?>
 2: <xsl:stylesheet version="1.0"
    xmlns:xsl="http://www.w3.org/1999/XSL/Transform">
 3:   <xsl:template match="/">
 4:     <html>
 5:       <head>
 6:         <title>Used Vehicles</title>
 7:       </head>
 8:
 9:       <body background="money.jpg">
10:         <h1 style="background-color:#446600;
11:           color:#FFFFFF; font-size:20pt; text-align:center;
12:           letter-spacing: 12pt">Used Vehicles</h1>
13:         <table align="center" border="2">
14:           <tr>
15:             <th>Year</th>
16:             <th>Make</th>
17:             <th>Model</th>
18:             <th>Mileage</th>
19:             <th>Color</th>
20:             <th>Price</th>
21:           </tr>
22:           <xsl:apply-templates/>
23:           <tr style="font-weight:bold">
24:             <td colspan="3"></td>
25:             <td colspan="2">Average price:</td>
26:             <td>
```

continues

LISTING 13.4 Continued

```
27:                    $<xsl:value-of select="round(sum(vehicles/vehicle/price) div
28:                    count(vehicles/vehicle))"/>
29:                </td>
30:             </tr>
31:          </table>
32:       </body>
33:    </html>
34: </xsl:template>
35:
36: <xsl:template match="vehicles">
37:    <xsl:apply-templates select="vehicle">
38:       <xsl:sort select="@price" order="descending"/>
39:    </xsl:apply-templates>
40: </xsl:template>
41:
42: <xsl:template match="vehicle">
43:   <xsl:choose>
44:     <xsl:when test="@model = 'Discovery'">
45:       <tr style="color:#446600; font-weight:bold">
46:         <td><xsl:value-of select="@year"/></td>
47:         <td><xsl:value-of select="@make"/></td>
48:         <td><xsl:value-of select="@model"/></td>
49:         <td><xsl:value-of select="mileage"/></td>
50:         <td><xsl:value-of select="color"/></td>
51:         <td>$<xsl:value-of select="price"/></td>
52:       </tr>
53:     </xsl:when>
54:
55:     <xsl:otherwise>
56:       <tr>
57:         <td><xsl:value-of select="@year"/></td>
58:         <td><xsl:value-of select="@make"/></td>
59:         <td><xsl:value-of select="@model"/></td>
60:         <td><xsl:value-of select="mileage"/></td>
61:         <td><xsl:value-of select="color"/></td>
62:         <td>$<xsl:value-of select="price"/></td>
63:       </tr>
64:     </xsl:otherwise>
65:   </xsl:choose>
66: </xsl:template>
67: </xsl:stylesheet>
```

13

Although the code is a little long compared to the other style sheets you've seen, it does some pretty neat things with the vehicle data. First of all, the XHTML Web page is set up and a table is created with a caption for the vehicle list; this all takes place in the first part of the root template (lines 4–21). On line 22 the xsl:apply-templates element is used to invoke the other templates in the style sheet, which results in the vehicle data getting transformed and formatted into XHTML table data. The root template then continues by calculating and displaying the average price of the vehicles on the last row of the table (lines 23–30). Notice that the round(), sum(), and count() functions are all used in this calculation, along with the div operator.

There are only two other templates defined in this style sheet: vehicles and vehicle. The vehicles template simply invokes the vehicle template, but it also sorts the vehicle elements using the xsl:sort element (line 38). The sort is a descending sort according to the price attribute of the vehicle elements.

The vehicle template is intriguing in that it uses the xsl:choose, xsl:when, and xsl:otherwise elements to set up two branches of code that are conditionally carried out based upon the value of the model attribute in each vehicle element. In this case the Land Rover Discovery vehicle is targeted for highlighting, so the test attribute of the xsl:when element looks for the model attribute being equal to Discovery (line 44). If there is a match with this attribute, the details of the vehicle are displayed in a green, bold font (lines 45–52); if there is no match, the vehicle details are displayed in a normal font, as indicated in the xsl:otherwise element (lines 56–63).

You now have a pretty good idea regarding what the resulting Web page should look like given the code in the vehicles.xsl style sheet. Figure 13.3 shows the vehicles.xml document as viewed in Internet Explorer using this style sheet.

FIGURE 13.3

The Vehicles example document is displayed in Internet Explorer using the vehicles.xsl style sheet.

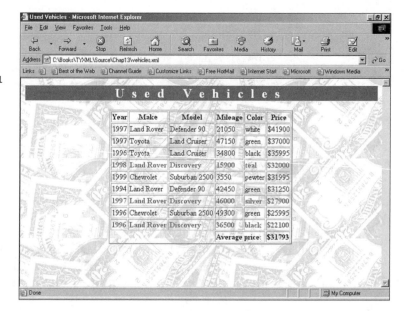

The figure reveals how the XSLT style sheet manipulates the Vehicles XML document in several ways. First off, the vehicles are sorted according to decreasing price, which allows you to quickly determine their different price points. Secondly, all of the Land Rover Discovery vehicles are highlighted with a bold font in a different color to make them stand out. Finally, the average price of the vehicles is calculated and displayed as the last item in the table, which would be useful information for a buyer trying to gauge how much vehicles cost.

Summary

Although XSLT style sheets can be used in conjunction with CSS to perform basic XML document formatting, the real power of XSLT is revealed when you actually manipulate the content of a document in order to facilitate a more meaningful presentation. Fortunately, XSLT includes rich features for carrying out a variety of different transformation tasks. Some of the XSLT features that make it so flexible are patterns and expressions, along with the ability to use them to process and sort nodes. Of course, at the core of every XSLT style sheet is a set of templates that are used to transform different parts of XML documents.

This hour taught you a great deal about templates and how they are created and applied in XSLT style sheets. You also learned how to process and sort nodes, not to mention how to use patterns and expressions. The hour culminated in a couple of complete XSLT example style sheets, which hopefully gave you some practical knowledge that can help you get started on your own XSLT projects.

Q&A

Q Are there any limitations regarding the use of literals in an XSLT style sheet?

A Yes. Because XSLT style sheets are coded in XML, everything in them must adhere to the syntax rules of XML. This applies to literals as well, which means that tags must be nested properly, start tags must have end tags, etc.

Q What happens to nodes in an XML document that aren't matched by a template in an XSLT style sheet?

A If nodes in a document aren't matched by a template in an XSLT style sheet, those nodes aren't processed or transformed. Keep in mind that it isn't necessary for a style sheet to address every single piece of information in an XML document; it's perfectly acceptable to pick out highly specific information from a document if so

13

desired. The degree to which document content is processed is entirely dependent on each specific application of XSLT.

Q Are there any other functions I can use with XSLT beyond the standard functions mentioned in this hour?

A Yes. There are several other standard XSLT functions that weren't covered in this hour; you can learn more about them by visiting the XSLT page at the W3C Web site, which is located at `http://www.w3.org/TR/xslt`. Additionally, XSLT supports the inclusion of extended functions in different implementations of XSLT. For example, a Web browser vendor could add browser-specific functions to their implementation of XSLT. You'll have to check with the specific browser you are targeting to see if extended XSLT functions are supported.

Q In regard to an XSLT style sheet, what happens if a document doesn't validate against a DTD/XSD schema?

A If a document doesn't validate against a provided schema, a Web browser will still apply the style sheet and display the document. However, if the document isn't well formed, then the style sheet is never processed and the document isn't displayed.

Workshop

The Workshop is designed to help you anticipate possible questions, review what you've learned, and begin learning how to put your knowledge into practice.

Quiz

1. What is the difference between instructions and literals in XSLT style sheets?

2. What is the significance of a forward slash (/) when used by itself in the `match` attribute of an XSLT element such as `xsl:template`?

3. If you use the `xsl:choose`, `xsl:when`, and `xsl:otherwise` elements to create a conditional section of a style sheet, when does the code within the `xsl:otherwise` element get carried out?

4. How do you reference the current node in the `select` attribute of an XSLT element such as `xsl:value-of`?

Quiz Answers

1. Instructions are the XSLT elements and attributes that describe how XML content is to be transformed, whereas literals are static pieces of information that are placed directly in the output document without being processed.

2. A forward slash (/) identifies the root node of a document when specified in the match attribute of an XSLT element such as xsl:template.

3. The code in an xsl:otherwise element gets carried out when none of the xsl:when conditionals apply.

4. A period (.) is used to reference the current node in the select attribute of an XSLT element such as xsl:value-of.

Exercises

1. Modify the vehicles.xml document so that it includes several more vehicles of varying model years and prices. Open the document in a Web browser to see how the vehicles.xsl style sheet automatically sorts the vehicles, identifies the Land Rover Discovery vehicles, and calculates an average price.

2. Modify the vehicles.xsl style sheet so that only vehicles with model years greater than 1995 are highlighted. Hint: You must use the > comparison operator to determine if each vehicle's year attribute is greater than 1995.

13

PART IV

Processing and Managing XML Data

Hour

HOUR 14

SAX: The Simple API for XML

Which painting in the National Gallery would I save if there was a fire?
The one nearest the door of course.

—George Bernard Shaw (writer, political activist, and philosopher)

If you share Mr. Shaw's propensity for practicality, then you will probably
find this lesson quite interesting. Through most of this book, the discussion
on XML has focused on its use as a structured document format. However,
XML is also often used as a format for data storage. Unlike proprietary file
formats, XML documents follow consistent structural rules and can be tested
not only for well-formedness but also for compliance with specific structural
rules. In this hour, I'm going to discuss an API that can be used to extract
data from an XML document called SAX, the simple API for XML.

In this hour, you'll learn

- What SAX is and how it works
- How to get a SAX parser for your favorite programming language
- How to write a Java program that uses a SAX parser to process an XML file

What Is SAX?

SAX is an interface for event-based parsing of XML files. Let me explain what that means. As you already learned in Hour 8, XML documents are processed using parsers. The parser reads the XML document; verifies that it is well formed; and, if it's a validating parser, validates it against a schema or DTD. What happens next depends on the parser you're using. In some cases, it might copy the data into a data structure that's native to the programming language you're using. In other cases, it might transform the data into a presentation format or apply styles to it. The SAX parser doesn't do anything to the data other than trigger certain events. It's up to the user of the SAX parser to determine what happens when those events occur.

What I mean when I say that SAX is an interface is that it isn't a program, it's a document—a standard—that describes how a SAX parser should be written. It explains which events must be supported in a compliant SAX parser and leaves it up to the implementers to make sure that the parsers they write comply.

 An interface is basically a contract offered by someone who writes a program or specifies how a program should work. It says that as long as you implement all of the features specified in the interface, any programs written to use that interface will work as expected. When someone writes a parser that implements the SAX interface, it means that any program that supports all of the events specified in the SAX interface can use that parser.

Where SAX Came From

Most of the time when you're dealing with XML, one standards body or another developed the various technologies. With SAX, that isn't the case. SAX was developed by members of the xml-dev mailing list in order to provide XML developers with a way to deal with XML documents in a simple and straightforward manner.

You can find out more about it at

```
http://www.megginson.com/SAX/index.html
```

The original version of SAX, 1.0, was released in May, 1998. The most recent version is SAX 2.0, which was released in May, 2000. Both methods were initially implemented as Java interfaces. You can write a SAX parser in any language, and indeed, there are SAX parsers available for most popular programming languages. However, I'm going to talk about the methods that were made available in the Java version—you can assume they'll also be available under whatever implementation you choose to use. Let's look at the specifics of these two releases.

SAX 1.0

SAX 1.0 provides support for triggering events on all of the standard content in an XML document. Rather than telling you everything it does support, it's easier to tell you that SAX 1.0 does not support namespaces.

A program that uses a SAX 1.0 parser must support the following methods:

- `characters()`—Returns the characters found inside an element
- `endDocument()`—Triggered when parsing of the document is complete
- `endElement()`—Triggered when the closing tag for any element is encountered
- `ignorableWhitespace()`—Triggered when white space is encountered between elements
- `processingInstruction()`—Triggered when a processing instruction is encountered in the document
- `startElement()`—Triggered when the opening tag for an element is encountered

SAX 1.0 also handles attributes of elements by providing them through its interface when the `startElement()` method of the document handler is called. SAX 1.0 has been deprecated now that SAX 2.0 has been implemented. In the Java world, the new SAX 2.0 libraries (such as Xerces 2) generally still support SAX 1.0 so that they'll work with existing SAX 1.0 applications, but if you're writing a new application, you should use SAX 2.0.

SAX 2.0

SAX 2.0 is an extension of SAX 1.0 that provides support for namespaces. As such, programs which communicate with a SAX 2.0 parser must support the following methods:

- `startPrefixMapping()`—Triggered when a prefix mapping (mapping a namespace to an entity prefix) is encountered
- `endPrefixMapping()`—Triggered when a prefix mapping is closed
- `skippedEntity()`—Triggered whenever an entity is skipped for any number of reasons

14

Writing Programs That Use SAX Parsers

Chances are you won't be writing a SAX parser. Rather, you'll be writing a program that interacts with a SAX parser. Writing a program that works with a SAX parser is in some ways similar to writing a GUI program. When you write a GUI program, the GUI library turns actions that the user takes into events that are returned to you by the library. For example, with JavaScript, certain elements on a Web page can generate events that can be handled by JavaScript. Links generate onClick() and onMouseOver() events. There are also document-wide events such as onLoad().

SAX works the same way. When a SAX parser parses the data in an XML document, it fires events based on the data that it is currently parsing. All of the methods listed previously that are associated with SAX are called by the parser when the associated event occurs. It's up to the application programmer to decide what action to take when those events are caught.

For example, you might want to print out just the contents of all of the title elements in a document, or you might want to construct a complex data structure based on all of the information you find in the document. The SAX parser doesn't care; it just provides you with all of the data in the document in a linear manner so that you can do whatever you like with it.

Obtaining a SAX Parser

If you want to write an application that uses SAX, the first thing you have to do is obtain a SAX parser. There's a partial list of SAX implementations at

http://www.megginson.com/SAX/applications.html

You'll need to look at the documentation for the parser that you choose in order to figure out how to integrate the parser with your applications. I'm going to explain how to download and install several of the more popular SAX parsers.

Xerces

Xerces is the XML parser from the Apache Software Foundation. It's used as part of several other Apache XML and Java-related projects and can be used by itself as well. In addition to supporting SAX, it also supports DOM Level 2, which I'll discuss in Hour 15. One thing that Xerces does not support is XML Schemas—if you want to validate your documents against a schema, you'll have to use another parser.

You can obtain Xerces, along with lots of other open source XML-related software, at http://xml.apache.org/. Xerces is completely free as it is released under the Apache Software License.

The Xerces library is available in both `.tar.gz` and `.zip` formats—download the one that's appropriate for your platform. Included in the package are `xerces.jar`, which contains the compiled class files for the library itself, and `xercesSamples.jar`, compiled versions of the sample programs that come with Xerces. The package also includes documentation, source code for the sample programs, and some sample data files.

In order to use the Xerces library, you just need to include the jar file in your class path when compiling and running programs that use it.

libxml

`libxml` is a package of Perl modules that contains a number of XML processing libraries. One of these is `XML::Parser::PerlSAX`. The easiest way to install it is to download it from CPAN (`http://www.cpan.org/`) and follow the instructions to install it on your local system. The methods provided by the `PerlSAX` module are basically identical to those in the Java version of SAX—they both implement the same interface in ways appropriate to Perl and Java, respectively.

Python

If you're a Python programmer, things are particularly easy for you. Recent versions of Python (from 2.0 on) provide support for SAX without any additional software. To use the SAX library in your programs, you just need to include the line

```
from xml.sax import saxutils
```

A Note on Java

The example program in this chapter is written in Java and uses the Xerces SAX parser, which I mentioned earlier. If you're a Java programmer, I'm sure you're perfectly happy with this state of affairs. If you have no interest in Java, this probably isn't to your liking. However, the purpose of this chapter is to explain how SAX works, and while there are SAX parsers available for many languages, it started out in the Java world.

If you're not interested in Java specifically, my advice is to look at the code as pseudo-code. The syntax for this program is relatively simple, and I've commented the code to make it as clear as possible.

Running the Example Program

Even if you don't care about Java programming, you may still want to see the output of the example program on your own computer. To run the program, you'll need Sun's Java

14

Development Kit and the Xerces library mentioned previously. I already explained how to get Xerces; to get the JDK, just go to

```
http://java.sun.com/j2se/
```

You'll need to download the SDK and install it. Once it's installed, you can run the example program. Just put the sample program in the directory where you put xerces.jar (you can put it anywhere you like, but this route is probably easiest), open a command prompt in that directory, and type the following:

```
javac -classpath xerces.jar;. DocumentPrinter.java
```

If your copy of the code for DocumentPrinter.java is correct and xerces.jar is really in the current directory, the DocumentPrinter class will be compiled, and a file called DocumentPrinter.class will result. To run the program, use the following command:

```
java -classpath xerces.jar;. DocumentPrinter file.xml
```

You should replace file.xml with the name of the XML file that you want to process.

A Working Example

Let's look at a program that uses a SAX parser to parse an XML document. The program just prints out messages that explain what it's doing. You could easily replace that code with code that actually performs useful tasks, but since the purpose of this program is just to illustrate how the SAX parser works, the diagnostic messages are fine.

Even though there are SAX parsers for many popular programming languages, SAX is generally associated with Java. This program uses the Xerces package, which I discussed earlier. Let's jump right into the program. Here are the first 12 lines.

```
import org.xml.sax.Attributes;
import org.xml.sax.ContentHandler;
import org.xml.sax.ErrorHandler;
import org.xml.sax.Locator;
import org.xml.sax.SAXParseException;
import org.xml.sax.XMLReader;

public class DocumentPrinter implements ContentHandler, ErrorHandler
{
    // A constant containing the name of the SAX parser to use.
    private static final String PARSER_NAME
        = "org.apache.xerces.parsers.SAXParser";
```

This code imports classes that will be used later on and declares the class (program) that I'm currently writing. The import statements indicate which classes will be used by this program. In this case, all of the classes that will be used are from the org.xml.sax package and are included in the xerces.jar archive.

This class, called `DocumentPrinter`, implements two interfaces—`ContentHandler` and `ErrorHandler`. These two interfaces are part of the standard SAX 2.0 package and are included in the `import` list. A program that implements `ContentHandler` is set up to handle events passed back in the normal course of parsing an XML document, and a program that implements `ErrorHandler` can handle any error events generated during SAX parsing.

In the Java world, an interface is a framework that specifies a list of methods that must be defined in a class. An interface is useful because they guarantee that any class that implements it meets the requirements of that interface. If you fail to include all of the methods required by the interface, your program will not compile. Because this program implements `ContentHandler` and `ErrorHandler`, the parser can be certain that it is capable of handling all of the events it triggers as it parses a document.

Once the class has been declared, I instantiate one member variable for this class, `PARSER_NAME`. This variable is a constant that contains the name of the class that I'm going to use as the SAX parser. There are any number of SAX parsers available; I'm using this one because it comes with the Xerces package.

The `main()` Method

Not only will this class handle all of the SAX-generated events, but it also has a `main` method. In the Java world, the `main` method indicates that a class is a standalone program, as opposed to one that just provides functionality used by other classes. It's the method that gets run when you start the program. The purpose of this method is to set up the parser and get the name of the document to be parsed from the arguments passed in to the program. Here's the code:

```
public static void main(String[] args)
{
    // Check to see whether the user supplied any command line
    // arguments. If not, print an error message and exit the
    // program.
    if (args.length == 0)
    {
        System.out.println("No XML document path specified.");
        System.exit(1);
    }

    // Create a new instance of the DocumentPrinter class.
    DocumentPrinter dp = new DocumentPrinter();

    try
    {
        // Create a new instance of the XML parser.
```

14

```
XMLReader parser
    = (XMLReader)Class.forName(PARSER_NAME).newInstance();

// Set the parser's content handler to the instance of the
// DocumentPrinter object that I created earlier.
parser.setContentHandler(dp);

// Set the parser's error handler to the instance of the
// DocumentPrinter object that I created earlier.
parser.setErrorHandler(dp);

// Parse the file named in the command line argument.
parser.parse(args[0]);
}
// Normally it's a bad idea to catch generic exceptions like this.
catch (Exception ex)
{
    System.out.println(ex.getMessage());
    ex.printStackTrace();
}
}
```

This program expects that the user will specify the path to an XML document as its only command-line argument. If no such argument is submitted, then the program will exit and instruct the user to supply that argument when running the program.

Next, the program creates an instance of the DocumentPrinter object and assigns it to the variable dp. We'll need this object later when we tell the parser which ContentHandler and ErrorHandler to use. After I instantiate dp, I open a try...catch block. This is necessary because some of the methods that I call can throw exceptions that must be caught within my program. All of the real work in the program takes place inside the try block.

The try...catch block is the standard way in which Java handles errors that crop up during the execution of a program. It enables the program to compensate and work around those errors if the user chooses to do so. In this case, I simply print out information about the error and allow the program to exit gracefully.

First, I create a new parser object. Let me talk about how this works. I refer to the object as an XMLReader object, but XMLReader is just an interface. The object is actually an instance of the class named in the variable PARSER_NAME. The fact that I am using it through the XMLReader interface means that I can call only those methods included in that interface. For this application, that's fine. I load the class specified in the

PARSER_NAME variable and assign that to my variable—parser. Because SAX 2.0 parsers must implement XMLReader, I can refer to it as an object of that type rather than referring to the class by its own name—SAXParser.

Once the parser has been created, I can start setting its properties. Before I can actually parse the document, I have to specify the content and error handlers that the parser will use. Since DocumentPrinter, the class I wrote, can play both of those roles, I simply set both of those properties to dp (the DocumentPrinter object I created). At this point, all I have to do is run the parse() method on the URI passed in on the command line, which I do.

Implementing the ContentHandler Interface

The skeleton for the program is in place. The rest of it consists of methods that fulfill the requirements of the ContentHandler and ErrorHandler interfaces. In this program, the methods just print out the content that they receive.

```java
public void characters(char[] ch, int start, int length)
{
    String chars = "";
    for (int i = start; i < start + length; i++)
    {
        chars = chars + ch[i];
    }

    System.out.println("Received characters: " + chars);
}
```

The first method is characters(), which receives content found within elements. It accepts three arguments: an array of characters, the position in the array where the content starts, and the amount of content received. In this method, I use a for loop to extract the content from the array, starting at the position in the array where the content starts and iterating over each element until the position of the last element is released. I then print out the characters that I received.

> It's important not to just process all of the characters in the array of characters passed in. The array can contain lots of padding on both sides of the relevant content, and including it all will read in a lot of extra characters along with the content that you actually want.

14

The next two methods are called when the beginning and end of the document are encountered. They accept no arguments and are called only once each during document parsing, for obvious reasons.

```
public void startDocument()
    {
        System.out.println("Start document.");
    }
public void endDocument()
    {
        System.out.println("End of document reached.");
    }
```

Next let's look at the startElement() method, which accepts the most complex set of arguments of any of the methods that make up a ContentHandler.

```
public void startElement(String namespaceURI, String localName,
                         String qName, Attributes atts)
    {
        System.out.println("Start element: " + localName);

        for (int i = 0; i < atts.getLength(); i++)
        {
            System.out.println("   Attribute: " + atts.getLocalName(i));
            System.out.println("       Value: " + atts.getValue(i));
        }
    }
```

The startElement() method accepts four arguments from the parser. The first is the namespace URI, which you'll see elsewhere as well. The namespace URI is the URI for the namespace associated with the element. If a namespace is used in the document, the URI for the namespace is provided in a namespace declaration. The local name is the name of the element without the namespace prefix. The qualified name is the name of the element including the namespace prefix if there is one. Finally, the attributes are provided as an instance of the Attributes object.

SAX parsers must have namespace processing turned on in order to populate all of these attributes. If that option is deactivated, any of the arguments (other than the attributes) may be populated with empty strings. The method for turning on namespace processing varies depending on which parser you use.

Let's look at attribute processing specifically. Attributes are supplied to this method as an instance of the `Attributes` object. In my code, I use three methods of the `Attributes` object: getLength(), getLocalName(), and getValue(). I use the getLength() method in iterating over the attributes supplied to the method call. getLocalName() and getValue() accept the index of the attribute being retrieved as arguments. My code retrieves each attribute and prints out its name and value. The full list of methods of the `Attributes` object appears in Table 14.1.

TABLE 14.1   Methods of the `Attributes` Object

Method	Purpose
getIndex(String qName)	Retrieves an attribute's index using its qualified name
getIndex(String uri, String localPart)	Retrieves an attribute's index using its namespace URI and the local portion of its name
getLength()	Returns the number of attributes in the element
getLocalName(int index)	Returns the local name of the attribute associated with the index
getQName(int index)	Returns the qualified name of the attribute associated with the index
getType(int index)	Returns the type of the attribute with the supplied index
getType(String uri, String localName)	Looks up the type of the attribute with the namespace URI and name specified
getURI(int index)	Looks up the namespace URI of the attribute with the index specified
getValue(int index)	Looks up the value of the attribute using the index
getValue(String qName)	Looks up the value of the attribute using the qualified name
getValue(String uri, String localName)	Looks up the value of the attribute using the namespace URI and local name

The method that follows is endElement(), which is called whenever the closing tag for an element is found. Here's the method:

```
public void endElement(String namespaceURI, String localName,
                       String qName)
{
    System.out.println("End of element: " + localName);
}
```

14

`endElement()` accepts three arguments from the parser—the URI of the namespace used in the element, the local name of the element, and the qualified name of the element. Its operation is basically the same as that of `startElement()` except that it doesn't accept the attributes of the element as an argument. The next two methods have to do with prefix mappings:

```
public void startPrefixMapping(String prefix, String uri)
{
    System.out.println("Prefix mapping: " + prefix);
    System.out.println("URI: " + uri);
}

public void endPrefixMapping(String prefix)
{
    System.out.println("End of prefix mapping: " + prefix);
}
```

These methods are used to report the beginning and end of prefix mappings when they are encountered in a document. The next method, `ignorableWhitespace()`, is just like `characters()`, except that it returns whitespace from element content that can be ignored.

```
public void ignorableWhitespace(char[] ch, int start, int length)
{
    System.out.println("Received whitespace.");
}
```

The next method is `processingInstruction()`, which reports processing instructions to the content handler. For example, a style sheet can be associated with an XML document using the following processing instruction:

```
<?xml-stylesheet href="mystyle.css" type="text/css"?>
```

The method that handles such instructions is:

```
public void processingInstruction(String target, String data)
{
    System.out.println("Received processing instruction:");
    System.out.println("Target: " + target);
    System.out.println("Data: " + data);
}
```

The next method, `setLocator()` is called when every event is processed. I don't use it in this program, but I'll explain what its purpose is anyway. Whenever an entity in a document is processed, the parser should call `setLocator()` with a `Locator` object. The `Locator` object contains information about where in the document the entity currently being processed is located. Here's the source code for the method:

```
public void setDocumentLocator(Locator locator)
{
    // Not used in this program.
}
```

The methods of a Locator object are in Table 14.2.

TABLE 14.2 The Methods of a Locator Object

Method	Purpose
getColumnNumber()	Returns the column number of the current position in the document being parsed
getLineNumber()	Returns the line number of the current position in the document being parsed
getPublicId()	Returns the public identifier of the current document event
getSystemId()	Returns the system identifier of the current document event

Implementing the ErrorHandler Interface

As you know, the DocumentPrinter class implements two interfaces, ContentHandler and ErrorHandler. Let's look at the methods that are used to implement the ErrorHandler interface. There are three types of errors that a SAX parser can generate—errors, fatal errors, and warnings. Classes that implement the ErrorHandler interface must provide methods to handle all three types of errors. Here's the source code for the three methods:

```
public void error(SAXParseException exception)
{
    System.out.println("Parsing error on line "
                        + exception.getLineNumber());
}

public void fatalError(SAXParseException exception)
{
    System.out.println("Fatal parsing error on line "
                        + exception.getLineNumber());
}

public void warning(SAXParseException exception)
{
    System.out.println("Warning on line "
                        + exception.getLineNumber());
}
```

As you can see, each of the three methods accepts the same argument—a SAXParseException object. The only difference between them is that they are called under different circumstances. In my code, I simply print out the line number of the document being parsed where the exception occurred. The full list of methods supported by SAXParseException appears in Table 14.3.

14

TABLE 14.3 Methods of the SAXParseException Interface

Method	Purpose
getColumnNumber()	Returns the column number of the current position in the document being parsed
getLineNumber()	Returns the line number of the current position in the document being parsed
getPublicId()	Returns the public identifier of the current document event
getSystemId()	Returns the system identifier of the current document event

Running the DocumentPrinter Class

Let's look at the output of the DocumentPrinter class when it's run against a simple XML document. Here's the XML document that I'm going to process:

```
<?xml-stylesheet href="mystyle.css" type="text/css"?>
<dealership>
  <automobile make="Buick" model="Century" color="blue">
    <options>
      <option>cruise control</option>
      <option>CD player</option>
    </options>
  </automobile>
  <automobile make="Ford" model="Thunderbird" color="red">
    <options>
      <option>convertible</option>
      <option>leather interior</option>
      <option>heated seats</option>
    </options>
  </automobile>
</dealership>
```

Here's the output of the program:

```
Start document.
Received processing instruction:
Target: xml-stylesheet
Data: href="mystyle.css" type="text/css"
Start element: dealership
Start element: automobile
   Attribute: make
       Value: Buick
   Attribute: model
       Value: Century
```

```
       Attribute: color
           Value: blue
Start element: options
Start element: option
Received characters: cruise control
End of element: option
Start element: option
Received characters: CD player
End of element: option
End of element: options
End of element: automobile
Start element: automobile
      Attribute: make
          Value: Ford
      Attribute: model
          Value: Thunderbird
      Attribute: color
          Value: red
Start element: options
Start element: option
Received characters: convertible
End of element: option
Start element: option
Received characters: leather interior
End of element: option
Start element: option
Received characters: heated seats
End of element: option
End of element: options
End of element: automobile
End of element: dealership
End of document reached.
```

The source code for the `DocumentPrinter` class can be found at the Web site for this book.

Summary

In this hour, I explained one of the two popular APIs for parsing XML files—SAX. SAX is an event-driven parser that is usually combined with a program set up to process the events generated by the parser. I demonstrated how such a program is written by creating a simple Java program that uses the Xerces SAX parser to iterate over the entities in an XML document and print out what they are. In the next hour, I'll explain how to use another popular API for parsing XML documents, the document object model.

14

Q&A

Q I didn't get any of that Java stuff; how am I supposed to use SAX?

A If you found the Java syntax confusing, you may be better off looking at the documentation for the SAX implementation for the language you're using. Check out the list of implementations above and investigate the one that's appropriate for you. If you're using JavaScript, or Visual Basic, you may prefer using the DOM for XML processing, which we discussed in Hour 15.

Q How do I access the data structure created by SAX?

A The catch with SAX is that it doesn't create its own data structure; it's up to the programmer who writes the content handler to generate a data structure, print the XML, or do whatever it is they want to with the data as it's processed by the SAX parser.

Workshop

The Workshop is designed to help you anticipate possible questions, review what you've learned, and begin learning how to put your knowledge into practice.

Quiz

1. What is an event-driven parser?

2. What standards body was responsible for the creation of SAX?

3. Which important feature was added when SAX was upgraded from version 1.0 to 2.0?

Quiz Answers

1. An event-driven parser iterates over a document and calls specific methods in another program as it processes entities in the document being parsed.

2. This was a trick question; a standards body did not create SAX. Rather, members of the xml-dev mailing list created it through a grassroots effort.

3. SAX 2.0 added support for namespaces.

Exercises

1. Modify the example program in this hour so that it reproduces the XML document that is supplied as input.

2. Reproduce the example program in the language that you do your development in (if it's not Java).

3. Find an alternate SAX parser and try it out in the example program (by changing the value of the PARSER_NAME variable).

HOUR 15

Understanding the XML Document Object Model (DOM)

A tree's a tree. How many more do you need to look at?

—Ronald Reagan

In the previous hour, you learned about SAX, which is an API for processing an XML document in a linear fashion. This hour discusses the Document Object Model, or DOM, which provides a set of interfaces that can be used to represent an entire XML document programmatically. This hour discusses

- What the Document Object Model is
- The interfaces that make up the DOM
- How to build programs that traverse the DOM
- How to access specific data inside an XML document using the DOM
- How to modify an XML document using the DOM

What Is the DOM?

If you're a seasoned HTML or JavaScript expert, you might already be familiar with the Document Object Model. When you're creating dynamic Web pages, it's common to access elements on a Web page from JavaScript using the DOM. The principles involved are basically the same for XML documents.

The DOM is just a standard method for exposing the elements in a structured document as a data structure in your programming language of choice. A program, called a DOM parser, reads through the XML in a file (or from some other source of input), and provides a data structure that you can access from your application. In the XML world, the DOM parser can also write its data structure out as XML so that you can save any changes that you make to the data structure.

Like XML itself, DOM is a standard developed by the World Wide Web Consortium (W3C). Most of the details of how the DOM works are left up to the specific implementations. It's important to understand that there are multiple levels of the DOM. DOM level 1 is concerned with basic XML and HTML. DOM level 2 adds specifications for XML namespaces, cascading stylesheets, events, and various traversal schemes. DOM level 3, which is currently at the Working Draft stage of the W3C standards process, will round out its XML coverage, include support for more user interface events, and support XPath. This hour is going to discuss how to use level 1 of the DOM, since it is the most widely implemented. You can find the DOM specifications online at

```
http://www.w3.org/DOM/
```

How the DOM Works

The DOM is really a collection of interfaces (I'll discuss each interface in the DOM a bit later), all of which extend a basic interface called a Node. The DOM represents an XML document as a tree structure, where each "thing" in the document is a node on the tree. Each node is associated with an interface that is more specific than the generic Node interface. Some nodes are Elements, others are Attributes, and still others are Comments. Each interface has its own properties and methods.

For example, the top-level node in the DOM model is a Document object. It can have exactly one Element object as a child (the root element of the document), one DocumentType object, and one DOMImplementation object. When you're dealing with XML, the various interfaces supplied correspond to the structural entities in XML documents. If you're dealing with XHTML (or HTML), then interfaces associated with them are also included in the DOM hierarchy.

Let's look at a simple XML document and then look at how that document is represented by the DOM. The document is provided in Listing 15.1, and the DOM representation appears in Figure 15.1.

LISTING 15.1   A Simple XML Document

```
 1: <?xml-stylesheet href="mystyle.css" type="text/css"?>
 2: <dealership>
 3:   <automobile make="Buick" model="Century" color="blue">
 4:     <options>
 5:       <option>cruise control</option>
 6:       <option>CD player</option>
 7:     </options>
 8:   </automobile>
 9:   <automobile make="Ford" model="Thunderbird" color="red">
10:     <options>
11:       <option>convertible</option>
12:       <option>leather interior</option>
13:       <option>heated seats</option>
14:     </options>
15:   </automobile>
16: </dealership>
```

FIGURE 15.1

The DOM representation of an XML document.

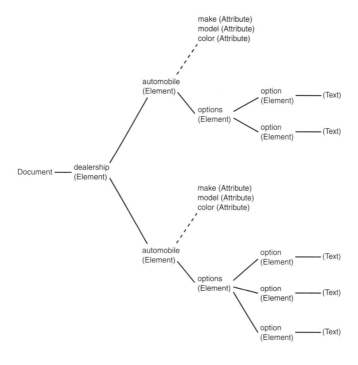

As you can see, the DOM representation of the document mirrors the structure of the XML document. Figure 15.1 contains a subset of the interfaces available in the DOM. For example, the `dealership` node expresses the `Element` interface, and the `make` nodes express the `Attribute` interface.

Language Bindings

The implementation of the DOM in a particular language is referred to as a language binding. The *language binding* is the set of objects native to the language in question that implements each of the interfaces in the DOM specification. When a DOM parser parses an XML document, it copies the document's data and structure into a data structure implemented using the language mapping associated with the parser.

The DOM specification includes bindings for Java and ECMAScript (the standardized version of JavaScript managed by ECMA). Developers can create language bindings from the DOM to their language simply by following the *IDL (Interface Definition Language)* in the DOM specification.

The language mapping is the most important part of the DOM specification. It is not concerned with the actual act of parsing the document. As long as a valid DOM tree is generated by the parser, it can work in any way that the developer of the parser chooses. For example, you could write a SAX application that produces a DOM tree. You can find more information about DOM language bindings at

```
http://www.w3.org/DOM/Bindings/
```

Using the DOM Tree

Once the parser has created the DOM tree, you can use it within your application. In many cases, you'll use other libraries that accept the DOM tree as input. You will be able to obtain the object that represents the DOM tree from the parser and then pass it along to whatever method uses it. For example, you might have a program that applies styles to a document using XSLT that accepts a parsed DOM tree as input.

Alternately, you can write your own programs that access the data in a document using the DOM. That's what the examples in this hour will do.

DOM Interfaces

As I've already mentioned, in order to comply with the DOM, an implementation must include the interfaces required by the DOM specification. Each of the interfaces is associated with a particular type of node found in a DOM tree. Rather than listing and describing all of these interfaces, I'm going to talk about the interfaces that you will use frequently in the course of writing applications that use the DOM.

The Node Interface

The Node interface is the interface from which all other interfaces are derived. Regardless of whatever else a particular entity in a DOM tree is, it's still a Node. The Node interface exposes some attributes and methods that are generic to anything that's in a DOM tree. These attributes and methods are largely associated with keeping track of the parents, siblings, and children of the Node. Nodes also have attributes that contain their names, values, and a pointer to the Document with which they are associated.

The Document Interface

The Document interface is the root node of a DOM tree. There's one important thing to point out here: the Document node in a DOM tree is not the root element of the XML document—it's one level above that. Every Document has one child Element node that contains the root element of the XML document. Document nodes have other attributes that are associated with the document itself, rather than with the root element. That's why a DOM tree has one more level in its hierarchy than an XML document.

In addition to the root level element of the document, the Document node also contains a pointer to a DocumentType node and a DOMImplementation node. Neither of these nodes are commonly referenced on programs which use the DOM, so I'm not going to discuss them individually. For more information, check out the DOM specification at

http://www.w3.org/DOM/DOMTR

The Element Interface

The Element interface represents an element in an XML (or HTML) document. The only attribute specific to the Element node is the tag name (of course, it inherits all of the attributes of a standard Node, as well).

It includes methods that enable you to retrieve, add, and remove attributes from the element. It also enables you to retrieve child elements that have a specific name. (You can already fetch all of the children of an element using the methods it inherits from the Node interface.)

The Attr Interface

The Attr interface represents an attribute of an Element. Despite the fact that they inherit the Node interface, they are not actually nodes on the DOM tree because they are not children of an element. Rather, they are part of the element itself. What this means in practical terms is that any methods inherited from the Node interface that deal with traversing the DOM tree return null. You can't fetch the parents, siblings, or children of an attribute, because in terms of the DOM, they don't have any of those things.

Attributes have three properties—a name, a value, and a boolean flag indicating whether or not the attribute was explicitly included in the document that was parsed. They have no methods specific to themselves.

The `NodeList` Interface

The `NodeList` interface is different from the other interfaces I've discussed so far. It's not a pointer to an entity in a DOM tree; rather, it's an abstract data structure that enables DOM implementations to handle collections of nodes. For example, if you call the method of the `Element` interface that returns all the children of an element with a particular name, the collection of child elements is returned as a `NodeList`. You can then iterate over the `NodeList` and extract all of the `Element` nodes from it. The only interface it must implement is one that returns items by index. Its only attribute is the size of the collection. Using the size and the method, which returns items, you can iterate over the members of the collection.

Accessing the DOM within Internet Explorer

For the sake of simplicity, the examples in this hour are written in JavaScript. One of the huge advantages of the DOM is that the interfaces that make up the DOM are basically the same regardless of whether you write your program in Java, C++, Visual Basic, JavaScript, or any other language with a DOM implementation. JavaScript programs run within the context of a Web browser are interpreted (so they don't have to be compiled) and don't have a lot of overhead or structure that can require a lot of knowledge beforehand in order to be understood.

In this case, I'll be taking advantage of some features specific to Microsoft Internet Explorer (versions 5 and above). Internet Explorer has some XML-related features that make it perfect for this job. The main thing it has is a built-in DOM parser for XML. Turning an XML data structure into a DOM-based data structure is, well, a zero step process. Thanks to a feature called XML data islands, you can include an XML document within your HTML document (or provide a link to an external XML document), and Internet Explorer will automatically parse that XML document. Listing 15.2 contains a program containing one of these XML data islands. The XML data appears in boldface.

LISTING **15.2**   An HTML Page Containing XML Data

```
1: <html>
2: <head>
3: <title>test</title>
4: <xml id="cars">
5: <?xml version="1.0"?>
```

continues

LISTING 15.2   Continued

```
 6: <?xml-stylesheet href="Vehicles.xsl" type="text/xsl"?>
 7:
 8: <vehicles>
 9:    <vehicle year="1996" make="Land Rover" model="Discovery">
10:      <mileage>36500</mileage>
11:      <color>black</color>
12:      <price>22100</price>
13:      <options>
14:        <option>leather interior</option>
15:        <option>heated seats</option>
16:      </options>
17:    </vehicle>
18:
19:    <vehicle year="1998" make="Land Rover" model="Discovery">
20:      <mileage>15900</mileage>
21:      <color>teal</color>
18:      <price>32000</price>
19:      <options>
20:        <option>cruise control</option>
21:        <option>CD player</option>
22:      </options>
23:    </vehicle>
24:
25:    <vehicle year="1996" make="Chevrolet" model="Suburban 2500">
26:      <mileage>49300</mileage>
27:      <color>green</color>
28:      <price>25995</price>
29:      <options />
30:    </vehicle>
31: </vehicles>
32: </xml>
33: </head>
34: <body>
35: </body>
36: </html>
```

Lines 5–19 contain the XML data island embedded within this HTML document. Now let's look at how to use JavaScript to access the XML data using the DOM. One thing you might find a bit confusing at first is that the browser also supports accessing the HTML document itself through the DOM—the top level object for an HTML Web page is a document node, just as the top level node in the XML DOM uses the document interface. Any time I use an object that starts with document, I'm referring to the root object for the HTML page, not for the XML data island.

Accessing XML Data within a Page

There are a number of ways you can retrieve the XML document object. Internet Explorer provides an interface to every element in the document with an identifier. The following statement will assign the DOM representation of the XML data to a variable:

```
var xmlDocument = document.all("cars").XMLDocument;
```

Let's break the statement down into parts. The part of the statement to the left of the "equal" sign initiates a new varaible, called xmlDocument. Using var indicates that the variable is local, which just limits the scope of the variable—the parts of the page from which the variable is accessible. document.all("cars") is used to retrieve the node in the HTML document with the ID cars. The all property of the document object (the one associated with the HTML page) provides access to all of the named elements in a page. The XMLDocument property of the element with the ID cars is the DOM representation of that element. This works because that element happens to be an XML data island.

Once you have the xmlDocument variable set, you can call all of the methods associated with nodes in general or with document nodes in particular on it. Let's look at a script that I can insert into the document in Listing 15.2 to print out the names of all of the nodes in the document tree using a function named printNode().

```
<script language="JavaScript">
var xmlDocument = document.all("cars").XMLDocument;

printNode(xmlDocument);

function printNode(node)
{
    document.write("Node name: " + node.nodeName + "<br />\n");

    for (var i = 0; i < node.childNodes.length; i++)
    {
        printNode(node.childNodes.item(i));
    }
}
</script>
```

Let's look at this script in detail. It just needs to be placed within the head element of the HTML document in order to work. When you include JavaScript on a page, any code that's not inside a function will be executed as soon as the browser interprets it.

The following code will be executed immediately:

```
var xmlDocument = document.all("cars").XMLDocument;
printNode(xmlDocument);
```

The rest of the code inside the `script` tag is inside the `printNode` function, and will be executed when the `printNode` function is called. As you can see, I call `printNode` as soon as I have retrieved the XML document from the full page's DOM tree.

The first line of the script creates a new variable, called `xmlDocument`, and assigns the XML document node from the XML that I included in the page to that variable. It retrieves this value by referencing the top level `document` object associated with the page and by selecting the object with the ID `cars`, using the `all` object that I discussed earlier. By specifically referencing the `XMLDocument` property of `document.all("cars")`, I indicate that the object I want to receive is a parsed XML document.

As you know, a `document` node provides all of the methods of the `node` interface as well as those specific to the `document` interface. The `printNode()` function will work with any node, including a `document` node, so I call it and pass it the `xmlDocument` variable as its argument.

The `printNode()` Function

The `printNode()` function uses a technique called recursion. Recursion is to tree-like data structures what loops are to list data structures. When you want to process a number of similar things that are in a list, you simply process them one at a time until you've processed all of the items in that list. Recursion is a bit more complex. When you're dealing with tree-like data structures, you have to work your way down each branch in the tree until you reach the end.

Let's look at an example not associated with the DOM first. When you want to find a file on your computer's hard drive manually, and you have no idea where it is located, the fastest way to find it is to recursively search all of the directories on the hard drive. The process goes something like this (starting at the root directory):

1. Is the file in this directory? If so, we're finished.
2. If not, does this directory contain any subdirectories? If not, skip to step 4.
3. If there are subdirectories, move to the first subdirectory and go back to step 1.
4. Move up one directory. Move to the next subdirectory in this directory, and skip to step 1. If there are no additional subdirectories in this directory, repeat this step.

That's one recursive algorithm. The most important thing to understand about recursion is that all of the items being processed recursively must be similar enough to be processed in the same way.

This explains why all of the interfaces in the DOM are extensions of the basic `Node` interface. You can write one recursive function that will process all of the nodes in a DOM tree using the methods that they have in common. `printNode()` is one such function

```
function printNode(node)
{
    document.write("Node name: " + node.nodeName + "<br />\n");

    for (var i = 0; i < node.childNodes.length; i++)
    {
        printNode(node.childNodes(i));
    }
}
```

First, let's examine the function declaration. In JavaScript, you indicate that you're creating a function using the `function` keyword. The name of the function is supplied next, followed by the list of arguments accepted by the function. The name of this function is `printNode`, and it accepts one argument, which is given the name `node`. This argument is intended to be a node that's part of a DOM tree.

In the body of the function, the first thing that happens is the `nodeName` property of the node currently being processed is printed. Then, the function loops over the children of the node currently being processed and calls the `printNode()` function on each of the children. This is where the recursion comes in. The same function, `printNode()`, is called repeatedly to process every node in the tree. Figure 15.2 contains this page, rendered in Internet Explorer.

FIGURE 15.2

The output of a function that prints the names of all of the nodes in a DOM tree.

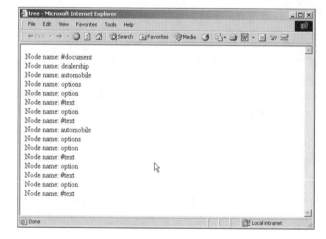

Another Example Program

Let's look at a slightly different program. In this program, if you type the name of a node in one field, the node type for that node will be printed in another form field. This example differs from the previous one in that it shows how to deal with the various types of nodes that can appear within a document and demonstrates how to process attributes as well as elements within an XML document.

First, let's look at the page's skeleton, without any JavaScript. It's in Listing 15.3.

LISTING 15.3 The Page Skeleton for Our Element Type Printing Program

```
 1: <html>
 2: <head>
 3: <title>show element type</title>
 4: <xml id="cars">
 5: <?xml version="1.0"?>
 6: <?xml-stylesheet href="Vehicles.xsl" type="text/xsl"?>
 7:
 8: <vehicles>
 9:   <vehicle year="1996" make="Land Rover" model="Discovery">
10:     <mileage>36500</mileage>
11:     <color>black</color>
12:     <price>22100</price>
13:     <options>
14:       <option>leather interior</option>
15:       <option>heated seats</option>
16:     </options>
17:   </vehicle>
18:
19:   <vehicle year="1998" make="Land Rover" model="Discovery">
20:     <mileage>15900</mileage>
21:     <color>teal</color>
18:     <price>32000</price>
19:     <options>
20:       <option>cruise control</option>
21:       <option>CD player</option>
22:     </options>
23:   </vehicle>
24:
25:   <vehicle year="1996" make="Chevrolet" model="Suburban 2500">
26:     <mileage>49300</mileage>
27:     <color>green</color>
28:     <price>25995</price>
29:     <options />
30:   </vehicle>
31: </vehicles>20: </xml>
32:
33: <script language="JavaScript">
```

continues

LISTING 15.3   Continued

```
34: </script>
35:
36: </head>
37: <body>
38: <form name="nodeform">
39: <table border="0">
40: <tr>
41:     <td>node name:</td>
42:     <td>
43:         <input name="nodename" />
44:         <input type="button" value="get type" onclick="printtype()" />
45:     </td>
46: </tr>
47: <tr>
48:     <td>node type:</td>
49:     <td><input type="text" name="nodetype" value="unknown" /></td>
50: </tr>
51: </table>
52: </form>
53:
54: </body>
55: </html>
```

As you can see, the script tag is in place (line 33), but I've left the script itself out. The XML data is the same as it was in the previous example program in this hour.

The main thing I want to look at right now is the form included on this page. It contains two text fields; the first accepts the name of a node as input, and the second prints the node's type, or a message indicating that no node with the name supplied was found. When the user clicks on the button, the `printtype()` function is called (using the `onclick` handler associated with button fields). Let's take a look at that function.

```
function printtype()
{
    var nodename = document.nodeform.nodename.value;

    var xml = document.all("cars").XMLDocument;

    nodefound = false;

    searchtree(nodename, xml);

    if (!nodefound)
    {
        document.nodeform.nodetype.value = "node not found";
    }
}
```

As you can see, this function accepts no arguments. It retrieves all of the data it needs from specific objects within the page. First, the function grabs the name of the node to search for from the nodename field in the form named nodeform. Then it retrieves the parsed XML from the DOM and assigns it to a variable called xml. At that point, the searchtree() function is called, and the node name we're looking for and parsed XML are passed in as arguments. The searchtree() function sets the nodefound variable to true if there's a node in the tree with a name matching the one the user supplied. If the node was not found, the value of the nodetype field is set to a message indicating so.

Finally, let's look at the searchtree() function itself. Let me explain what it does briefly before I include the source code. The first thing it does is retrieve the node's type and set the nodetype variable to a description of the node type using a switch statement. It then checks to see whether the name of the node currently being processed matches the name of the node that the user is searching for. If there's a match, then the function returns— it's finished. If not, then the script processes all of the child nodes for the current node. It also processes all of the attributes, if the node is of a type that supports attributes. Here's the code for the function:

```
 1: function searchtree(nodename, node)
 2: {
 3:     var nodetype = "unknown";
 4:
 5:     switch (node.nodeType)
 6:     {
 7:         case 1:
 8:             nodetype = "element";
 9:             break;
10:         case 2:
11:             nodetype = "attribute";
12:             break;
13:         case 3:
14:             nodetype = "text";
15:             break;
16:         case 4:
17:             nodetype = "cdata section";
18:             break;
19:         case 5:
20:             nodetype = "entity reference";
21:             break;
22:         case 6:
23:             nodetype = "entity";
24:             break;
25:         case 7:
26:             nodetype = "processing instruction";
27:             break;
28:         case 8:
29:             nodetype = "comment";
30:             break;
```

```
31:          case 9:
32:              nodetype = "document";
33:              break;
34:          case 10:
35:              nodetype = "document type";
36:              break;
37:          case 11:
38:              nodetype = "document fragment";
39:              break;
40:          case 12:
41:              nodetype = "notation";
42:              break;
43:          default:
44:              nodetype = "unknown";
45:      }
46:
47:      if (nodename == node.nodeName)
48:      {
49:          document.nodeform.nodetype.value = nodetype;
50:          nodefound = true;
51:          return;
52:      }
53:
54:      for (var i = 0; i < node.childNodes.length; i++)
55:      {
56:          searchtree(nodename, node.childNodes.item(i));
57:      }
58:
59:      if (nodetype == "element" || nodetype == "entity")
60:      {
61:          for (var i = 0; i < node.attributes.length; i++)
62:          {
63:              searchtree(nodename, node.attributes(i));
64:          }
65:      }
66: }
```

Let's look at the code. On line 5, the function determines the type of the node currently being processed. The nodeType property of node objects indicates which interface is associated with the node. The property contains an integer that is associated with a particular interface. A switch statement is used to set the nodetype variable based on the value of the nodeType property.

I used a switch statement for this to demonstrate that I could in fact run entire blocks of code based on the node type if I needed to. The break statement in each case indicates that the switch statement should exit once that case has been run. If you leave them out, it will run the code for the cases that follow the case that matches (until it encounters a break statement or runs out of cases). If I were just going for efficiency, I'd create a data structure mapping node types (which are integers) to node names and use a single line of code to fetch the name of the node from the mapping.

Once the node's type has been determined, I check to see whether the name of the node matches the name that the user is searching for. If so, then I go ahead and update the field on the form using the statement on line 49.

Then I set the nodefound variable to true, and use a return statement to stop executing the function. Once the node has been found, we're done. If the node we're looking for was not yet found, we use recursion to search all of the children of this node. The same process above is repeated for each of the children.

If the children of the current node do not contain a matching node, I deal with attributes of the current node. Remember, attributes are nodes, so you can handle them in exactly the same way. One added bit of complexity is that not all types of nodes can have attributes, so I have to make sure that I try to process only the attributes of element and entity nodes. The if statement on line 59 makes sure that I only check those node types for attributes. (Attempting to retrieve the attributes from nodes that do not support attributes will cause errors in JavaScript).

Once I've determined that the node being processed supports attributes, I retrieve and iterate over the attributes of the node just like I would the children of the node, using the loop which begins on line 61. The attributes property of a node returns a NamedNodeList of the attributes for that node. The only difference between a NamedNodeList and a regular NodeList is that items in a NamedNodeList can be retrieved by name. I won't be taking advantage of that feature in this program; instead, I just refer to the attributes by index on line 63.

That's it for this program. Figure 15.3 is a screen shot of this page at work.

FIGURE 15.3

A Web page that determines the type of a node when given its name.

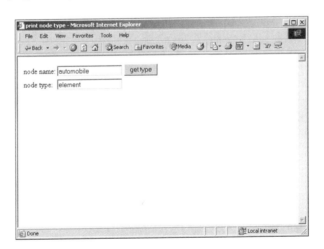

Updating the DOM Tree

Not only does the DOM enable you to access an XML data structure in a number of ways, but it also enables you to alter an XML data structure. Rather than providing you with a lengthy example program that explains how to alter the DOM tree, I'll just show you some specific examples that demonstrate how such tasks are performed. Note that if I were using a language other than JavaScript, I could store the updated DOM tree on disk once the tree has been updated. However, JavaScript runs within the context of a Web browser and has no access to the file system, so any changes you make to a DOM tree in a JavaScript program will be lost as soon as you leave that page.

First, let's look at how you can access a specific node in a tree. In the earlier examples in this hour, I've iterated over all of the children of a particular node. You will probably want to be more specific when you're updating the tree.

The key method here is the `item()` method of the `NodeList` interface. When you call the `item()` method and supply it with an index, it returns the node associated with that index. Let's say you have the document node of a DOM tree assigned to the variable `doc`. To access the root level element of the document, you can use the following code:

```
doc.childNodes.item(0);
```

Or, if you prefer, simply

```
doc.childNodes.firstChild;
```

In order to be valid XML, you can have only one element at the top level of your tree, so when you want to add a node, you need to add it to the root element. You can assign the root element to a variable like this:

```
var root = doc.childNodes.firstChild;
```

Once you've done that, you can add an element as its child. However, first you'll need an element node. You can create one using the document object, like this:

```
var newElement = doc.createElement("automobile");
```

Then, you can add it to your tree, like this:

```
root.appendChild(newElement);
```

If you want, you can then add an attribute to the node you just inserted into the tree

```
var attr = doc.createAttribute("make");
attr.text = "Suburu";
root.childNodes.lastChild.setAttributeNode(attr);
```

15

First, I create an attribute just like I created the element before. Then I set its value, and finally I add it to the element I just added to the tree. Note that I used the `lastChild` method to access the node I just added. Because I appended the node to the tree, I know that it's the last child of the root element.

It's just as easy to update and remove items in the DOM. Now I'll update the attribute I just added. To do so, I just need to access it in the DOM tree, and change its value, like so:

```
root.childNodes.lastChild.setAttribute("make", "BMW");
```

As you can see, there's a method specifically used to update a named attribute. To remove that attribute, I can call the following method:

```
root.childNodes.lastChild.removeAttribute("make");
```

Now let's look at updating and removing elements themselves. There are two ways to do so—you can replace child nodes or remove them. First, let's look at replacing them. In order to replace an element, I'll need to create a new element to put in place of the old one, and then call the method that swaps them

```
var replacementElem = doc.createElement("customer");
var oldNode = root.replaceChild(replacementElem, root.childNodes.lastChild);
```

As you can see, to replace a child of a node, you just have to pass in the new node and a reference to the node that will be replaced. The node that was replaced is assigned to the variable `oldNode`—if you want to do something else with it. Removing a node is even easier:

```
var anotherOldNode = root.removeChild(root.childNodes.lastChild);
```

The node that was removed is assigned to the variable `anotherOldNode`.

Summary

The DOM is a W3C standard that describes how the structure of XML and HTML documents can be expressed as a native data structure within various programming languages. The DOM standard is language neutral, and implementations exist for a number of languages, including JavaScript, Java, C++, and Visual Basic. In this hour, you learned about the various interfaces that make up the DOM and how you can access data stored within the DOM structure from JavaScript. Even though the syntax of the language you use with the DOM might differ significantly from the syntax used in these JavaScript examples, the means of accessing the DOM will be basically the same.

Q&A

Q Why didn't the example programs in this hour work in Netscape?

A Unfortunately, Microsoft Internet Explorer is the only browser that supports XML Data Islands, which are used by the examples in this hour.

Q Can large documents create performance issues when I use the DOM?

A Yes. As you know, DOM parsers create a data structure that contains all of the data in an XML document. If your XML document is really large (in comparison to the amount of RAM in the computer that your application runs on), performance issues can arise. In those cases, it may make more sense to use SAX because it does not deal with the document as a whole.

Workshop

The Workshop is designed to help you anticipate possible questions, review what you've learned, and begin learning how to put your knowledge into practice.

Quiz

1. From which interface in the DOM are all the others derived?
2. The DOM is specific to which programming language?
3. How do the `NodeList` and `NamedNodeList` interfaces differ?
4. Which interfaces support attributes?

Quiz Answers

1. All of the interfaces in the DOM are derived from the `Node` interface, with the exception of the `NodeList` interface.
2. The DOM is not specific to any programming language.
3. The `NamedNodeList` interface is an extension of the `NodeList` interface—it adds support for retrieval of members using the node name.
4. The `Element` and `Entity` interfaces support attributes.

Exercises

1. Write a program that converts all of the attributes in an XML document into child elements of the elements that they were associated with.
2. Write a program that allows you to rename elements by entering the old and new element names into a form.
3. Write a program that shows the names of only those elements that have attributes and no children.

HOUR 16

The XML Query Language

I have never been lost, but I will admit to being confused for several weeks.

—Daniel Boone (American pioneer)

I would be a little surprised if you aren't at least mildly confused by the sheer number of acronyms there are that go along with XML: DTDs, CSS, XSL, XSLT, XHTML, XPath, and the DOM—the list goes on and on. In today's lesson, I'm going to spring another one on you. This hour is about *XQL—the XML Query Language*. XQL is used when you want to retrieve particular pieces of data from a larger document.

In this hour, you'll learn the following:

- What XQL is
- How to write queries using XQL
- Where to find applications that support XQL

What Is XQL?

In order to explain what XQL is, I'll first talk about the problem it's designed to solve. As you already know all too well, XML documents have a treelike structure. Let's say you wanted to find all of the elements in a document named color. Given what you've learned so far, you'd probably use the DOM to read the document into your application and then iterate over the entire tree in order to extract all of the elements called color. Sounds easy enough, right? Let's say you wanted to find only the color elements that are inside elements called automobile or you want to return only those color elements that have the value blue. I think you can see where I'm going.

When you use XML for data storage, these sorts of problems are very common, so XQL was created to simplify handling them. If you have an application that supports XQL, you can write simple queries to perform all the tasks I mentioned in the previous paragraph and many, many more.

Before I get started on explaining how XQL works, I'll provide you with a bit of background on the language. XQL was originally created in 1998. It has not been adopted by any standards body but has become the de facto standard for querying XML data and has seen relatively wide adoption in the XML community.

Where XQL Is Going

Unfortunately, the future of XQL is somewhat cloudy. Despite the fact that it has been well received, it will likely be superseded by another query language. The language which is likely to become the most popular query language for XML is XQuery. Unlike XQL, XQuery is set to become a standard; currently it's at the working draft stage of the W3C standards process. You can view the XQuery specification at

http://www.w3.org/TR/xquery/

The good news is that Jonathan Robie, the creator of XQL, is also part of the working group that is definining XQuery. Much of XQL makes it into the XQuery specification intact. You can learn XQL now and you'll be prepared for applications which implement XQuery later, as well as being able to use those applications which implement XQL now. For more information on XQL and its history, check out the XQL FAQ at

http://www.ibiblio.org/xql/

Later on in this hour, I'll talk about some implementations of XQL that you can try out. Right now, though, let's jump right into using XQL to write queries for XML data.

Writing Queries in XQL

Let's look at how XQL is used to query an XML document. The sample XML document, an adapted version of a document included in earlier chapters, shown in Listing 16.1, is used in the examples that follow.

LISTING 16.1 A Sample XML Document

```
 1: <?xml version="1.0"?>
 2: <?xml-stylesheet href="Vehicles.xsl" type="text/xsl"?>
 3:
 4: <vehicles>
 5:   <vehicle year="1996" make="Land Rover" model="Discovery">
 6:     <mileage>36500</mileage>
 7:     <color>black</color>
 8:     <price>22100</price>
 9:     <options>
10:       <option>leather interior</option>
11:       <option>heated seats</option>
12:     </options>
13:   </vehicle>
14:
15:   <vehicle year="1998" make="Land Rover" model="Discovery">
16:     <mileage>15900</mileage>
17:     <color>teal</color>
18:     <price>32000</price>
19:     <options>
20:       <option>cruise control</option>
21:       <option>CD player</option>
22:     </options>
23:   </vehicle>
24:
25:   <vehicle year="1996" make="Chevrolet" model="Suburban 2500">
26:     <mileage>49300</mileage>
27:     <color>green</color>
28:     <price>25995</price>
29:     <options />
30:   </vehicle>
31: </vehicles>
```

Now let's take a look at some simple XQL queries that can be used to retrieve data from that document. The syntax for XQL is very spare. For example, the query that retrieves all of the color elements from the document is

`color`

which returns

```
<xql:result>
    <color>black</color>
    <color>teal</color>
    <color>green</color>
</xql:result>
```

> The queries are intended to be typed into an application which supports XQL, or to be used within XQL queries within a program. The results of the query are displayed afterward, to show what would be returned.

A / at the beginning of a query string indicates the root level of the document structure. For example, the query that follows wouldn't return anything, because color is not the root level element of the document.

`/color`

On the other hand, the results of the following query would be the same as the one above:

vehicles/vehicle/color

```
<xql:result>
    <color>black</color>
    <color>teal</color>
    <color>green</color>
</xql:result>
```

As you can see, only the color elements are returned by the query. Let's say you want to find color elements that exist anywhere inside a vehicles element. The // operator is used to return elements anywhere below another element. Let's look at how it works:

dealership//color

```
<xql:result>
    <color>black</color>
    <color>teal</color>
    <color>green</color>
</xql:result>
```

That's it for requesting specific elements from an XML document. As you can see, aside from a few wrinkles, requesting elements from an XML document using XQL isn't all that different from locating files in a file system using a command shell.

Using Wildcards

Let's say you want to find all of the `option` elements that are grandchildren of the `vehicle` element. To get them all from the example document, you could just use the query `vehicle/options/option`. However, let's say that you didn't know that the intervening element was `options` or that there were other elements that could intervene between `vehicle` and `option`. In that case, you could use the following query:

vehicle/*/option

```
<xql:result>
      <option>leather interior</option>
      <option>heated seats</option>
      <option>cruise control</option>
      <option>CD player</option>
</xql:result>
```

The wildcard (*) matches any element. You can also use it at the end of a query to match all of the children of a particular element. To retrieve all of the children of the `vehicle` element, use the following query:

vehicle/*

```
<xql:result>
    <mileage>36500</mileage>
    <color>black</color>
    <price>22100</price>
    <options>
       <option>leather interior</option>
       <option>heated seats</option>
     </options>
     <mileage>15900</mileage>
     <color>teal</color>
     <price>32000</price>
     <options>
       <option>cruise control</option>
       <option>CD player</option>
     </options>
     <mileage>49300</mileage>
     <color>green</color>
     <price>25995</price>
     <options />
</xql:result>
```

Using Subqueries

In XQL, expressions within square brackets ([ ]) are subqueries. Those expressions are not used to retrieve elements themselves but to qualify the elements that are retrieved.

For example, a query such as

```
vehicle/color
```

retrieves `color` elements that are children of `vehicle` elements. On the other hand, this query

```
vehicle[color]
```

retrieves `vehicle` elements that have a `color` element as a child. Later I'll demonstrate how to use subqueries with filters, which can be used to write very specific queries.

Using Filters to Query Specific Information

Once you've mastered the extraction of specific elements from XML files, you can move on to searching for elements that contain information you specify. To search for a particular value, you just specify that value using an equals sign after the element that should contain that value. Here's a simple example:

```
color='green'
```

```
<xql:result>
    <color>green</color>
</xql:result>
```

As you can see, only the `color` element that was set to `green` was actually returned. Of course, the previous query is nearly useless. Why would you want to write a query that retrieves individual elements with contents you already know are there? The only thing this query tells you is that the document does, in fact, contain a `color` element with the value red.

Let's say you want to find higher-level elements containing a particular value in a child element. The `[]` operator indicates that the expression within the square braces should be searched but that the element listed to the left of the square braces should be returned. For example, the expression below would read "return any `automobile` elements that contain a `color` element with a value of red":

```
vehicle[color='green']
```

```
<xql:result>
  <vehicle year="1996" make="Chevrolet" model="Suburban 2500">
<mileage>49300</mileage>
    <color>green</color>
    <price>25995</price>
    <options />
  </vehicle>
</xql:result>
```

The full `automobile` element is returned because it appeared to the left of the search expression enclosed in the square braces. You can also use Boolean operators to string multiple search expressions together. For example, to find all of the automobiles with a color of green or a mileage of 15900, you would use the following query:

```
vehicle[color='green' or mileage='15900']
```

```
<xql:result>
  <vehicle year="1998" make="Land Rover" model="Discovery">
    <mileage>15900</mileage>
    <color>teal</color>
    <price>32000</price>
    <options>
      <option>cruise control</option>
      <option>CD player</option>
    </options>
  </vehicle>
  <vehicle year="1996" make="Chevrolet" model="Suburban 2500">
    <mileage>49300</mileage>
    <color>green</color>
    <price>25995</price>
    <options />
  </vehicle>
</xql:result>
```

The `!=` operator is also available when you want to write expressions to test for inequality. Optionally, the = operator can be written as `$eq$`, and the `!=` operator can be written as `$neq$`.

Using Boolean Operators in Queries

XQL supports all three common Boolean operators, `$and$`, `$or$`, and `$not$` (the $ characters surrounding the operators are used to indicate that the word is an operator and not the name of an element). For example, you can write complex queries, such as

```
vehicle[$not$ (color='blue' $or$ color='green') $and$ make='Chevrolet']
```

In this case, the query wouldn't return any results because it returns only Chevrolet cars that are not blue or green. Now let's look at an even more complex query. What if you wanted to retrieve just the options for any black car in the document? Here's the query:

```
//vehicle[color='black']//options
```

```
<xql:result>
    <options>
      <option>leather interior</option>
      <option>heated seats</option>
    </options>
</xql:result>
```

Let's break down that query. Remember that `//` means "anywhere in the hierarchy." The `//vehicle` part indicates that we're looking for elements inside a `vehicle` element. The `[color='green']` part indicates that we're interested only in `vehicle` elements with a `color` element with a value of `green`. The part you haven't yet seen is `//options`. This indicates that the results should be any `options` elements under `vehicle` elements that contain a matching `color` element.

Dealing with Attributes

The next thing to look at is attributes. When you want to refer to an attribute, place an `@` sign before its name. So, to find the year attributes in a document, you refer to them as `@year`. A simple query that will do just that is

```
@year
```

To find all the `year` attributes of `vehicle` elements, use the following query:

```
vehicle/@year
```

You can write a slightly different query that returns all of the `vehicle` elements that have year attributes as well:

```
vehicle[@year]
```

This naturally leads up to writing a query that returns all of the `vehicle` elements that have a `year` attribute with a value of 1996. That query is

```
vehicle[@year='1996']
```

Requesting Items from a Collection

The total results of a query are referred to as a collection. For example, if you write a query that returns all of the `vehicle` elements in the document in Listing 16.1, you wind up with a collection of three elements. In the examples you've seen so far, the elements that are returned by a query are included in the results.

You can use subscripts at the end of your queries to limit the number of items included in the results. Items in a collection of results are indexed the same way arrays are in most programming languages—beginning with 0. In other words, the first element has the subscript 0, the second 1, and so on.

Looking back at an example that queried the XML document in Listing 16.1, we can see how subscripts are used. Take a look at these three queries:

```
color
```

```
<xql:result>
    <color>black</color>
```

```
    <color>teal</color>
    <color>green</color>
</xql:result>
```

color[0]

```
<xql:result>
    <color>black</color>
</xql:result>
```

color[1]

```
<xql:result>
    <color>teal</color>
</xql:result>
```

color[-1]

```
<xql:result>
    <color>green</color>
</xql:result>
```

The first query is just a repeat of the example from earlier in the hour, which I included for reference purposes. As you can see from the fourth example, you can specify elements using negative subscripts. In this case, –1 retrieves the last element in the collection. You can also specify ranges of elements using the to operator. For example, if a document contains five color elements, you can select the second, third, and fourth using this query:

```
color[2 to 4]
```

How Do I Use This Stuff?

Now that you've seen how XQL works, the next thing you're probably wondering is how you can use it. Unless you're open to writing your own parser for XQL, you'll need to find a product that enables you to execute XQL queries against XML documents.

There are a number of different types of products that provide this functionality. There are libraries that you can use in your own applications to query XML documents, databases that store data in XML format and allow you to retrieve it using XQL, or tools that allow you to enter XQL queries and retrieve results from XML documents.

Because XQL is not approved by any standards organization, there are slight differences between all of the XQL implementations that are available. When you choose an XQL implementation to use, you'll need to consult the documentation to clear up any syntax differences between the examples in this hour and those specific to your implementation.

16

Implementations

The GMD-ISPI XQL Engine is an XQL engine written in Java that allows you to run XQL queries on XML documents. You can download it at

`http://xml.darmstadt.gmd.de/xql/`

That site requires you to fill out a form with personal information to download the application, but it is free for noncommercial use. If you want to use it commercially, you can purchase it from Infonyte at

`http://www.infonyte.com/`

Tamino is an XML database from Software AG that supports XQL. You can find out more at

`http://www.softwareag.com/tamino/`

If you're a Perl programmer, you can use the `XML::XQL` module to perform XQL queries on XML documents. You can download it from CPAN at `http://www.cpan.org/`.

Fatdog Software (`http://www.fatdog.com/`) has a product called XML Query Engine that supports XQL. It's a Java bean that can be used within other programs to index XML documents, and it then allows you to search them using XQL queries.

Summary

XQL is a query language that makes it easy to extract specific elements from an XML document. It is analogous to SQL in the relational database world. In this hour, you've seen how to write queries in XQL ranging from simple to complex. I also pointed you toward some products that include support for XQL.

Q&A

Q Earlier in the chapter you talked about XQuery as the upcoming standard. Are there any early implementatations?

A Fatdog's XML Query Engine provides early support for XQuery. You can find out more about it at `http://www.fatdog.com/`

Q How does XQL differ from XPath?

A XPath is a language used for addressing within XML documents. XQL is a query language used to filter data within XML documents. XPath can also be used for pattern matching on XML documents and in that role is very similar to XQL. Fundamentally, the two languages differ more in purpose and syntax than in design. XQuery includes elements of both XPath and XQL. Chapter 19 covers XPath in detail.

Workshop

The Workshop is designed to help you anticipate possible questions, review what you've learned, and begin learning how to put your knowledge into practice. The answers to the quiz can be found in Appendix A, "Quiz Answers."

Quiz

1. How do the queries `automobile/color=red` and `automobile[color=red]` differ?

2. How do you indicate that an entity is an attribute rather than an element?

3. How do the queries `automobile//option` and `automobilie/*/option` differ?

Quiz Answers

1. The first of the two queries returns the `color` elements that are children of `automobile` elements and are set to `red`. The second of the two returns `automobile` elements that contain a `color` element set to `red`.

2. Names that begin with @ are treated as attributes; names with no qualifier are elements.

3. The query `automobile//option` returns any `option` elements that are found below an `automobile` element in the document hierarchy. The second query, `automobile/*/option`, returns any option elements that are grandchildren of `automobile` elements.

Exercises

Download an implementation of XQL and use it to write some queries against your XML documents.

16

HOUR 17

Using XML with Databases

Nothing you can't spell will ever work.

—Will Rogers

Most Web applications store their data in relational databases. As you've seen in the past few hours, XML can be used not only as a document format, but also as a way to store your data in a structured manner. In this hour, I'm going to explain how relational databases work and how you can integrate your XML applications with relational databases. In this hour you'll learn

- The basic theory behind the relational model
- What database normalization is
- How to use SQL, the query language for relational databases
- Some ways that XML and databases can be integrated
- How to write a program that retrieves XML data from a database and processes it

The Relational Model

Before I can discuss integrating XML data with databases, I need to talk about databases themselves. When most people think of databases, they're thinking specifically about relational databases. All of the popular database products—Microsoft SQL Server, Oracle, IBM DB/2, MySQL—use the relational model. In turn, most Web and business applications use one relational database or another for data storage.

Let's look at what the relational model is. Basically, the relational model is all about tables. All of the data is stored in a tabular format, and relationships between tables are expressed through data shared among those tables. Tables in relational databases are just like tables in HTML or tables in this book. They consist of rows and columns. Each row represents a record in the database, and each column represents one field in each of the records.

A group of tables is generally referred to as a *schema*. In a schema, some or all of the tables are generally related to one another. Let's look at how those relationships work. Ordinarily, every table contains a column (or group of columns) that contains data that uniquely identifies that row in the table. In most cases, this is an ID field that simply contains a number that sets that row apart from the others in the table. This value is referred to as the primary key. In relational database design, the primary key is extremely important because it is the root of relationships between tables. When a column in a table corresponds to the primary key of another table, it's referred to as a foreign key. These foreign keys define the relationship between two tables.

Relationships

Here's a simple example. Let's say you have a table called students. The students table contains, among other bits of data, a column called id_students. The table might also include the student's name, address, and phone number. You might also have a second table, called majors. This table contains the major and minor for all of the students, under the assumption that no student has more than one major or minor.

This is what is referred to as a one-to-one relationship. Each record in the students table can have one corresponding row in the majors table. There are two other types of relationships between tables—one-to-many and many-to-many. Before I discuss those relationships, I'll explain how a one-to-one relationship is implemented. As I already mentioned, the students table contains a column called id_students, which serves as its primary key. The majors table should contain a column that contains student IDs. This is referred to as a foreign key, since it's a reference to a primary key in another table. The foreign key is used to implement the one-to-one relationship between the records in the two tables.

Now let's look at a one-to-many relationship. In a one-to-many relationship, a record in one table can have a reference to many records in a second table, but each record in the second table can have a reference to only one record in the first table. Here's an example: let's say I create a table called grades, which contains a column for student IDs as well as columns for class names and the grades themselves. Since a student can take multiple classes, but each grade applies to only one student, the relationship between students and grades is a one-to-many relationship. In this case, id_students in the grades table is a foreign key relating to the students table.

Finally, let's look at a many-to-many relationship. An example of a many-to-many relationship is the relationship between students and classes. Each student is usually enrolled in several classes, and each class usually contains multiple students. In a relational database, such a relationship is expressed using what is sometimes referred to as a *joining table*—a table that exists solely to express the relationship between two pieces of data. Let's look at how this works. The schema contains two tables, students and classes. You already know about the students table; the classes table contains information about the classes offered—the name of the professor, the room where the class is held, and the time at which the class is scheduled.

In order to relate students to classes, we need a third table, called classes_students (or anything else that makes sense). At a bare minimum, this table must include two columns, id_students and id_classes, both of which are foreign keys pointing to the students and classes tables, respectively. These two columns are used to express the many-to-many relationship. In other words, both of the other two tables have one-to-many relationships with this table. Using this table, each student can be associated with several classes, and each class can be associated with any number of students. It may also contain properties that are specific to the relationship, rather than to either a student or a class specifically. For example, a student's grade or her attendance record for the class might be stored in this table. This table structure is illustrated in Figure 17.1.

Figure 17.1

The tables in a many-to-many relationship.

Normalization

Now that I've explained the basics of the relational model, let me explain a bit about relational design. The reason I'm going into all of this material is that before you can deal with integrating databases and XML, you need to understand both databases and XML. You've been learning about XML for awhile now, and this hour is a crash course in databases.

Normalization is a set of rules for relational database design. There are several levels of normalization, which are referred to as normal forms. Each normal form has a name; the most basic are first, second, and third normal form. There are a number of other, more esoteric normal forms, but I won't be going into them in this hour.

The normal forms are not rules in a formal sense, but rather guidelines that, if you adhere to them, enable you to avoid running into problems with your data later. The main problem they were formulated to avoid is redundancy. Redundancy is the bane of the existence of the relational database user. Any time you have redundant data, you must make sure that the values are in sync at all times. If you update the value in one place, you have to update it every other place it appears. If values do become inconsistent, then you can run into problems in data retrieval where some of the data is outdated, and the user might not know which data that is.

With that in mind, let's look at the normal forms. Bear in mind that the later normal forms build on the earlier ones. The first normal form simply states that the values in each field in a database must be atomic; list or array types are not allowed. The reason for this lies in the way that relational database queries work. The query language can't handle fields that contain more than one discrete value, and creating such fields would hamper data retrieval. Let's look at a simple example that violates the first normal form. Let's say I added a column to the `students` table called `classes`, and in that column I included a comma-separated list of class IDs for the classes that the student is taking. This design would violate the first normal form because the value in the column would not be "atomic," as it would contain multiple values, rather than just a single value.

The second normal form is focused on eliminating redundancy. Let's say you have a table called `schedule` that has the schema in Figure 17.2.

FIGURE 17.2

A table that does not satisfy the second normal form.

schedule
id_schedule
id_students
class_name
professor
department
room_number

As you can see, there's a lot of redundant data in this table. For every record in the table, the room number, department, and professor are listed. Unfortunately, that means that if the professor for a class changes, you have to update every record in the table associated with that class with the name of the new professor. You also won't be compliant with the second normal form, since it requires that redundant data be moved to a separate table. To properly normalize the data above, you'd need to create two tables, one called schedule and one called classes, with the structure shown in Figure 17.3.

FIGURE 17.3

Two normalized tables.

Now, let's look at the third normal form. The third normal form dictates that the tables must not contain any columns that are not directly dependent on the primary key. What does this mean? Again, it's probably easiest to explain with an example. I'll go with something really obvious so that you can you can see what I mean. Now, let's take a look at a table that does not satisfy the third normal form.

FIGURE 17.4

A table that does not satisfy the third normal form.

As you can see, in the student table, the columns parent_name, parent_address, and parent_employer are included. The information about the parent is not really dependent on the student's data at all; it's all about the parent. To make this table compliant with 3NF, you need to split it in two. The parent information should be included in the parents table, and the column id_parents should be included in the students table as a foreign key in order to create a relationship between students and their parents. The main advantage of changing the design of the database is to accommodate future data. Let's say that a student's brother enrolls at the college. If we don't optimize the table to 3NF, then the parent data will be redundant.

The World's Shortest Guide to SQL

OK, I'm almost done explaining all of the background information you need on relational databases in order to deal with integrating them with XML. SQL is an acronym for Structured Query Language—it's the language used to retrieve, add, modify, and delete records in databases. Let's look at each of these features in turn.

Retrieving Records Using SELECT

First, let's look at data retrieval. In SQL, the query used to retrieve data from a database is called the SELECT statement. It has several parts, not all of which are mandatory. The most basic SELECT statement is composed of two parts—the select list and the FROM clause. A very simple SELECT statement looks like this:

```
SELECT *
FROM students
```

```
+-------------+-------------------+---------------------+-------+----------------+---------+
| id_students | student_name      | city                | state | classification | tuition |
+-------------+-------------------+---------------------+-------+----------------+---------+
|           1 | Franklin Pierce   | Hillsborough        | NH    | senior         |    5000 |
|           2 | James Polk        | Mecklenburg County  | NC    | freshman       |   11000 |
|           2 | Warren Harding    | Marion              | OH    | junior         |    3500 |
+-------------+-------------------+---------------------+-------+----------------+---------+
3 rows in set (0.00 sec)
```

In this case, the * is the select list. The select list indicates which columns should be included in the query results. When a * is supplied, it indicates that all of the columns in the table or tables listed in the FROM clause should be included in the query results.

The FROM clause contains the list of tables from which the data will be retrieved. In this case, the data will be retrieved from just one table, students. I'll explain how to retrieve data from multiple tables in a bit.

Let's go back to the select list. If you use a select list that isn't simply *, you include a list of column names separated by commas. You can also rename columns in the query results (useful in certain situations), using the AS keyword, as follows:

```
SELECT id_students AS id, student_name, state
FROM students
```

```
+------+-----------------+-------+
| id   | student_name    | state |
+------+-----------------+-------+
|    1 | Franklin Pierce | NH    |
|    2 | James Polk      | NC    |
|    2 | Warren Harding  | OH    |
+------+-----------------+-------+
3 rows in set (0.01 sec)
```

The id_students column is renamed id in the query results. The utility of the AS keyword will become more apparent when I talk about retrieving rows from multiple tables in one query. The other modifier you'll often use in the select list is DISTINCT. When you include DISTINCT at the beginning of a select list, it indicates that no duplicates should be included in the query results. Here's a sample query:

```
SELECT DISTINCT city
FROM students
```

```
+--------------------+
| city               |
+--------------------+
| Hillsborough       |
| Mecklenburg County |
| Marion             |
+--------------------+
3 rows in set (0.08 sec)
```

Without DISTINCT, this query would return the city of every student in the students table. In this case, it returns only the distinct values in the table, regardless of how many of each of them there are. In this case, there are only three records in the table and each of them has a unique city, so the result set is the same as it would be if DISTINCT were left off.

The WHERE Clause

Both of the previous queries simply return all of the records in the students table. Often, you'll want to constrain the result set so that it returns only those records you're actually interested in. The WHERE clause is used to specify which records in a table should be included in the results of a query. Here's an example:

17

```
SELECT student_name
FROM students
WHERE id_students = 1

+-----------------+
| student_name    |
+-----------------+
| Franklin Pierce |
+-----------------+
1 row in set (0.00 sec)
```

When you use the WHERE clause, you must include an expression which filters the query results. In this case, the expression is very simple. Given that id_students is the primary key for this table, this query is sure to return only one row. You can use other comparison operators as well, like the > or != operators. For example, the following query retrieves all of the students with an ID less than or equal to 10:

```
SELECT student_name
FROM students
WHERE id_students <= 10

+-----------------+
| student_name    |
+-----------------+
| Franklin Pierce |
| James Polk      |
| Warren Harding  |
+-----------------+
3 rows in set (0.00 sec)
```

It's also possible to use Boolean operators to create compound expressions. For example, you can retrieve all of the students who pay over $10,000 per year in tuition and who are classified as freshmen using the following query:

```
SELECT student_name
FROM students
WHERE tuition > 10000
AND classification = 'freshman'

+--------------+
| student_name |
+--------------+
| James Polk   |
+--------------+
1 row in set (0.00 sec)
```

There are also several other functions you can use in the WHERE clause that enable you to write more powerful queries. The LIKE function allows you to search for fields containing a particular string. The BETWEEN function allows you to search for values between the two you specify, and IN allows you to test whether a value is a member of a list you specify. Let's look at each of them. First, here's LIKE:

```
SELECT student_name
FROM students
WHERE student_name LIKE James%'
```

```
+--------------+
| student_name |
+--------------+
| James Polk   |
+--------------+
1 row in set (0.00 sec)
```

This query retrieves any records in which the student_name field begins with James. If you want to retrieve all of the records where the James appears anywhere in the student_name field, use the following query:

```
SELECT student_name
FROM students
WHERE student_name LIKE '%James%'
```

```
+--------------+
| student_name |
+--------------+
| James Polk   |
+--------------+
1 row in set (0.00 sec)
```

The % character is a wildcard. Putting it before and after the string in question indicates that the field must contain James, but can be preceded or followed by any other characters.

The BETWEEN function allows you to specify two values and is true whenever the value being evaluated is between those values. Here's a simple example:

```
SELECT student_name
FROM students
WHERE tuition BETWEEN 5000 AND 10000
```

```
+-----------------+
| student_name    |
+-----------------+
| Franklin Pierce |
+-----------------+
1 row in set (0.00 sec)
```

Finally, the IN function enables you to write an expression that tests a value to see if it matches any member of a list. The syntax is as follows:

17

```
SELECT student_name
FROM students
WHERE classification IN ('junior', 'senior')

+-----------------+
| student_name    |
+-----------------+
| Franklin Pierce |
| Warren Harding  |
+-----------------+
2 rows in set (0.00 sec)
```

If you're thinking that you could just as easily write the above query using two expressions combined with an OR, you're right. However, tackling the problem that way becomes tedious when you have 10 items in your list rather than two.

Joins

Now, let's look at what happens when you want to retrieve records from multiple tables and include them in one result set. First, I'll provide an example of a query that uses a join.

```
SELECT student_name, major
FROM students, majors
WHERE students.id_students = 1
AND students.id_students = majors.id_students

+-----------------+-----------+
| student_name    | major     |
+-----------------+-----------+
| Franklin Pierce | Chemistry |
+-----------------+-----------+
1 row in set (0.00 sec)
```

As I mentioned earlier, there's a relationship between students and majors. In order to take advantage of that relationship, I have to be able to join the two tables in order to produce meaningful query results. First, take a look at the FROM clause. As you can see, I include both tables in the list. That's half of the join.

The other half is the following expression:

```
students.id_students = majors.id_students
```

It's called the joining condition because it establishes the conditions under which the two tables are joined. If you leave out the joining condition, then the query results include all of the possible combinations of records from the two tables. In other words, if both tables have 10 records in them, the results will include 100 rows of data. In order to pare this down, I include only the records from the combined table in which the id_students fields match. This ensures that the results include each student's own major only, not the major for every student with each student record.

One thing it's important to notice about the joining condition is that I have to qualify the names of the columns in the condition because the column id_students appears in both tables. If a column name is unique to one of the tables in the join, there's no need to qualify it. In this case, however, I must. If you include a column name that's not unique to one table in the select list, it must be qualified there as well.

> The join I described is referred to as an inner join. There isn't enough space left this hour to go into the other types of joins which you can use. You can find out more about other types of joins in a SQL book like *Sams Teach Yourself SQL in 24 Hours, Second Edition* by Ryan Stephens.

17

Inserting Records

The INSERT statement is used to insert records into a table. The syntax is simple, especially if you plan on populating every column in a table. To insert a record into majors, use the following statement:

```
INSERT INTO majors
VALUES (115, 50, 'Math', 'English')
```

The values in the list correspond to the id_majors, id_students, major, and minor columns respectively. If you only want to specify values for a subset of the columns in the table, you must specify the names of the columns as well, as in the following:

```
INSERT INTO students
(id_students, student_name)
VALUES (50, 'Rafe Colburn')
```

When you create tables, you can specify whether values are required in certain fields, and you can also specify default values for fields. For example, the classification column might default to freshman since most new student records being inserted will be for newly enrolled students, who are classified as freshmen.

Updating Records

When you want to modify one or more records in a table, the UPDATE statement is used. Here's an example:

```
UPDATE students
SET classification = 'senior'
```

The previous SQL statement will work, but I bet you can figure out what's wrong with it. Nowhere is it specified which records to update. If you don't tell it which records to update, it just assumes that you want to update all of the records in the table, thus the previous query would turn all of the students into seniors. That's probably not what you have in mind. Fortunately, the UPDATE statement supports the WHERE clause, just like the SELECT statement.

```
UPDATE students
SET classification = 'senior'
WHERE id_students = 1
```

That's more like it. This statement updates the classification of only one student. You can also update multiple columns with one query, as in the following:

```
UPDATE students
SET classification = 'freshman', tuition = 7500
WHERE id_students = 5
```

As you can see from the example, you can supply a list of fields to update with your UPDATE statement, and they will all be updated by the same query.

Deleting Records

The last SQL statement I'll discuss is the DELETE statement, which is similar to the UPDATE statement. It accepts a FROM clause, and optionally a WHERE clause. If you leave out the WHERE clause, it deletes all of the records in the table. Here's an example:

```
DELETE FROM students
WHERE id_students = 1
```

Integrating XML with a Database

Now that I've given you a broad sense of how relational databases work, I can explain how to integrate XML into your database applications or database storage into your XML applications, depending on how you look at things. Clearly, the simplest approach in integrating XML and relational databases is just to stick an XML document into a field in a table in the database. You can then retrieve the document from the field, feed it to your favorite parser, and then apply XSLT transformations to it, process it using SAX, or create a data structure for the document using the DOM.

However, there are trade-offs involved with taking this approach. When you put all of the data in your document into one field, you lose a ton of the capabilities of a relational database. On the other hand, if you break up your XML documents into normalized tables, restoring them to the data structures that they were in originally can be a lot of work.

When you integrate XML applications with databases, the first question that you must look at is how you're using XML in your application. There are two broad categories of XML applications—those that use XML for data storage, and those that use XML as a document format. The approach for database integration depends on which category your application falls into.

Using XML for Data Storage

Although XML is commonly thought of as a document format, it's also very popular as a format for data storage. Many applications are now using XML files to store their configuration, and remote procedure calling services like XML-RPC and SOAP format the messages that they exchange using XML. The fact that XML is highly structured and can be tested to ensure that it's both well-formed and valid in a standardized, programmatic fashion takes a lot of the burden of reading and modifying the data file off of the application developer when he or she is writing a program.

Let's look at a couple of real world examples where XML might need to be integrated with a relational database. The structured nature of XML makes it a good choice to use as a data interchange format. Let's say that a company periodically receives inventory information from a supplier. That information might be stored in an Oracle database on a server in the supplier's system but might need to be imported into an Access database when the company receives it. XML would make a good intermediate format for the data because it's easy to write programs that import and export the data and because, by using XML, the data can be used in future applications that require it as well.

Another example might be a service that syndicates news articles. The news articles could be distributed via XML files so that they could easily be transformed for presentatation on the Web, or they could be imported into a relational database and published from there.

The question you face when you integrate applications that use XML for data storage with relational databases is the degree to which you want to take advantage of the features of the relational database. As I demonstrated earlier, using both complex expressions in the WHERE clause and joins, you can write queries to retrieve very specific information. If you simply insert entire XML documents into the database, you can't use these features to retrieve specific bits of information from the XML documents.

Here's an XML document that I've used in previous examples:

```
<dealership>
  <automobile make="Buick" model="Century" color="blue">
    <options>
      <option>cruise control</option>
      <option>CD player</option>
```

```
      </options>
    </automobile>
    <automobile make="Ford" model="Thunderbird" color="red">
      <options>
        <option>convertible</option>
        <option>leather interior</option>
        <option>heated seats</option>
      </options>
    </automobile>
</dealership>
```

Now, let's look at how you might design a database to store this information. As I mentioned earlier, the path of least resistance is just to stick the whole XML document in a field. However, that probably isn't a good idea for this file, since it contains more than one automobile "record."

Instead, let's look at what a properly normalized database schema for the information in the XML file would look like. A diagram of the schema appears in Figure 17.5.

FIGURE 17.5

The schema that corresponds to the cars.xml *file.*

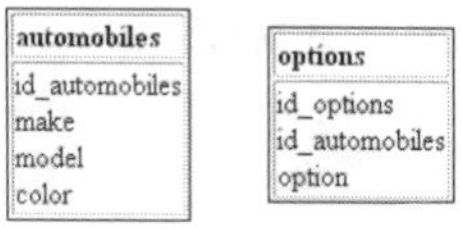

As you can see, I turned the XML document into two tables, automobiles and options. The automobiles table contains all of the information stored in the attributes of the automobile tag in the XML document. Because automobiles have a one-to-many relationship to options, I've created a separate table for them. id_automobiles is a foreign key in the options table.

Storing Documents in a Database

If you're storing documents in a database, then you don't need to worry about normalizing the XML document format as a data structure. Instead, you just need to extract the information from the document that you need to use in the relational database world and create columns for that. Let's look at what I mean. If you store newspaper articles as XML documents, the headline, writer, body, sections of the paper, and perhaps more information will all be included in the XML document.

If you store those documents in a database and plan on publishing them on the Web from that database, you'll want to copy some of that information into the table directly so that you can retrieve the information easily. For example, you might want columns for the writer and section, so that you can write simple SQL statements that retrieve the documents based on those values.

An Example Program

Let's look at an example program that retrieves an XML document from a database, parses it using the DOM, and then extracts information from the document object. If any errors occur in parsing the document, the program reports them. If no errors are encountered, it prints out a message indicating successful parsing and the name of the root element in the document.

The example program is written using Active Server Pages. It connects to the database using ODBC and uses the MSXML component to parse the XML documents stored in the database. The table that I'm using in this example is called documents and has two columns, id_documents and document. id_documents is an integer field, and documents is just a big text field for holding XML documents. In order to run this example yourself, you need a Windows system with Internet Explorer version 5.0 or higher and Microsoft Internet Information Server installed. You'll also need to set up an ODBC data source and create the example table that I use. Even if you don't have a database, you can use ODBC to create a database that's compatible with Microsoft Access.

This example relies on two components, ODBC and MSXML. ODBC is a common means of connecting to databases supported by many applications and databases. If both an application and a database support ODBC, then they can communicate with one another. MSXML is a general purpose XML processing component which comes with many Microsoft products, including Microsoft Internet Information Server, and Microsoft Internet Explorer.

The program itself consists of two chunks of code surrounded by some HTML. I'll just explain the code in detail. The first thing the program does is retrieve all of the records from the documents table. Here's the code that accomplishes that task:

```
Set conn = Server.CreateObject("ADODB.Connection")
conn.Open "DSN=xml"
sql = "SELECT * FROM documents"
Set rs = conn.Execute(sql,,adOptionUnspecified)
```

The first line of code creates a new Connection object and assigns it to a variable named conn. This object contains the methods required to open a connection to the database and execute SQL commands. In fact, on the next line, I do open a connection to the database using the Open method of the conn object. In my case, I have a system DSN defined using ODBC, so the connect string (simply DSN=xml, in this case) is very short. Depending on the database that you're using, your connect string might be completely different.

> DSN stands for Data Source Name; it's the identifier assigned to ODBC resources on Windows systems.

Next, I assign my SQL statement to a variable. In this case, the SQL is very simple, so I just select all of the rows from the table in question. On the line that follows, I execute that SQL statement. To do so, I call the Execute method of the connection object, and assign the results of that method to the variable rs. The output of the Execute method is a Resultset object that contains all of the data returned by the query. I'll use the Resultset in the next chunk of code, which I'll explain in a bit.

The Execute method accepts three arguments, an SQL statement, the number of rows affected by the SQL statement, and any options specific to the statement being executed. In this case, I pass in the sql variable as the first argument, since it contains my SQL statement, and pass basically nothing in for the other two arguments. The second argument, the number of rows affected, is optional, so I leave it out. For the final argument, I pass in an option that means "no options set."

> The options argument is a bitmask. To set more than one option, you add up the value of each of the options and pass in that value. There are constants defined for all of the options, so it's not necessary to remember the numbers. You can just add up the constants associated with the options you want to set. Anyway, all you need to know in this case is that I'm not setting any options.

Once this block of code is complete, you should have the entire contents of the documents table safely tucked away in a Resultset object named rs. Now let's look at the next block of code. Here's the source:

```
Set docID = rs("id_documents")
Set doc = rs("document")
Do Until rs.EOF
    response.write "<p>Document ID: " + CStr(docID) + "</p>"
    set xmlobj = Server.CreateObject("Microsoft.FreeThreadedXMLDOM")
    xmlobj.loadXML doc

    if xmlobj.parseError.errorCode <> 0 then
        response.write "<p>A parse error occurred on line "
        response.write CStr(xmlobj.parseError.line) + ". "
        response.write "The reason given was: "
        response.write xmlobj.parseError.reason + "</p>"
```

```
else
    response.write "<p>Document successfully parsed.</p>"
    response.write "<p>The name of the root element in this document is: "
    response.write xmlobj.firstChild.nodeName + "</p>"
end if

rs.MoveNext

Response.write("<hr>")
Loop
```

Let me get one thing out of the way first. `response.write` is basically a print statement. Whatever is passed into the `write` method of the `response` object is sent directly to the browser for rendering. Now, let's delve into this code.

The first thing I do is create objects that contain references to the columns in the `Resultset`. `docID` is a reference to the `id_documents` column, and `doc` is a reference to the `document` column. These references will contain the current values in those columns as I iterate over all of the records in the result set.

Next, I start the loop that iterates over the result set. It's a `Do Until` loop that stops executing when it runs out of records to process—this is indicated by the `rs.EOF` property. Now I'll delve into the body of the loop. The code inside the loop, which ends when the `Loop` statement is reached, is executed once for every record in the result set. The first thing this code does is print out the ID of the record currently being processed, just so I can keep track of what's going on.

The next two lines are the most important in this block of code:

```
set xmlobj = Server.CreateObject("Microsoft.FreeThreadedXMLDOM")
xmlobj.loadXML doc
```

First, I create a new object, called `xmlobj`, which contains an instance of the DOM. I do so by calling the `CreateObject` method of the `Server` object and instructing it to create an instance of the `Microsoft.FreeThreadedXMLDOM` object. I parse the value currently stored in the `doc` variable on the next line using the `loadXML` method of this object. The `loadXML` method is specifically designed for parsing a string that you pass in as an argument. If you want to parse a file on disk, you have to use another method.

Once you've run the `loadXML` method, the XML is parsed and stored in the variable `xmlobj`. The next step is to determine whether the parsing of the XML was successful. I check this by looking at the value of `xmlobj.parseError.errorCode`. If the error code is 0, it means that parsing was successful. Any other code indicates that an error occurred while the document was being parsed. If an error did occur, then I print out the line number on which the parsing error was encountered and the reason for the error provided by the parser.

17

If no error occurred, I print a message indicating that the document was successfully parsed and the name of the top level element in the document. I retrieve the name of the top level document using the DOM methods that you're familiar with from Hour 15. Specifically, the name of the first element is retrieved using this property: `xmlobj.firstChild.nodeName`. Once I'm done processing the XML document, I print out a horizontal rule to separate the records and move to the next record in the result set using `rs.moveNext`.

Let's look at the output that results from executing this page when the database contains three records, two of which contain errors. The page is included in Figure 17.6.

FIGURE 17.6

The output of the example program.

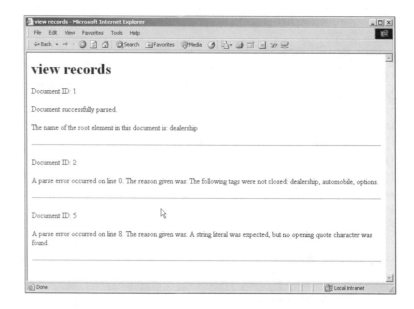

As you can see, the first record in the database was a valid XML document with a root element named `dealership`. The next two records both had problems. In the case of the second record, the root element was not closed properly (nor were several others in the document). In the third, an attribute was missing an opening quotation mark around its value.

The full source code for the page is included in Listing 17.1.

LISTING 17.1 The Source Code for the `view.asp` Page

```
 1: <%@ Language=VBScript %>
 2:
 3: <%
 4: Set conn = Server.CreateObject("ADODB.Connection")
 5: conn.Open "DSN=xml"
 6: sql = "SELECT * FROM documents"
 7: Set rs = conn.Execute(sql,,adOptionUnspecified)
 8: %>
 9:
10: <html>
11: <head>
12: <title>view records</title>
13: </head>
14:
15: <body>
16: <h1>view records</h1>
17:
18: <%
19: Set docID = rs("id_documents")
20: Set doc = rs("document")
21: Do Until rs.EOF
22:     response.write "<p>Document ID: " + CStr(docID) + "</p>"
23:     set xmlobj = Server.CreateObject("Microsoft.FreeThreadedXMLDOM")
24:     xmlobj.loadXML doc
25:
26:     if xmlobj.parseError.errorCode <> 0 then
27:         response.write "<p>A parse error occurred on line "
28:         response.write CStr(xmlobj.parseError.line) + ". "
29:         response.write "The reason given was: "
30:         response.write xmlobj.parseError.reason + "</p>"
31:     else
32:         response.write "<p>Document successfully parsed.</p>"
33:         response.write "<p>The name of the root element in this document is: "
34:         response.write xmlobj.firstChild.nodeName + "</p>"
35:     end if
36:
37:     rs.MoveNext
38:
39:     Response.write("<hr>")
40: Loop
41: %>
42:
43: </body>
44: </html>
```

17

Summary

The purpose of this hour was to introduce the concepts behind relational databases and explain how to integrate them with your XML applications. First, I provided a brief introduction to the theory behind relational databases, which is important to understand when you're mixing them with a different sort of data structure, like the one provided by XML. I then provided a very brief overview of SQL, which is the language used to query all relational databases. I then described the issues that arise when you're integrating relational databases with XML applications, and explained how using XML for data storage and XML as a document format differ. Finally, I included an example program that demostrates how to retrieve XML data from a database and parse it using a DOM parser.

Q&A

Q Don't some databases provide features specifically for handling XML?

A Most major relational databases (like Oracle, Microsoft SQL Server, and IBM's DB2) support XML natively. The problem is that none of them support XML in the same way. If you use a database that provides XML support, you should look at the vendor documentation and decide whether you want to use it. There's no room in this hour to explain how XML is supported in each of those databases.

Q What about object-oriented databases? Aren't they better suited to use with XML?

A Object-oriented databases are more appropriate for storing XML data than relational databases, generally speaking. They're designed explicitly to handle the tree-like data structures associated with object-oriented design. Treelike is also the best way to describe most XML data structures. However, object-oriented databases have not displaced relational databases on the market and are not standardized in the same manner as relational databases.

Workshop

The Workshop is designed to help you anticipate possible questions, review what you've learned, and begin learning how to put your knowledge into practice.

Quiz

1. What is the primary reason for normalizing relational databases?

2. What method is used to include the records from multiple tables in one set of query results?

3. Why is it a good idea to break down XML documents used for data storage into normalized tables when storing the data in a relational database?

Quiz Answers

1. Databases are ordinarily normalized in order to eliminate redundancy in the data stored in them.

2. Joins are used to include records from multiple tables in one set of query results.

3. When you use XML documents for data storage, it's a good idea to convert them into normalized tables when using a relational database so that you can take advantage of SQL when you're retrieving data from the database.

Exercises

1. Modify the `view.asp` script so that only records with an ID less than 100 are included in the results.

2. Write an ASP page that allows you to insert records into the `view.asp` script. If you're up for a challenge, have your script verify that the XML parses correctly before inserting the data into the database.

3. Convert the DOM iteration program from Hour 15 into an ASP subroutine and modify the script to print out the full data structure of documents retrieved from the database.

17

PART V

XML and the Web

Hour

HOUR 18

Getting to Know XHTML

I generally avoid temptation unless I can't resist it.

—Mae West (actress and writer)

One form of temptation many Web developers have been unable to resist is that of hacking together Web pages with poorly coded HTML. Fortunately, XML is aiming to add some structure to the Web by ushering in a new version of HTML called XHTML, which represents a merger of XML and HTML. Considering that there is a lot of confusion surrounding the relationship between XML and HTML, XHTML often serves only to muddy the water in terms of how people perceive XML. XHTML is ultimately quite simple in that it is a version of HTML reformulated to meet the strict structural and syntax requirements of XML. XHTML makes use of the same elements and attributes as HTML, but it enforces XML rules, such as quoting all attribute values and requiring empty elements to end with />. It still isn't clear if, how, or when the Web will transition from HTML to XHTML, but it is a likely prospect given the benefits of XML. This hour introduces you to XHTML and examines some of the consequences of migrating Web pages from HTML to XHTML.

In this hour, you'll learn

- What XHTML is and why it was created
- About the differences between XHTML and HTML
- How to create and validate XHTML documents
- How to convert existing HTML documents to XHTML

XHTML: A Logical Merger

XHTML is an XML-based markup language that carries out the functionality of HTML in the spirit of XML. As you may know, HTML is not a descendent of XML; this would be tricky considering that XML was created after HTML. HTML is actually a descendent of an older markup language technology known as SGML (Standard Generalized Markup Language), which is considerably more complex than XML. Along with being much more compact than SGML, XML is also much easier to learn and process. So, XML is beneficial from the perspective of both application developers and document developers. But what exactly does this have to do with HTML? Or, to pose the question more generally, why exactly do we need XHTML?

To answer the "Why XHTML?" question, you have to first take stock of the Web and some of the problems surrounding it. Currently, the Web is a jumbled mess of hacked HTML code that has very little structure. Poor coding, browser leniency, and proprietary browser extensions have all combined to create a Web of HTML documents that are extremely unstructured, which is a bad thing. Web browser vendors have had to create HTML processors that are capable of reading and displaying even the most horrendous HTML code so that Web users never have to witness the underlying bad code in many Web pages. Although this is good in terms of the Web experience, it makes it very difficult to glean information from Web pages in an automated manner because their structure is so inconsistent.

You know that XML documents can't suffer from bad coding because XML simply won't allow it. Knowing this, a logical answer to the HTML problem is to convert Web pages to XML documents and then use style sheets to render them. It would also be nice to have peace on earth, tasty fat-free foods, and lower taxes, but life just doesn't work that way. What I'm getting at is that HTML will likely always have a place on the Web simply because it is too deeply ingrained to replace. Besides, even though XML paired with CSS/XSLT has huge structural benefits over a purely presentational HTML Web page, it involves more work. There are certainly situations where it doesn't matter too much if content is separated from how it is displayed, in which case HTML represents a more efficient solution.

The point I'm trying to make is that HTML, in one form or another, is here to stay. The solution to the problem then shifts to improving HTML in some way. The most logical improvement to solve the structural problems of HTML is to express HTML as an XML language (XHTML), which allows us to reap many of the benefits of XML without turning the Web on its ear. The primary benefit of XHTML is obviously structure, which would finally force browser vendors and Web developers alike to play by the rules. Browsers could strictly enforce an HTML schema to ensure that documents are both well formed and valid. Just requiring HTML documents to be well formed would be a significant step in the right direction; checking them for validity is just icing on the cake.

The latest version of XHTML is version 1.1. You can learn more about XHTML 1.1 by visiting the W3C Web site at http://www.w3.org/MarkUp/#xhtml11.

Even if XHTML catches on and Web developers migrate their HTML code to it, Web browsers will still have to support the old, unstructured versions of HTML for the foreseeable future. However, over time these legacy HTML documents could eventually be supplanted by valid, well-formed XHTML documents with plenty of structure. One thing that will perhaps make the migration to XHTML smoother is the fact that a great deal of Web page development is carried out with visual authoring tools that automatically generate HTML code. If these tools start generating XHMTL code instead of HTML code, then it will be virtually painless for developers to make the move to XHTML.

18

You might not realize it, but another compelling reason to move the Web toward XHTML is so that new types of browsers with limited processing capabilities can avoid the hassles of trying to process unstructured HTML code. These browsers are becoming prevalent on Internet devices, such as mobile phones and handheld computers, and would benefit from highly structured XHTML documents to minimize processing overhead.

Comparing XHTML and HTML

You probably know that the latest version of HTML is version 4.0, which is in wide use across the Web. XHTML is a version of HTML 4.0 that plays by the more rigid rules of XML. Fortunately, most of the differences between XHTML and HTML 4.0 are syntactic, which means that they don't dramatically impact the overall structure of HTML documents. Migrating an HTML 4.0 document to XHTML is more a matter of cleaning and tightening up the code than converting it to a new language. If you have any Web pages that were developed using HTML 4.0, you'll find that they can be migrated to XHTML with relative ease. You learn how to do this later in the hour in the section titled, "Migrating HTML to XHTML."

Even though XHTML supports the same elements and attributes as HTML 4.0, there are some significant differences that are due to the fact that XHTML is an XML-based language. You probably have a pretty good idea regarding some of these differences, but the following list will help you to understand exactly how XHTML documents differ from HTML documents:

- XHTML documents must be well formed.
- Element and attribute names in XHTML must be in lowercase.
- End tags in XHTML are required for nonempty elements.
- Empty elements in XHTML must consist of a start-tag/end-tag pair or an empty element.
- Attributes in XHTML cannot be used without a value.
- Attribute values in XHTML must always be quoted.
- An XHTML namespace must be declared in the root html element.
- The head and body elements cannot be omitted in XHTML.
- The title element in XHTML must be the first element in the head element.
- In XHTML, all script and style elements must be enclosed within CDATA sections.

Given your knowledge of XML, these differences between XHTML and HTML 4.0 shouldn't come as too much of a surprise. Fortunately, none of them are too difficult to find and fix in HTML documents, which makes the move from HTML 4.0 to XHTML relatively straightforward. However, Web pages developed with previous versions of HTML typically require more dramatic changes. This primarily has to do with the fact that HTML 4.0 does away with some formatting attributes such as background and instead promotes the usage of style sheets. Since XHTML doesn't support these formatting attributes, it is necessary first to convert legacy HTML (prior to 4.0) documents to HTML 4.0, which quite often involves replacing formatting attributes with CSS equivalents. Once you get a Web page up to par with HTML 4.0, the move to XHTML is pretty straightforward.

Creating and Validating XHTML Documents

Because XHTML is an XML-based markup language, creating XHTML documents is little different than creating any other kind of XML document. You must first learn the XHTML language, after which you use a text editor or other XML development tool to construct a document using XHTML elements and attributes. If you've always created Web pages using visual authoring tools, such as FrontPage or Dreamweaver, then the concept of assembling a Web page in a text editor might be new. On the other hand, if you aren't a seasoned Web developer and your only experience with markup languages is XML, then you'll feel right at home. The next few sections explore the basics of creating and validating XHTML documents.

Preparing XHTML Documents for Validation

Just as it is beneficial to validate other kinds of XML documents, it is also important to validate XHTML documents to ensure that they adhere to the XHTML language. As you know, validation is carried out through a schema, which can be either a DTD or an XSD. Both kinds of schemas are available for use with XHTML. I'll focus on the usage of an XHTML DTD to validate XHTML documents because DTDs are still more widely supported than XSDs. Before getting into the specifics of using a DTD to validate XHTML documents, it's necessary to clarify the different versions of XHTML and how they impact XHTML document validation.

The first version of XHTML was version 1.0, which focused on a direct interpretation of HTML 4.0 as an XML-based markup language. Since HTML 4.0 is a fairly large and complex markup language, the W3C decided to offer XHTML 1.0 in three different flavors, which vary in their support of HTML 4.0 features:

- Strict—No HTML presentation elements are available (`font`, `table`, and so on)
- Transitional—HTML presentation elements are available for formatting documents
- Frameset—Frames are available, as well as HTML presentation elements

These different strains of XHTML are listed in order of increasing functionality, which means that the Frameset feature set is richer and therefore more complex than the Strict feature set. These three different strains of XHTML 1.0 are realized by three different DTDs that describe the elements and attributes for each feature set. The idea is that you can use a more minimal XHTML DTD if you don't need to use certain XHTML language features, or you can use a more thorough DTD if you need additional features, such as frames.

The Strict DTD is a minimal DTD that is used to create very clean XHTML documents without any presentation markup. Documents created from this DTD require style sheets in order to be formatted for display because they don't contain any presentation markup. The Transitional DTD builds on the Strict DTD by adding support for presentation markup elements. This DTD is useful in performing a quick conversion of HTML documents to XHTML when you don't want to take the time to develop style sheets. The Frameset DTD is the broadest of the three DTDs and includes support for creating documents with frames.

18

The three DTDs associated with XHTML 1.0 can certainly be used to validate XHTML documents, but there is a newer version of XHTML known as XHMTL 1.1 that includes a DTD of its own. The XHTML 1.1 DTD is a reformulation of the XHTML 1.0 Strict DTD that is designed for modularity. The idea behind the XHTML 1.1 DTD is to provide a means of expanding XHTML to support other XML-based languages, such as MathML. Since the XHTML 1.1 DTD is based upon the Strict XHTML 1.0 DTD, it doesn't include support for presentation elements or framesets. The XHTML 1.1 DTD is therefore designed for pure XHTML documents that adhere to the XML adage of separating content from how it is formatted and displayed.

Regardless of which XHTML DTD you decide to use to validate XHTML documents, there are a few other validity requirements to which all XHTML documents must adhere:

- There must be a document type declaration (DOCTYPE) in the document that appears prior to the root element

- The document must validate against the DTD declared in the document type declaration; this DTD must be one of the three XHTML 1.0 DTDs or the XHTML 1.1 DTD

- The root element of the document must be html

- The root element of the document must designate an XHTML namespace using the xmlns attribute

You must declare the DTD for all XHTML documents in a document type declaration at the top of the document. A Formal Public Identifier (FPI) is used in the document type declaration to reference one of the standard XHTML DTDs. Following is an example of how to declare the Strict XHTML 1.0 DTD in a document type declaration:

```
<!DOCTYPE html PUBLIC "-//W3C//DTD XHTML 1.0 Strict//EN"
  "DTD/xhtml1-strict.dtd">
```

It isn't terribly important that you understand the details of the FPI in this code. The main point is that it identifies the Strict XHTML 1.0 DTD and therefore is suitable for XHTML documents that don't require formatting or frameset features. The XHTML 1.0 Transitional DTD is specified using similar code, as the following example reveals:

```
<!DOCTYPE html PUBLIC "-//W3C//DTD XHTML 1.0 Transitional//EN"
  "DTD/xhtml1-transitional.dtd">
```

The XHTML 1.0 Frameset DTD is also specified with similar code, as in the following example:

```
<!DOCTYPE html PUBLIC "-//W3C//DTD XHTML 1.0 Frameset//EN"
  "DTD/xhtml1-frameset.dtd">
```

Finally, the XHTML 1.1 DTD is specified with a document type declaration that is a little different from the others:

```
<!DOCTYPE html PUBLIC "-//W3C//DTD XHTML 1.1//EN"
  "http://www.w3.org/TR/xhtml11/DTD/xhtml11.dtd">
```

The decision regarding which XHTML DTD to use really comes down to what features your documents require. If you can get by without the presentation or frameset
features, then the XHTML 1.0 Strict DTD or the XHTML 1.1 DTD are your best bet.
Between the two, it's probably better to go with the newer XHTML 1.1 DTD because
it represents the future direction of XHTML. If your documents require some presentation features, then the XHTML 1.0 Transitional DTD is the one for you. And finally,
if you need the whole gamut of XHTML features, including framesets, then the
XHTML 1.0 Frameset DTD is the way to go.

In addition to declaring an appropriate DTD in the document type declaration, a valid
XHTML document must also declare the XHTML namespace in the root html element,
and it must declare the language. Following is an example of declaring the standard
XHTML namespace and the English language in the html element for an XHTML document:

```
<html xmlns="http://www.w3.org/1999/xhtml" xml:lang="en">
```

Putting Together an XHTML Document

XHTML documents are created in much the same way as any other XML document, or
any HTML document for that matter. As long as you keep in mind the differences
between XHTML and HTML, you can develop XHTML Web pages just as you would
create HTML Web pages, assuming you don't mind creating Web pages by hand. To give
you a better idea as to how an XHTML document comes together, check out the code for
a skeletal XHTML document in Listing 18.1.

LISTING 18.1 A Skeletal XHTML Document

```
01: <?xml version="1.0" encoding="UTF-8"?>
02: <!DOCTYPE html PUBLIC "-//W3C//DTD XHTML 1.1//EN"
03:   "http://www.w3.org/TR/xhtml11/DTD/xhtml11.dtd">
04:
05: <html xmlns="http://www.w3.org/1999/xhtml" xml:lang="en">
06:   <head>
07:     <title>Skeletal XHTML Document</title>
08:   </head>
09:
10:   <body>
11:     <p>
```

continues

18

LISTING 18.1   Continued

```
12:      This is a skeletal XHTML document.
13:    </p>
14:   </body>
15: </html>
```

The `skeleton.xhtml` document admittedly doesn't do much in terms of being a useful Web page, but it does demonstrate how to create a legal XHTML document. In other words, the skeletal document declares an XHTML DTD and namespace and adheres to all of the structural and syntax rules of XML. It can also be viewed directly in a Web browser. The main significance of the skeletal XHTML document is that it serves as a great template for creating other XHTML documents. Figure 18.1 shows the skeletal XHTML document as viewed in Internet Explorer.

FIGURE 18.1

The skeletal XHTML document serves as a great template for developing other XHTML documents.

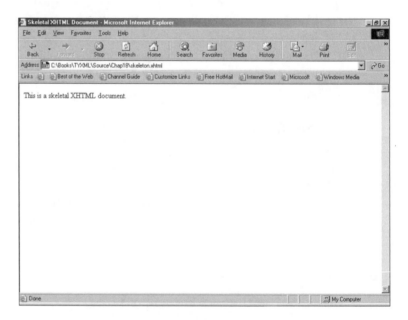

Validating an XHTML Document

As with any XML document, it's very important to be able to validate XHTML documents. You've already learned about the DTDs that factor into XHTML validation, but you haven't learned exactly when XHTML documents are validated. Keep in mind that it takes processing time for any XML document to be validated, and in the case of XHTML, this could hinder the speed at which Web pages are served and displayed. The ideal scenario in terms of performance is for developers to validate XHTML documents before making them publicly available, which alleviates the need for browsers to perform any validation. On the other hand, there currently is a lot of HTML code generated on the fly by scripting languages and other interactive technologies, in which case it might be necessary for a browser to sometimes validate XHTML documents.

Although there are no rules governing the appropriate time for XHTML documents to be validated, it's generally a good idea for you to take the initiative to validate your own documents before taking them live. Fortunately, the W3C provides a free online validation service known as the W3C Validator that can be used to validate XHTML documents. This validation service is available online at `http://validator.w3.org/` and is shown in Figure 18.2.

FIGURE 18.2

The W3C Validator service is capable of validating XHTML documents as well as HTML documents.

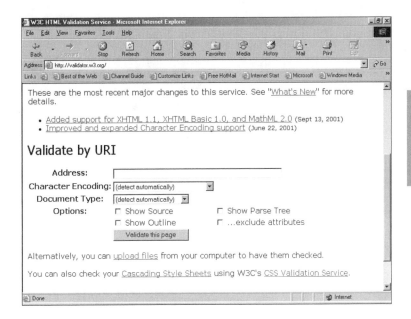

You can see in the figure that the W3C Validator is used by entering the URI of an XHTML document. Of course, there is a little problem if you haven't published your documents to a Web server that makes them available on the Internet—the Validator can't access them. The W3C considered this problem and provided a solution in the form of another page that allows you to validate files that are stored on your local file system. This page is located at `http://validator.w3.org/file-upload.html` and is shown in Figure 18.3.

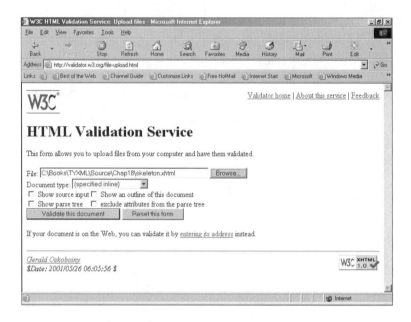

In the figure, I've specified the `skeleton.xhtml` document as the document to be validated. Figure 18.4 shows the results of validating this document using the W3C
Validator.

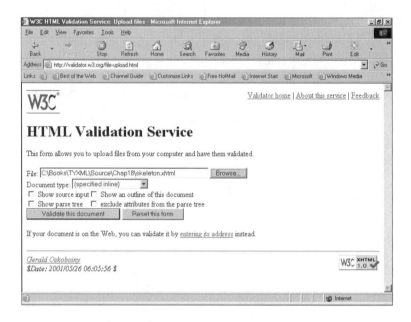

As the figure reveals, the skeletal document passed the W3C Validator with flying colors, which isn't too much of a surprise. This is a handy service to have around when creating XHTML documents, especially when you consider that it is always up to date with the latest standards set forth by the W3C.

Migrating HTML to XHTML

Throughout the hour thus far I've focused on the concept of creating XHTML documents from scratch. This sounds great in theory, but the reality is that there are gazillions of HTML-based Web pages in existence that could benefit from being migrated to XHTML. Fortunately, it isn't too terribly difficult to bring HTML 4.0 documents up to par with the XHTML specification. You've already learned about the ways in which XHTML documents differ from HTML 4.0 documents; these differences are your guide to converting HTML to XHTML. There are two fundamental approaches available for converting HTML documents to XHTML documents:

- Convert the documents by hand (more work, more accurate)
- Convert the documents using an automated conversion tool (less work, less accurate)

The former approach requires some elbow grease, but it yields the best results because you're carrying out the migration process with considerable attention to detail. On the other hand, the latter approach has the obvious benefit of automating the conversion process and saving you a lot of tedious work. However, as in any automated process, the conversion from HTML to XHTML doesn't always go perfectly smooth. That's why the first approach is the more accurate of the two, even though it requires much more effort. A middle ground hybrid approach involves first using an automated conversion tool and then making fine-tuned adjustments by hand.

Hands-On HTML to XHTML Conversion

Converting HTML documents to XHTML can be a tedious process, but if you have a strategy for the conversion process it can make things go much more smoothly. In fact, it helps to have a checklist to use as a guide while hand-coding the conversion. Following are the main steps you'll need to take to convert HTML code to XHTML code:

1. Add (or modify) a document type declaration that declares an appropriate XHTML DTD
2. Declare the XHTML namespace in the html element
3. Convert all element and attribute names to lowercase

18

4. Match every start-tag with an end-tag

5. Replace > with /> at the end of all empty tags

6. Make sure all required attributes are set

7. Make sure all attributes have values assigned to them

8. Enclose all attribute values in quotes (" ")

9. Make sure all elements and attributes are defined in the XHTML DTD used by the document

If you carry out each of these steps, you should be able to arrive at a valid XHTML document without too much difficulty. A simple example will help explain the relevance of these steps a little better. Listing 18.2 contains the code for an HTML document that describes a Web page chronicling a mountain bike trip. Figure 18.5 shows the mountain biking Web page as viewed in Internet Explorer.

LISTING 18.2   The Mountain Biking Example HTML Document

```
01: <!DOCTYPE HTML PUBLIC "-//IETF//DTD HTML//EN">
02:
03: <HTML>
04:   <HEAD>
05:     <TITLE>Mountain Biking at Tsali</TITLE>
06:   </HEAD>
07
08:   <BODY STYLE=background-image:url(dirt.gif)>
09:     <H2>Mountain Biking at Tsali</H2>
10:     <P>
11:     Last year I took a trip to Bryson City, North Carolina, the location
12:     of an amazing system of mountain bike trails known as Tsali. Tsali is
13:     positioned in western North Carolina on the edge of the Smoky Mountains.
14:     The Tsali trails wind around a lake called Fontana Lake, which offers
15:     plenty of scenery when you slow down enough to take notice. Following
16:     are a couple of pictures from the trip:
17:     <P>
18:     <A HREF=jump_lg.jpg><IMG SRC=jump.jpg STYLE=align:left></A>
19:     <A HREF=cruise_lg.jpg><IMG SRC=cruise.jpg STYLE=align:left></A>
20:     <P>
21:     In these photos, I'm catching a little air off of a jump located on the
22:     Right Loop of the Tsali trail, as well as cruising by
23:     <A HREF=http://www.greatsmokies.com/community/fontana.htm>Fontana
24:     Lake</A> on the Left Loop. The jump picture shows the last in a series
25:     that provided a change of pace from the fast descents and smooth climbs.
26:     The cruise picture shows how the water in the lake was lowered due to
27:     dam maintenance.
28:     <P>
29:     If you'd like to learn more about the Tsali trails, contact my
```

continues

LISTING 18.2   Continued

```
30:     <A HREF=mailto:christheyeti@thetribe.com>Chris the Yeti</A>:
31:     <A HREF=mailto:christheyeti@thetribe.com><IMG SRC=yeti.jpg
32:        STYLE=align:middle></A>
33:   </BODY>
34: </HTML>
```

FIGURE 18.5

The mountain biking example HTML document as viewed in Internet Explorer.

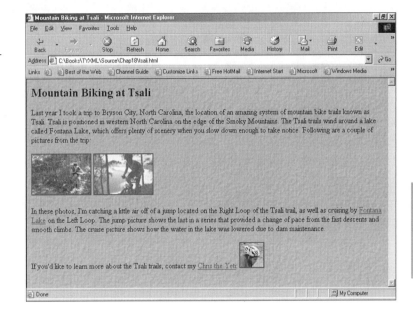

18

If you study the code for the mountain biking example HTML document, you'll notice that it doesn't meet the high standards of XHTML in terms of structure and syntax. Granted, the code is cleanly organized but it definitely doesn't qualify as a valid or even well-formed document under the rules of XHTML. Following are the major problems with this code that need to be resolved in order for the document to comply with XHTML rules:

- The document type declaration doesn't refer to one of the XHTML DTDs (line 1)
- The XHTML namespace isn't declared
- The elements and attributes are all in uppercase
- Not every start-tag (`<P>`) has an end tag (lines 10 and 17, among others)
- Empty elements (`IMG`) don't end with `/>` (lines 18, 19, and 31)
- Some elements (`IMG`) are missing required attributes (`ALT`)
- The attribute values aren't enclosed in quotes (lines 8, 18, and 19, among others)

You might be thinking that this list of problems is uncannily similar to the list of HTML to XHTML conversion steps I mentioned earlier in the hour. This is not mere coincidence—I arrived at the list of conversion steps by addressing the most common HTML coding problems that conflict with XHTML. If you go through the document and fix all of these problems, the resulting XHTML code will look like the code shown in Listing 18.3.

LISTING 18.3   The Mountain Biking Example XHTML Document That Was Converted by Hand

```
01: <?xml version="1.0" encoding="UTF-8"?>
02: <!DOCTYPE html PUBLIC "-//W3C//DTD XHTML 1.1//EN"
03:   "http://www.w3.org/TR/xhtml11/DTD/xhtml11.dtd">
04:
05: <html xmlns="http://www.w3.org/1999/xhtml" xml:lang="en">
06:   <head>
07:     <title>Mountain Biking at Tsali</title>
08:   </head>
09:
10:   <body style="background-image:url(dirt.gif)">
11:     <h2>Mountain Biking at Tsali</h2>
12:     <p>
13:     Last year I took a trip to Bryson City, North Carolina, the location
14:     of an amazing system of mountain bike trails known as Tsali. Tsali is
15:     positioned in western North Carolina on the edge of the Smoky Mountains.
16:     The Tsali trails wind around a lake called Fontana Lake, which offers
17:     plenty of scenery when you slow down enough to take notice. Following
18:     are a couple of pictures from the trip:
19:     </p>
20:     <p>
21:     <a href="jump_lg.jpg"><img src="jump.jpg" alt="Here I am catching a
22:       little air." style="align:left"/></a>
23:     <a href="cruise_lg.jpg"><img src="cruise.jpg" alt="Here I am cruising
24:       by Fontana Lake." style="align:left"/></a>
25:     </p>
26:     <p>
27:     In these photos, I'm catching a little air off of a jump located on the
28:     Right Loop of the Tsali trail, as well as cruising by
29:     <a href="http://www.greatsmokies.com/community/fontana.htm">Fontana
30:     Lake</a> on the Left Loop. The jump picture shows the last in a series
31:     that provided a change of pace from the fast descents and smooth climbs.
32:     The cruise picture shows how the water in the lake was lowered due to
33:     dam maintenance.
34:     </p>
35:     <p>
36:     If you'd like to learn more about the Tsali trails, contact my
37:     <a href="mailto:christheyeti@thetribe.com">Chris the Yeti</a>:
38:     <a href="mailto:christheyeti@thetribe.com"><img src="yeti.jpg"
39:       alt="Chris the Yeti" style="align:middle"/></a>
40:     </p>
41:   </body>
42: </html>
```

If you study this document carefully, you'll see that it meets all of the requirements of a valid XHTML document. For example, the <p> tags all have matching </p> closing tags (lines 19, 25, 34, and 40). If you're a skeptic and want to make sure that the document is really valid, you can run it through the W3C Validator just to make sure. Actually, I already did it for you and the document checked out fine, which means that it is a bona-fide XHTML document.

Automated HTML to XHTML Conversion

If you don't like getting your hands dirty, you might consider an automated approach to converting HTML documents to XHTML. Or you might decide to go for a hybrid conversion approach that involves using an automated tool and then a little hand coding to smooth out the results. Either way, there are a few tools out there that automate the HTML to XHTML conversion process. One such tool is HTML Tidy, which was developed by Dave Raggett, an engineer at Hewlett Packard's UK Laboratories.

HTML Tidy is a command-line tool that was originally designed to clean up sloppy HTML code, but it also supports converting HTML code to XHTML code. When you think about it, converting HTML to XHTML really is nothing more than cleaning up sloppy code, which is why HTML Tidy works so well. The HTML Tidy tool is available for free download from the HTML Tidy Web site at http://www.w3.org/People/Raggett/tidy/. There are also a few graphical HTML applications that serve as front-ends for HTML Tidy just in case you aren't comfortable using command-line applications.

18

If you run HTML Tidy without any command-line options, it will process an HTML document and clean it up. However, the resulting document won't be an XHTML document. In order for HTML Tidy to generate an XHTML document, you must use the -asxml command-line option, which indicates that HTML Tidy is to convert the HTML document to an XHTML document. The output of HTML Tidy defaults to standard output, which is usually just your command-line window. Although this works if you just want to see what a converted document looks like, it doesn't help you in terms of generating a converted document file. You must specify that you want the output to be in XHTML format by redirecting the output of the tool. Following is an example command that converts the tsali.html mountain biking HTML document to XHTML using HTML Tidy:

```
tidy -asxml tsali.html > tsaliT.xhtml
```

This command directs the output of the HTML Tidy application to the file tsaliT.xhtml. Listing 18.4 contains the code for the resulting XHTML document generated by HTML Tidy.

LISTING 18.4   The Mountain Biking Example XHTML Document That Was
Converted by HTML Tidy

```
01: <!DOCTYPE html PUBLIC "-//W3C//DTD XHTML 1.0 Strict//EN"
02:     "http://www.w3.org/TR/xhtml1/DTD/xhtml1-strict.dtd">
03: <html xmlns="http://www.w3.org/1999/xhtml">
04: <head>
05: <meta name="generator" content="HTML Tidy, see www.w3.org" />
06: <title>Mountain Biking at Tsali</title>
07: </head>
08:
09: <body style="background-image:url(dirt.gif)">
10: <h2>Mountain Biking at Tsali</h2>
11:
12: <p>Last year I took a trip to Bryson City, North Carolina, the
13: location of an amazing system of mountain bike trails known as
14: Tsali. Tsali is positioned in western North Carolina on the edge of
15: the Smoky Mountains. The Tsali trails wind around a lake called
16: Fontana Lake, which offers plenty of scenery when you slow down
17: enough to take notice. Following are a couple of pictures from the
18: trip:</p>
19:
20: <p><a href="jump_lg.jpg"><img src="jump.jpg"
21: style="align:left" /></a> <a href="cruise_lg.jpg"><img
22: src="cruise.jpg" style="align:left" /></a></p>
23:
24: <p>In these photos, I'm catching a little air off of a jump located
25: on the Right Loop of the Tsali trail, as well as cruising by <a
26: href="http://www.greatsmokies.com/community/fontana.htm">Fontana
27: Lake</a> on the Left Loop. The jump picture shows the last in a
28: series that provided a change of pace from the fast descents and
29: smooth climbs. The cruise picture shows how the water in the lake
30: was lowered due to dam maintenance.</p>
31:
32: <p>If you'd like to learn more about the Tsali trails, contact my
33: <a href="mailto:christheyeti@thetribe.com">Chris the Yeti</a>: <a
34: href="mailto:christheyeti@thetribe.com"><img src="yeti.jpg"
35: style="align:middle" /></a></p>
36: </body>
37: </html>
```

If you look carefully, you'll notice that this code looks surprisingly similar to the hand-coded conversion of the HTML document, with the exception of the lack of indentations. Notice that the document type declaration and namespace declaration are both present, not to mention that all element and attribute types have been converted to lowercase. The empty img elements have been fixed with a trailing />. Also, all attribute values are quoted.

There is still an important aspect of the generated XHTML document that has to be modified by hand. I'm referring to the img elements, none of which provide alt attributes. The alt attribute is a required attribute of the img element in HTML 4.0 and XHTML, so you must specify values for them in all images in order to make the document a valid XHTML document. Fortunately, the HTML Tidy tool caught this problem and output an error message indicating that the change needed to be made by hand (Figure 18.6).

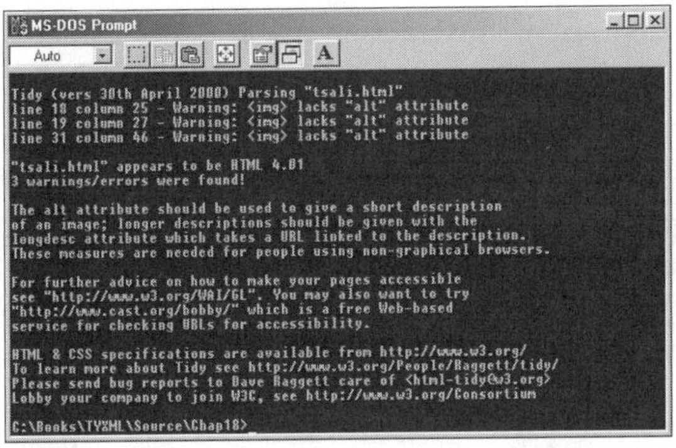

FIGURE 18.6

HTML Tidy was able to detect conversion errors in the mountain biking example HTML document so that you can repair them by hand.

Finalizing the conversion of the mountain biking example document involves adding alt attributes to the img elements. Once that's done, the new XHTML document is good to go. As you can see, the HTML Tidy tool significantly improves the HTML to XHTML conversion process, leaving you with very minor changes to make by hand.

Summary

HTML has served its eventual purpose well by allowing people to build Web pages with relative ease, but its lack of structure is limiting when it comes to intelligently processing Web content. For this reason, the architects of the Web have focused significant efforts on charting the future of the Web with a more structured markup language for creating Web pages. This markup language is XHTML, which is a reformulated version of HTML that meets the high structural and organizational standards of XML. XHTML is still in many ways a future technology in terms of becoming a standard used by all Web developers, but it is nonetheless important to XML developers and HTML developers alike.

This hour introduced you to XHTML and then explored the relationship between HTML and XHTML. You learned about the origins of both languages and why XHTML has long-term benefits that make it an ideal successor to HTML. The hour shifted gears toward the practical by showing you how to create and validate XHTML documents. You then finished up the hour by learning how to migrate legacy HTML documents to XHTML.

Q&A

Q If Web browsers don't know how to display XML documents, how is it that XHTML documents can be viewed in Web browsers?

A XHTML represents the one exception to the rule about XML documents not being viewable without the aid of style sheets. Because HTML documents are directly viewable in Web browsers, even without the help of style sheets, it only makes sense that XHTML documents should be viewable as well. However, you still must use style sheets if you want control over the layout and formatting details of XHTML documents.

Q What happens if I don't validate my XHTML documents?

A Nothing happens, as least for now. Web browsers currently treat XHTML documents with the same leniency that they handle HTML documents, so you can get away with creating invalid documents if you want. However, this goes against the whole premise of XHTML, which is to demand the creation of highly accurate documents. The idea is that browsers and future Web-based applications may at some point validate XHTML documents. So you should make an effort to police your own documents and make sure they are valid before publishing them on the Web.

Workshop

The Workshop is designed to help you anticipate possible questions, review what you've learned, and begin learning how to put your knowledge into practice.

Quiz

1. What is the relationship between HTML and XHTML?

2. How do XHTML attributes differ from typical HTML attributes?

3. What is the root element of XHTML documents?

Quiz Answers

1. XHTML is an XML-based markup language that carries out the functionality of HTML in the spirit of XML. More specifically, XHTML is a version of HTML 4.0 that plays by the more rigid rules of XML.

2. Attributes in XHTML cannot be used without a value, and all XHTML attribute values must appear within quotes.

3. The root element of XHTML documents is html, which is the same root element used in HTML documents.

Exercises

1. Using the `skeleton.xhtml` document as a template, create an XHTML document for a personal Web page. A good example of a personal Web page is an XHTML document that stores your resume. After creating the XHTML document, use the W3C Validator to validate the document.

2. Find an existing HTML document and convert it to XHTML using the list of conversion steps presented in this hour. It's up to you whether you convert the document entirely by hand or take advantage of an automated tool, such as HTML Tidy.

18

HOUR 19

Addressing XML Documents with XPath

Did you ever walk in a room and forget why you walked in? I think that's
how dogs spend their lives.

—Sue Murphy (comedian and actress)

Forgetfulness is certainly something I can relate to, but fortunately I'm not
too forgetful when it comes to remembering the location of information
within my XML documents. That's because there is a technology called
XPath that makes it possible to specify exactly where XML content is
located. Just as your mailing address helps you to remember where you live,
XPath provides a means of remembering where nodes are located in XML
documents. OK, you probably don't rely on your mailing address to remember where you live, but you will rely on XPath if you use technologies such
as XSLT, XLink, or XPointer, which must reference parts of XML documents. XPath is the enabling technology that allows you to drill down into
XML documents and reference individual pieces of information.

In this hour, you'll learn

- The significance of the XPath technology
- How to navigate through an XML document using XPath patterns
- How to build powerful expressions using XPath patterns and functions
- The role that XPath plays with other XML technologies such as XSLT and XLink

Understanding XPath

XPath is a technology that enables you to address parts of an XML document, such as a specific element or set of elements. XPath is implemented as a non-XML expression language, which makes it suitable for use in situations where XML markup isn't really applicable, such as within attribute values. As you know, attribute values are simple text and therefore can't contain additional XML markup. So, although XPath expressions are used within XML markup, they don't directly utilize tags and attributes themselves. This makes XPath considerably different from its XSL counterparts (XSLT and XSL-FO) in that it isn't implemented as an XML language. XPath's departure from XML also makes it both flexible and compact, which are important benefits when you consider that XPath is typically used in constrained situations such as attribute values.

XPath is a very important XML technology in that it provides a flexible means of addressing XML document parts. Any time you need to reference a portion of an XML document, such as with XSLT, you ultimately must rely on XPath. The XPath language is not based upon XML, but it is somewhat familiar nonetheless because it relies on a path notation that is commonly used in computer file systems. In fact, the name XPath stems from the fact that the path notation used to address XML documents is similar to path names used in file systems to describe the locations of files. Not surprisingly, the syntax used by XPath is extremely concise because it is designed for use in URIs and XML attribute values.

You'll find that XPath is similar in many ways to XQL, which you learned about in Hour 16. The primary difference between the two is that XQL is implemented as an XML-based language, while XPath is used to create expressions within attribute values of XML code. Since XQL actually includes its own elements and attributes, it is somewhat more powerful than XPath. However, XPath is always coupled with another technology, such as XSLT, which makes for an extremely powerful combination.

Similar to XSLT, XPath operates under the assumption that a document has been parsed into a tree of nodes. XPath defines different types of nodes that are used to describe nodes that appear within a tree of XML content. There is always a single root node that serves as the root of an XPath tree, and that appears as the first node in the tree. Every element in a document has a corresponding element node that appears in the tree under the root node. Within an element node there are other types of nodes that correspond to the element's content. Element nodes may have a unique identifier associated with them that is used to reference the node with XPath. Figure 19.1 shows the relationship between different kinds of nodes in an XPath tree.

FIGURE 19.1

XPath is based upon the notion of an XML document consisting of a hierarchical tree of nodes.

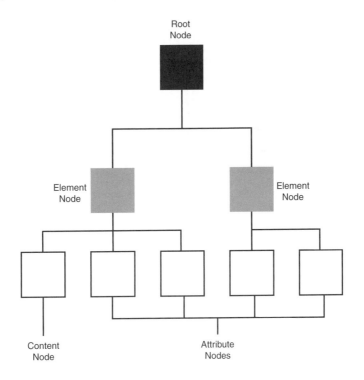

Nodes within an XML document can generally be broken down into element nodes, attribute nodes, and text nodes. Some nodes have names, in which case the name can consist of an optional namespace URI and a local name; a name that includes a namespace is known as an *expanded name*. Following is an example of an expanded element name:

```
<xsl:value-of select="."/>
```

In this example, the local name is value-of and the namespace is xsl. If you were to declare the XSL namespace as the default namespace for a document, you could get away with dropping the namespace part of the expanded name, in which case the name becomes this:

```
<value-of select="."/>
```

If you declare more than one namespace in a document, you will have to use expanded names for at least some of the elements and attributes. It's generally a good idea to use them for all elements and attributes in this situation just to make the code clearer and eliminate the risk of name clashes.

Getting back to node types in XPath, following are the different types of nodes that can appear in an XPath tree:

- Root node
- Element nodes
- Text nodes
- Attribute nodes
- Namespace nodes
- Processing instruction nodes
- Comment nodes

You should have a pretty good feel for these node types, considering that you've learned enough about XML and have dealt with each type of node throughout the book thus far. The root node in XPath serves the same role as it does in the structure of a document: it serves as the root of an XPath tree and appears as the first node in the tree. Every element in a document has a corresponding element node that appears in the tree under the root node. Within an element node appear all of the other types of nodes that correspond to the element's content. Element nodes may have a unique identifier associated with them, which is useful when referencing the node with XPath.

The point of all this naming and referencing with nodes is to provide a means of traversing an XML document to arrive at a given node. This traversal is accomplished using expressions, which you learned a little about back in Hour 13. You use XPath to build expressions, which are typically used in the context of some other operation, such as a document transformation. Upon being processed and evaluated, XPath expressions result in a data object of one of the following types:

- Node set—A collection of nodes
- String—A text string
- Boolean—A true/false value
- Number—A floating-point number

Similar to a database query, the data object resulting from an XPath expression can then be used as the basis for some other process, such as an XSLT transformation. For example, you might create an XPath expression that results in a node set that is transformed by an XSLT template. On the other hand, you can also use XPath with XLink, where a node result of an expression could form the basis for a linked document.

To learn more about the formal XPath specification, please visit the XPath section of the W3C Web site at http://www.w3.org/TR/xpath.

Navigating a Document with XPath Patterns

XPath expressions are usually built out of *patterns,* which describe a branch of an XML tree. A pattern therefore is used to reference one or more hierarchical nodes in a document tree. Patterns can be constructed to perform relatively complex pattern matching tasks and ultimately form somewhat of a mini-query language that is used to query documents for specific nodes. Patterns can be used to isolate specific nodes or groups of nodes and can be specified as absolute or relative. An *absolute pattern* spells out the exact location of a node or node set, whereas a *relative pattern* identifies a node or node set relative to a certain context.

The next few sections examine the ways in which patterns are used to access nodes within XML documents. To better understand how patterns are used, it's worth seeing them in the context of a real XML document. Listing 19.1 contains the code for the familiar training log example document that you saw earlier in the book, which serves as the example document in this hour for XPath.

19

LISTING 19.1 The Training Log Example XML Document

```
01: <?xml version="1.0"?>
02: <!DOCTYPE trainlog SYSTEM "etml.dtd">
03:
04: <trainlog>
05:   <!-- This session was part of the marathon training group run. -->
06:   <session date="11/19/01" type="running" heartrate="158">
07:     <duration units="minutes">45</duration>
08:     <distance units="miles">5.5</distance>
09:     <location>Warner Park</location>
10:     <comments>Mid-morning run, a little winded throughout.</comments>
11:   </session>
12:
13:   <session date="11/21/01" type="cycling" heartrate="153">
```

continues

LISTING **19.1**   Continued

```
14:      <duration units="hours">2.5</duration>
15:      <distance units="miles">37.0</distance>
16:      <location>Natchez Trace Parkway</location>
17:      <comments>Hilly ride, felt strong as an ox.</comments>
18:    </session>
19:
20:    <session date="11/24/01" type="running" heartrate="156">
21:      <duration units="hours">1.5</duration>
22:      <distance units="miles">8.5</distance>
23:      <location>Warner Park</location>
24:      <comments>Afternoon run, felt reasonably strong.</comments>
25:    </session>
26: </trainlog>
```

Be sure to keep this listing handy, as several of the XPath examples throughout the next section rely on it.

Referencing Nodes

The most basic of all patterns is the pattern that references the current node, which consists of a simple period:

.

If you're traversing a document tree, a period will obtain the current node. The current node pattern is therefore a relative pattern because it makes sense only in the context of a tree of data. As a contrast to the current pattern, which is relative, consider the pattern that is used to select the root node of a document. This pattern is known as the root pattern and consists of a single forward slash:

/

If you were to use a single forward slash in an expression for the training log example document, it would refer to the trainlog element (line 4) because this element is the root element of the document. Since the root pattern directly references a specific location in a document (the root node), it is considered an absolute pattern. The root pattern is extremely important to XPath because it represents the starting point of any document's node tree.

As you know, XPath relies on the hierarchical nature of XML documents to reference nodes. The relationship between nodes in this type of hierarchy is best described as a familial relationship, which means that nodes can be described as parent, child, or sibling nodes, depending upon the context of the tree. For example, the root node is the parent of all nodes. Nodes might be parents of some nodes and siblings of others. If you think of a family tree for people as a logical comparison, the concept of a node tree makes much more sense. To reference child nodes using XPath, you use the name of the child node as the pattern. So, in the training log example, you can reference a `session` element (line 6, for example) as a child of the root node by simply specifying the name of the element: `session`. Of course, this assumes that the root node (line 4) is the current context for the pattern, in which case a relative child path is OK. If the root node isn't the current context, then you should fully specify the child path as `/session`. Notice in this case that the root pattern is combined with a child pattern to create an absolute path.

If there are child nodes then there must also be parent nodes. To access a parent node, you must use two periods:

```
..
```

As an example, if the current context is one of the `distance` elements (line 15, for example) in the training log document, the `..` parent pattern will reference the parent of the node, which is a `session` element (line 13). You can put patterns together to get more interesting results. For example, to address a sibling node, you must first go to the parent and then reference the sibling as a child. In other words, you use the parent pattern (`..`) followed by a forward slash (`/`) followed by the sibling node name, like this:

```
../duration
```

This pattern assumes that the context is one of the child elements of the `session` element (other than `duration`). Assuming this context, the `../duration` pattern will reference the `duration` element (line 14) as a sibling node.

Thus far I've focused on referencing individual nodes. However, it's also possible to select multiple nodes. For example, you can select all of the child nodes (descendants) of a given node using the double slash pattern:

```
//
```

As an example, if the context is one of the `session` elements in the training log document (line 20, for example), then you can select all of its child nodes by using double slashes. This results in the `duration` (line 21), `distance` (line 22), `location` (line 23), and `comments` (line 24) elements being selected.

Another way to select multiple nodes is to use the wildcard pattern, which is an asterisk:

```
*
```

The wildcard pattern selects all of the nodes in a given context. So, if the context was a `session` element and you used the pattern `*/distance`, all of the `distance` elements in the document would be selected. This occurs because the wildcard pattern first results in all of the sibling `session` elements being selected, after which the selection is limited to the child `distance` elements.

19

To summarize, following are the primary building blocks used to reference nodes in XPath:

- Current node—.
- Root node—/
- Parent node—..
- Child node—*Child*
- Sibling node—/*Sibling*
- All child nodes—//
- All nodes—*

These pattern building blocks form the core of XPath, but they don't tell the whole story. The next section explores attributes and subsets and how they are referenced.

Referencing Attributes and Subsets

Elements aren't the only important pieces of information in XML documents; it's also important to be able to reference attributes. Fortunately, XPath makes it quite easy to reference attributes through the usage of the "at" symbol:

```
@
```

The "at" symbol is used to reference attributes by preceding an attribute name:

```
*/distance/@units
```

This code selects all of the `units` attributes for `distance` elements in the training log document, assuming that the context is one of the `session` elements. As you can see, attributes fit right into the path notation used by XPath and are referenced in the same manner as elements, with the addition of the "at" (`@`) symbol.

One other important feature of XPath expressions is support for the selection of subsets of nodes. You select a subset by appending square brackets (`[]`) to the end of a pattern and then placing an expression within the brackets that defines the subset. As an example, consider the following pattern that selects all of the `session` elements in the training log document:

```
*/session
```

It's possible that you might want to limit the `session` elements to a certain type of training session, such as running. To do this, you add square brackets onto the pattern, and you create an expression that checks to see if the session type is set to `running`:

```
*/session[@type='running']
```

This pattern results in selecting only the session elements whose type attribute is set to running. Notice that an "at" symbol (@) is used in front of the attribute name (type) to indicate that it is an attribute.

Using XPath Functions

Back in Hour 13, you learned about some of the more commonly used XPath functions and how they can be used to create expressions for XSLT style sheets. I'd like to revisit the standard XPath functions and go into a little more detail regarding their usage in creating expressions. Before getting into the specifics of the XPath functions at your disposal, it's worth taking a look at their general usage. The functions supported by XPath, which are available for use in creating XPath expressions, can be roughly divided along the lines of the data types on which they operate:

- Node functions
- String functions
- Boolean functions
- Number functions

The next few sections explore the functions in each of these categories in more detail. For a complete XPath function reference, please visit the XPath page at the W3C Web site at http://www.w3.org/TR/xpath#corelib.

Node Functions

Node functions are XPath functions that relate to the node tree. Although all of XPath technically relates to the node tree, node functions are very direct in that they allow you to ascertain the position of nodes in a node set, as well as how many nodes are in a set. Following are the most common XPath node functions:

- position()—Determine the numeric position of a node
- last()—Determine the last node in a node set
- count()—Determine the number of nodes in a node set

Although these node functions might seem somewhat abstract, keep in mind that they can be used to carry out some interesting tasks when used in the context of a broader expression. For example, the following code shows how to use the count() function to calculate the total distance in the training log document for sessions whose distances are recorded in miles:

```
count(*/distance[@units='miles'])
```

19

Following is another example that shows how to reference a child node based solely upon its position within a document:

```
child::item[position()=3]
```

Assuming there are several child elements of type `item`, this code references the third child `item` element of the current context. To reference the last child item, you use the `last()` function instead of an actual number, like this:

```
child::item[position()=last()]
```

String Functions

The XPath string functions are used to manipulate strings of text. With the string functions you can concatenate strings, slice them up into substrings, and determine the length of them. Following are the most popular string functions in XPath:

- `concat()`—Concatenate two strings together
- `starts-with()`—Determine if a string begins with another string
- `contains()`—Determine if a string contains another string
- `substring-before()`—Retrieve a substring that appears before another string
- `substring-after()`—Retrieve a substring that appears after another string
- `substring()`—Retrieve a substring of a specified length starting at an index within another string
- `string-length()`—Determine the length of a string

These XPath string functions can come in quite handy when it comes to building expressions, especially when you consider the fact that XML content is always specified as raw text. In other words, it is possible to manipulate most XML content as a string, regardless of whether the underlying value of the content is numeric or some other data type. Following is an example that demonstrates how to extract the month of a training session from a `date` attribute in the training log document:

```
substring-after(@date, "/")
```

In this example, the `substring-after()` function is called and passed the `date` attribute. Since a forward slash (/) is passed as the second argument to the function, it is used as the basis for finding the substring. If you look back at one of the `date` attributes in the document (line 6, for example), you'll notice that the month appears just after the first forward slash. As a comparison, you could extract the year as a substring by providing the same arguments but instead using the `substring-before()` function:

```
substring-before(@date, '/')
```

Another usage of the string functions is in finding nodes that contain a particular substring. For example, if you wanted to analyze your training data and look for training sessions where you felt strong, you could use the `contains()` function to select `session` elements where the `comments` child element contains the word "strong":

```
*/session[contains(comments, 'strong')]
```

In this example, the second and third `session` elements (lines 13 and 20) would be selected because they both contain the word "strong" in their `comments` child elements.

Boolean Functions

Boolean functions are pretty simple in that they operate solely on Boolean (true/false) values. Following are the two primary Boolean functions that you may find useful in XPath expressions:

- `not()`—negate a Boolean value
- `lang()`—determine if a certain language is being used

The `not()` function is pretty straightforward in that it simply reverses a Boolean value. The `lang()` function is a little more interesting because it actually queries a node to see what language it uses. As an example, many English-language XML documents set the `xml:lang` attribute to `en` in the root element. Although this value typically cascades down to all elements within the document, it's possible for a document to use multiple languages. The `lang()` function allows you to check the language setting for any node. Following is an example of how to use the `not()` and `lang()` functions to determine if the English language is not being used in a document:

```
not(lang("en"))
```

19

Number Functions

The XPath number functions should be somewhat familiar to you since you saw them in action back in Hour 13 when you created XSLT style sheets that relied on the number functions. Following are the most commonly used number functions in XPath:

- `ceiling()`—Round up a decimal value to the nearest integer
- `floor()`—Round down a decimal value to the nearest integer
- `round()`—Round a decimal value to the nearest integer
- `sum()`—Add a set of numeric values

Following is an example of how to use the sum() function to add up a bunch of attribute values:

```
sum(cart/item/@price)
```

Of course, you can make nested calls to the XPath number functions. For example, you can round the result of the sum() function by using the round() function, like this:

```
round(sum(cart/item/@price))
```

The Role of XPath

Throughout this hour you've learned how to create abstract patterns and expressions that can be used to reference specific parts of XML documents. I've used the word "select" a lot in this hour because when you create an XPath expression you are effectively selecting part of a document. However, this selection process doesn't take place within XPath alone. What I'm saying is that XPath is always used in the context of another technology such as XSLT, XPointer, or XLink. The examples of XPath that you've seen in this hour must therefore be used in conjunction with additional code. For example, the following code shows how one of the training log expressions from earlier in the hour might be used in an XSLT style sheet:

```
<xsl:value-of select="*/session[@type='running']" />
```

In this code, the XPath expression appears within the select attribute of the xsl:value-of element, which is responsible for inserting content from a source XML document into an output document during the transformation of the source document. Please refer back to Hours 12 and 13 for more information on XSLT style sheets and how they are used. The point I'm making is that the XSLT xsl:value-of element is what makes the XPath expression useful. XPath plays a critical role in XSLT, as you probably remember from Hour 13.

Similar to its role in XSLT, XPath serves as the addressing mechanism in XPointer. XPointer is the component of the larger XLink technology that is used to address parts of XML documents. XPointer uses XPath to provide a means of navigating the tree of nodes that comprise an XML document to address a specific node or nodes. Sounds familiar, right? XPointer takes XPath a step further by defining a syntax for *fragment identifiers,* which are in turn used to specify parts of documents. In doing so, XPointer provides a high degree of control over the addressing of XML documents. When coupled with XLink, the control afforded by XPointer makes it possible to create interesting links between documents that simply aren't possible in HMTL. You learn exactly how XPath fits into XLink in the next hour.

Summary

If you think of an XML document as a hierarchical tree of data, which it is, then it's not too hard to make a comparison between XML documents and the family trees used in genealogy. This comparison is useful because it turns out that one of the best ways to interact with XML data is by thinking in terms of nodes of data that are related to each other as family members. For example, there are parent, child, and sibling nodes at most points in a document's node tree. XPath is a technology that takes advantage of this hierarchical nature of XML by allowing you to reference parts of XML documents as nodes within a node tree.

Although you've heard mention of XPath earlier in the book, this hour formally introduced you to it. You began by learning what XPath is along with what it has to offer in terms of referencing XML documents. From there you learned how to use XPath patterns and expressions, as well as the standard XPath functions. The hour concluded with a quick explanation of the role of XPath in other important XML technologies.

Q&A

Q What is the difference between a pattern and an expression?

A A pattern is simply a reference to a location within an XML document or a node in the node tree. An expression is somewhat of an equation that uses patterns to carry out some kind of comparison or more advanced node selection based upon how it is evaluated within the context of a document.

Q What is the relationship between XPath and XPointer?

A XPath is a simple path language that uses patterns and expressions to reference portions of an XML document tree. XPointer extends XPath by offering more specific referencing capabilities within XML documents. XPointer also serves as the basis for identifying link sources and targets in XLink, which is the standard linking technology for XML.

19

Workshop

The Workshop is designed to help you anticipate possible questions, review what you've learned, and begin learning how to put your knowledge into practice.

Quiz

1. How do you reference the current node in an XML document using XPath?

2. What is the difference between the / and // patterns in XPath?

3. How would you go about using XPath to select all of the elements in a document whose attribute named location includes the text "Florida"?

Quiz Answers

1. To reference the current node in an XML document, you use a single period (.) as the pattern.

2. The / pattern in XPath is used to reference the root node of a document, whereas the // pattern selects all of the child nodes of a particular node.

3. To select all of the elements in a document whose attribute named location includes the text "Florida", you must use the expression */[contains(@location, 'Florida')].

Exercises

1. Now that you understand XPath a little better, modify the vehicles template in the vehicles.xsl style sheet from Hour 13 so that only green vehicles are selected and displayed.

2. While you're at it, modify the root template in the contacts.xsl style sheet from Hour 12 so that only contacts from New York City are displayed. Hint: You'll need to add a few new contacts from other places for testing purposes.

Hour 20

XML Linking with XLink and XPointer

Never offend people with style when you can offend them with substance.

—Sam Brown (writer)

Hopefully there is nothing in this hour that you'll find offensive, and I can all but guarantee that you'll appreciate the substance behind XLink and XPointer, the two technologies that make it possible to carry out advanced linking between XML documents. You are no doubt familiar with HTML hyperlinks, which are ultimately responsible for the interconnections between all of the pages on the Web; the Web simply wouldn't exist without hyperlinks. XML linking builds on the premise of HTML hyperlinks but goes several steps further in supporting advanced linking features such as two-way links. Although XML linking is still a new technology, it will likely have a dramatic impact on how information is connected on the Web. This hour explores XLink and XPointer, the two XML technologies that facilitate the linking of XML documents.

In this hour, you'll learn

- About the XML approach to linking documents
- What technologies come together to support linking in XML
- How to reference document fragments with XPointer
- How to link XML documents with XLink

HTML, XML, and Linking

Similar to HTML Web pages, XML documents can also benefit greatly from links that connect them together. Knowing this, the architects of XML set out to create a linking mechanism for XML that would provide support for traditional one-way links, such as those you may be familiar with in HTML, along with more advanced links, such as two-way links. Links in XML are in fact considerably more powerful than HTML links, as you will learn in a moment when you begin exploring XLink and XPointer. Before getting into that, however, it's worth taking a moment to assess the role of links in HTML.

HTML links (*hyperlinks*) are based upon the concept of connecting one resource to another resource—a *source* is linked to a *target*. The source of an HTML link is typically displayed on a Web page (via text or an image) so as to call out the fact that it links to another resource. Text links are typically displayed with an underline, and the mouse pointer usually changes when the user drags it over a link source. Traversing a link in HTML typically involves clicking the source resource, which results in the Web browser navigating to the target resource. This navigation can occur in the same browser window, in which case the target resource replaces the current page, or in a new browser window.

The important thing to understand about HTML links is that although they always involve two resources, they always link in one direction. In other words, one side of the link is always the source and the other side is always the target, which means you can follow a link only one way. You might think that the Back button in a Web browser allows HTML links to serve as two-way links, but the Back button has nothing to do with HTML. The Back button in a Web browser is a browser feature that involves keeping a running list of Web pages so that the user can back through them. There is nothing inherent in HTML links that supports backing up from the target of a link to the source. So, HTML links are somewhat limited in that they can link only in one direction. You might be wondering how it could possibly be useful to link in two directions—we'll get to that in a moment.

It's worth pointing out that many of the conventions we've come to expect in terms of HTML linking aren't directly related to HTML. For example, an HTML link doesn't specify anything about how it is to be displayed to the user (colored, underlined, and so forth). It is up to specific browsers and user preferences to determine how links are presented. Although this may not seem like a big deal right now, the browser's role in displaying links will become more significant as browsers start supporting XLink. This is because XLink supports links between multiple resources and in multiple directions, which makes them difficult to visualize with a simple underline or mouse pointer.

If you've spent any time coding Web pages with HTML, then you're no doubt familiar with the a element, also known as the anchor element, which is used to create HTML links. The anchor element identifies the target resource for an HTML link using the href attribute, which contains a URI. The href attribute can either reference a full URI or a relative URI. HTML links can link to entire documents or to a document fragment. The following is an example of an HTML link that uses a relative URI to link to a document named fruit.html:

```
Click <a href="fruit.html">here</a> for fruit!
```

This code assumes the document fruit.html is located in the same path as the document in which the code appears. If you want to link to a document located somewhere else, you'll probably take advantage of a full URI, like this:

```
Click <a href="http://www.michaelsgroceries.com/veggies.html">here</a> for
veggies!
```

Document fragments are a little more interesting in terms of how they are linked in HTML. When linking to a document fragment, the href attribute uses a pound symbol (#) in between the URI and the fragment identifier. The following is an example of how you create an HTML link to a specific location within a document:

```
Click <a href="fruit.html#bananas">here</a> for bananas!
```

In this code, the fragment identifier bananas is used to identify a portion of the fruit.html document. You associate a fragment identifier with a portion of a document using the anchor element (a) and the name attribute in the link target. This attribute value is the name used to the right of the pound symbol (#) in the anchor element that serves as the link source. The following is an example of an HTML link that establishes a banana document fragment for a link target:

```
<a name="bananas">We have the freshest bananas for $0.99 per pound.</a>
```

20

This code shows how a sentence of text can be marked as a link target by setting the name attribute of the a tag with a unique fragment identifier.

> If you're already an HTML guru, then I apologize for boring you with this recap of HTML links. Boring or not, it's important to have a solid grasp of HTML links because they serve as the basis for simple XML links.

As the previous examples demonstrate, HTML links are both very useful and very easy to create. Simply based on the power and usefulness of the Web, it's hard to make an argument against the strength of HTML's simplistic approach to linking documents. However, there are many ways that it can be improved, some of which you might have never thought about. For one, it would be nice if links could be bi-directional, which means that you wouldn't be dependent on a browser's implementation of a Back button in order to navigate backwards to a previous resource. Although this may seem trivial, it could be extremely useful to be able to traverse a link in either direction, thereby eliminating the need for fixed source and target resources. A bi-directional link would treat the two resources as both sources and targets depending on the context.

In addition to bi-directional links, it could be extremely beneficial to have links that reference multiple target resources. This would keep Web developers from having to duplicate content for the sole purpose of providing link sources. More specifically, a link with multiple targets could present a pop-up menu with the target selections from which the user selects. An example of this type of link might be a book listing on Amazon.com. A multiple-target link for the cover image of a book could present a pop-up menu containing links to documents such as a book summary, reviews, and a sample chapter. This tightens up the user interface for the Web site by reducing the content used purely for navigational purposes. It also provides a logical grouping of related links that would otherwise be coded as unrelated links using HTML anchors.

If your only exposure to document linking is HTML, then you probably regard link resources as existing completely separate of one another, at least in terms of how they are displayed in a Web browser. XML links shatter this notion by allowing you to use links to embed resources within other resources. In other words, the contents of a target resource are inserted in place of the link in a source document. Granted, images are handled much like this in HTML, but XML links offer the possibility of embedding virtually any kind of data in a document, not just an image. Traversing embedded links in this manner ultimately results in compound documents that are built out of other resources, which has some interesting implications for the Web. For example, you could build a news Web page out of paragraphs of text that are pulled from other documents around the Web.

Speaking of link traversal, HTML links are limited in that the user must trigger their traversal. For example, the only way to invoke a link on a Web page is to click the linked text or image, as shown in Figure 20.1. You may be wondering why it would be desirable to have it any other way. Well, consider the situation where a linked resource is to be embedded directly in a document to form a compound document. You might want the embedding to take place immediately upon opening the document, in which case the user would have nothing to do with the link being invoked. In this sense, the link is serving as a kind of connective tissue for components of a compound Web document (Figure 20.2), which is far beyond the role of links in HTML. Again, images already work like this in HTML, but XML links open the door for many other possibilities with flexible linking.

FIGURE 20.1

In order to traverse an HTML link, the user must click on linked text or a linked image, which points to another document or resource.

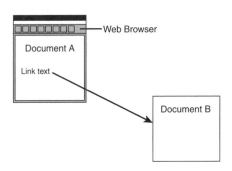

FIGURE 20.2

XML links are flexible enough to allow you to construct compound documents by pulling content together from other documents.

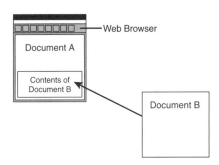

20

As you're starting to see, XML links, which are made possible by the XLink technology, are much more abstract than HTML links, and therefore can be used to serve more purposes than just providing users a way of moving from one Web page to the next. XLink fully aims to change the fundamental connections between resources on the Web. Admittedly, you almost have to take a few steps back and think of links in a more abstract sense to fully understand what XML links are all about. The up side to this shift in thinking is that when the significance of XLink fully sinks in, you will probably view the Web quite differently.

Yet another facet of XLink worth pointing out is its support for creating links that reside outside of the documents they link. In other words, you can create a link in one document that connects two resources contained in other documents (Figure 20.3). This can be particularly useful when you don't have the capability of editing the source and target documents. These kinds of links are known as *out-of-line links* and will probably foster the creation of link repositories. A *link repository* is a database of links that describe useful connections between resources on the Web. One example of such a repository might be an intricately cross-referenced legal database, where court cases are linked in such a way that a researcher in a law office could quickly find and verify precedents and track similar cases. Though it's somewhat possible to create such a database and incorporate it into HTML Web pages, it is extremely cumbersome. XLink provides the exact feature set to make link repositories a practical reality.

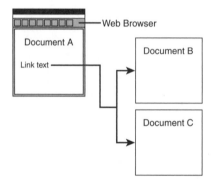

FIGURE 20.3

XML links allow you to do interesting things such as referencing multiple documents from a link within another document.

One of the side benefits of out-of-line links is the fact that the links are maintained separately from the documents that they link. This separate storage of links and resources makes it possible to dramatically reduce broken links, which are otherwise difficult to track down and eliminate.

Getting to Know XML Linking Technologies

You now understand that XML linking is considerably more powerful than its HTML counterpart. Perhaps more interesting is the fact that XML links involve a concert of technologies working together. XLink is the primary technology that makes XML links possible, but it requires the help of two other technologies—XPointer and XPath. The following are the three technologies that come together to make links in XML possible:

- XPath—A non-XML language used to address parts of an XML document via patterns and expressions, which you learned about in the previous hour

- XPointer—A non-XML language that builds on XPath by allowing you to address the internal structures of XML documents
- XLink—An XML-based language that specifies constructs for advanced linking in XML documents (XPointer is used to specify link sources and targets)

As you can see in this list, it isn't sufficient to discuss XML links in terms of XLink alone. If you traced the history of XLink in the W3C, you'd learn that it originally consisted of only two components, XPointer and XLink. However, the W3C realized that XPointer wasn't the only XML technology that needed a means of addressing parts of a document. XSLT also needed a means of addressing document parts, so it was decided to separate document addressing into XPath. XPointer builds on XPath to provide support for addressing the internal structure of XML documents. XLink in turn utilizes XPointer to describe flexible links to specific structures within XML documents.

Perhaps the biggest drawback of XLink and XPointer is that they aren't currently supported in major browsers. The good news is that they have reached formal recommendation status with the W3C, which is a big deal because it means that they have the official endorsement required for industry adoption. Now it's just a matter of waiting to see how fast they make their way into Web browsers and XML applications.

You learned a great deal about XPath in the previous hour. For this reason, I don't get into too many specifics of XPath in this hour, other than its relationship to XPointer and XLink. Moving on to XPointer, you now know that XPointer is a non-XML language based upon XPath that is used to address internal structures in XML documents. XPointer is an important part of XLink because it specifies the syntax used to create *fragment identifiers,* which are used to reference internal document constructs.

XLink is designed to support simple one-way links similar to those in HTML, as well as a variety of different extended links that offer interesting new ways of linking documents. XLink is implemented as an XML language, which means that it can be easily integrated into XML applications. This is a very important aspect of XLink because it allows XML developers to work within a familiar language to create links.

20

Addressing with XPointer

XPointer is the facet of XML linking that allows you to reference the internal parts of an XML document. More specifically, XPointer allows you to walk the tree of nodes that an XML document is comprised of to address a specific node or nodes. XPointer expands the syntax set forth by XPath to provide a means of creating fragment identifiers, which are used to specify parts of documents. XPointer provides considerably more control over the referencing of XML document data than the hyperlink approach employed by HTML. For example, XPointer allows you to do things such as address an element with a given value within a list of elements of a given type. You use XPointer expressions in XML links by appending them onto the end of URIs with a pound symbol (#), as in the separation between a URI and an XPointer expression. The next few sections break down XPointer into further detail and demonstrate exactly how to create XPointer expressions.

Building XPointer Expressions

The most important component of XPointer expressions is the *location path*, which is a construct used to describe the path that must be followed to arrive at a node within an XML document tree. Location paths are the building blocks of XPointer expressions, which are evaluated to arrive at a specific location within a tree. More specifically, location paths allow you to traverse siblings, ancestors, children, and descendants of nodes, not to mention attributes. Location paths are broken down into two basic types—absolute paths and general paths.

Absolute location paths point to a specific location within an XML tree, and therefore aren't dependent on context. Following are the different absolute location paths defined in XPointer:

- `/`—Locates the root node, which is the parent node for the entire document tree
- `id(Name)`—Locates the element with an attribute ID value of *Name*
- `here()`—Locates the node containing the current XPointer expression
- `origin()`—Locates the sub-resource from which the user initiated a link (used with out-of-line links)

The most important absolute location paths are the root and `id()` paths. The root path is represented by a forward slash (`/`), and is often used at the start of an XPointer expression as the basis for absolute location paths. The `id()` location path is used to locate an element with a specific attribute value.

In addition to absolute location paths, XPointer also defines a rich set of relative location paths. Relative location paths are always relative to some node, which is known as the *context node* for the path. Following are the relative location paths available for use in XPointer expressions:

- `child`—locates child nodes of the context node
- `descendant`—locates nodes within the context node

- descendant-or-self—same as descendant except the context node is also included
- parent—locates nodes one level above the context node that contain the context node
- ancestor—locates all nodes above the context node that contain the context node
- ancestor-or-self—same as ancestor except the context node is also included
- preceding-sibling—locates sibling nodes that precede the context node
- following-sibling—locates sibling nodes that follow the context node
- preceding—locates nodes that precede the context node
- following—locates nodes that follow the context node
- self—locates individual context nodes within a list of context nodes
- attribute—locates attributes of the context node

If you're totally confused by all this context node talk, don't worry because it will all make sense in a moment. As confusing as it may seem, the relative location paths in the previous list really are quite useful and are much easier to use than you might think. The next section shows you how to use these location paths to create expressions in XPointer.

Creating XPointers

Though the hour thus far has admittedly been a little on the reference side, I promise things will get better as you start looking at XPointer examples. Seeing a few examples of XPointer expressions can make all the difference in understanding how XPointer is used to define document fragment identifiers. The following is an example of a simple XPointer expression:

```
child::factoid
```

This example uses the child relative location path to locate all of the children of the context node that are of element type factoid. Just in case you didn't get that, let me rephrase it in a different way: the example expression locates element nodes of type factoid that are child nodes of the context node. Keep in mind that the context node is the node from which you are issuing the expression, which is a lot like the current path of a file system when you're browsing for files. Also, it's worth clarifying that the XPointer expression child::factoid simply describes the fragment identifier for a resource and is not a complete resource reference. When used in a complete expression, you would pair this fragment identifier with a URI that is assigned to an href attribute, like this:

```
href="http://www.gashoundgames.com/factoids.xml#child::factoid"
```

20

In this example, a URI is specified that references the XML document named `factoids.xml`. The XPointer expression is then provided as a fragment identifier, which is separated from the URI by a pound symbol (#). This is the typical way in which XPointers are used, although expressions can certainly get more complex than this. For example, the following code shows how to use location paths to create a more elaborate expression that carries out a more intricate reference:

```
child::factoid/following-sibling::legend
```

This example first locates all child elements that are of type `factoid` and then finds the second siblings following each of those element nodes that are of type `legend`. To understand how this code works, let's break it down. You begin with the familiar `child::factoid` expression, which locates element nodes of type `factoid` that are child nodes of the context node. Adding on the `following-sibling::legend` location path causes the expression to locate sibling elements of type `legend`. Granted, this may seem like a strange usage of XPointer, but keep in mind that it is designed as an all-purpose language for addressing the internal structure of XML documents. It's impossible to say how different applications might want to address document parts, which is why XPointer is so flexible.

In addition to location paths, XPointer defines several functions that perform different tasks within XPointer expressions. One class of functions is known as *node test functions,* which are used to determine the type of a node. Of course, you can use the name of an element to check if a node is of a certain element type, but the node test functions allow you to check and see if a node contains a comment, text, or processor instruction. The following is an example of how to use one of these functions:

```
/child::processing-instruction()
```

This expression results in the location of any processing instructions that are children of the root element. The reason the expression results in children of the root element is because the root element (`/`) is specified as the basis for the expression.

As you can see in these few examples, XPointer is a comprehensive yet flexible technology that is capable of doing some pretty interesting things. I'll readily admit that there is more to XPointer than I've touched on here; I mainly wanted to provide a solid overview and demonstrate how basic expressions are created. I encourage you to explore XPointer more on your own and experiment with creating XPointer expressions. However, before you do that you need to learn how XPointer fits into XLink.

Linking with XLink

The whole point of XPointer (no pun intended) is to provide a means of referencing portions of XML documents for the purpose of creating powerful XML links. XLink ultimately makes links possible through *linking elements,* which are elements that describe the characteristics of links. The anchor element in HTML is a good example of a linking element. Although linking elements form the basis of XLink, there are no predefined linking elements in the XLink language. Although it may seem strange at first, you won't find any standard element in the XLink language. The reason is because XML is all about the creation of custom tags (elements), which precludes the usage of a fixed linking element in XLink. In other words, you are encouraged to define your own linking elements specific to a particular XML-based language, as opposed to being locked into a fixed element, such as HTML's anchor element (a).

Even though HTML's anchor element is somewhat limiting in the context of XML, there still must be some kind of mechanism in XLink that identifies links. This mechanism comes in the form of standard linking attributes that can be associated with any element. There are several of these attributes, which you learn about in the next section. For now, just understand that the presence of XLink attributes is sufficient to identify an element as a *linking element.*

A linking element uses a construct called a *locator* to connect resources involved in a link. In both HTML and XML, the href attribute serves as the locator for links. Although HTML and XML share this attribute, links in XML are described in much more detail than their HTML counterparts. Perhaps the most important difference is the fact that XML links completely describe the resources involved, even if a target resource is just a document fragment. In HTML, it is necessary to place an anchor element in a target fragment resource and identify it using the name attribute. This is not the case in XML because XLink provides the necessary ingredients to fully describe the resources involved in a link.

There are two types of linking elements supported in XLink:

- Inline links
- Out-of-line links

An *inline link* is a link whose content serves as one of the link's participating resources. Typically, an inline link has a linking element that contains content that serves as the source for the link. HTML anchor links are good examples of inline links because an anchor link contains text that acts as the source for the link. Due to HTML's usage of inline links, you may be curious as to how a link could work any other way. Out-of-line links extend the concept of linking in XML by allowing you to create links that are independent of the linked resources.

20

An *out-of-line link* is a link whose content doesn't serve as one of the link's participating resources. This means that out-of-line links are independent of their participating resources and therefore serve a very different purpose than inline links. Out-of-line links are useful for linking information in documents that you can't modify for one reason or another. For example, if you wanted to create a link between two resources that reside on other Web sites, then you'd use an out-of-line link. How can such a link be possible? This is possible because out-of-line links are geared toward opening up interesting new opportunities for how links are used on the Web. More specifically, it will be possible to create link databases that describe relationships between information spread across the Web.

Out-of-line links partially form the concept of extended links in XML. *Extended links* are basically any links that extend the linking functionality of HTML. Out-of-line links obviously are considered extended links since HTML doesn't support any type of out-of-line linking mechanism. Extended links also support the association of more than one target resource with a given link. With extended links, you could build a table of contents for a Web site that consists solely of extended links that point to the various pages in the site. If the links were gathered in a single document separate from the table of contents page itself, then they would also be considered out-of-line links.

Understanding XLink Attributes

Hopefully I've sold you on the fact that XLink offers some interesting opportunities for creating XML links that are impossible in HTML. Now it's time to look at exactly how such interesting linking is made possible by XLink. Earlier I mentioned that XLink defines standard attributes that are used to establish linked elements in XML documents. The following are the XLink attributes that can be used to create linked elements:

- `type`—A string that specifies the type of link
- `href`—A locator that addresses a target resource using a URI
- `from`—A string that identifies the resource being linked from when describing an arc
- `to`—A string that identifies the resource being linked to when describing an arc
- `show`—A string that determines how a target resource is to be revealed to the user
- `actuate`—A string that determines how a link is initiated
- `role`—An application-specific string used to describe the function of a link's content
- `title`—A string that serves as a name for a link

The `type` attribute determines the type of a link and can have one of the following values: `simple`, `extended`, `locator`, `arc`, or `group`. The `href` attribute is one with which you are already familiar, based on its usage in HTML. The `from` and `to` attributes are used by *arcs*, which describe the traversal behavior of links. More specifically, an arc defines where a two-way link comes from and where it goes. Arcs can be used to establish Web rings, where Web pages are linked from one to the next using the `from` and `to` attributes to traverse the ring.

The `show` attribute determines how a target resource for a link is revealed to the user. There are three possible values for the `show` attribute:

- `replace`—The target resource replaces the current document (default value).
- `new`—The target resource is shown in a new window.
- `parsed`—The target resource is inserted into the current document in place of the link.

The functionality of the `show` attribute follows that of HTML anchor links until you get to the last possible value, `parsed`. If you set the `show` attribute to `parsed`, the link will be replaced by the target resource. This type of link allows you to divide a document into subdocuments and then link them together, which can help improve the organization of data.

The `actuate` attribute determines how a link is initiated and can have one of the following values:

- `user`—The link must be manually traversed by the user (default value).
- `auto`—The link is automatically traversed upon loading the source document.

Setting the `actuate` attribute to `user` makes a link act like an HTML link, which means that you have to click the link in order to activate it. The `auto` value offers functionality not available in HTML by allowing a link to be traversed when a document is first loaded. The `auto` value is particularly useful when used in conjunction with the `parsed` value for the `show` attribute; this results in a resource being automatically loaded and placed directly in a document.

The last two XLink attributes are `role` and `title`, which are used primarily for descriptive purposes. The `role` attribute describes the role of the content in a link, whereas `title` provides a human-readable title for the link that may be displayed in a browser.

20

Creating Links with XLink

You're now finally ready to put all of your XPointer and XLink knowledge to work and create some links that would never be possible in HTML. As an example, consider an element named `employees` that is used to identify a group of employees for a company. The following is an example of how you might create a simple link for the `employees` element:

```
<employees xmlns:xlink="http://www.w3.org/1999/xlink"
  xlink:href="employees.xml">
  Current Employees
</employees>
```

This example is the simplest possible link you can create using XLink, and it actually carries out the same functionality as an HTML anchor link. In other words, an HTML link is known as a *simple link* in XML. Notice in the code that the XLink namespace is declared and assigned to the xlink prefix, which is then used to reference the href attribute; this is the standard approach used to access all of the XLink attributes. What you may not realize is that this link takes advantage of some default attribute values. The following is another way to express the exact same link by spelling all of the pertinent XLink attribute values:

```
<employees xmlns:xlink="http://www.w3.org/1999/xlink"
  xlink:type="simple"
  xlink:href="employees.xml"
  xlink:show="replace"
  xlink:actuate="user"
  xlink:role="employees"
  xlink:title="Employee List">
  Current Employees
</employees>
```

In this code, you can more clearly see how the XLink attributes are specified in order to fully describe the link. The type attribute is set to simple, which indicates that this is a simple link. The show attribute has the value replace, which indicates that the target resource is to replace the current document when the link is traversed. The actuate attribute has the value user, which indicates that the link must be activated by the user for traversal to take place. And finally, the role and title attributes are set to indicate the meaning of the link and its name.

The previous example demonstrated how to create a link that imitates the familiar HTML anchor link. You can dramatically change a simple link just by altering the manner in which it is shown and activated. For example, take a look at the following link:

```
<resume xmlns:xlink="http://www.w3.org/1999/xlink"
  xlink:type="simple"
  xlink:href="resume_e1.xml"
  xlink:show="parsed"
  xlink:actuate="auto"
  xlink:role="employee1 resume"
  xlink:title="Employee 1 Resume"/>
```

This code shows how to effectively embed another XML document into the current document at the position where the link is located. This is accomplished by simply setting the show attribute to parsed and the actuate attribute to auto. When a Web browser or XML application encounters this link, it will automatically load the resume_e1.xml document and insert it into the current document in place of the link. When you think about it, the img element in HTML works very much like this link except that it is geared solely toward images; the link in this example can be used with any kind of XML content.

In this discussion of Xlink, I haven't really clarified how XPointer fits into links. XPointer impacts links through the `href` attribute, which is where you specify the location of a source or target resource for a link. All of the flexibility afforded by XPointer in specifying document parts can be realized in the `href` attribute of any link.

Although simple links such as the previous example are certainly important, they barely scratch the surface in terms of what XLink is really capable of doing. Links get much more interesting when you venture into extended links. A powerful usage of extended links is the *linkset,* which allows you to link to a set of target resources via a single source resource. For example, you could use an extended link to establish a link to each individual employee in a company. To create an extended link, you must create child elements of the linking element that are set to type `locator`; these elements are where you set each individual target resource via the `href` attribute. The following is an example of an extended link, which should help clarify how they work:

```
<employees xmlns:xlink="http://www.w3.org/1999/xlink"
  xlink:type="extended"
  xlink:role="employees"
  xlink:title="Employee List"
  xlink:show="replace"
  xlink:actuate="user">

  <employee xlink:type="locator" xlink:href="employee1.xml">
    Chuck Cinelli
  </employee>

  <employee xlink:type="locator" xlink:href="employee2.xml">
    Brian Briggs
  </employee>

  <employee xlink:type="locator" xlink:href="employee3.xml">
    Scott Kozicki
  </employee>
</employees>
```

This example creates an extended link out of the `employees` element, but the most interesting thing about the link is that it has multiple target resources that are identified in the child `employee` elements. This is evident by the fact that each of the `employee` elements has an `href` attribute that is set to their respective target resources.

Of course, you might be wondering exactly how a link like the extended link shown here is used. In Web pages, links are usually identified by colored, underlined text, and are activated simply by clicking them with the mouse. When there are multiple targets associated

20

with a link, as in the example, it somehow becomes necessary to specify which target you want when you traverse the link. Since XLink currently isn't supported in any Web browsers, it's hard to say exactly how this target resource selection will be carried out. My hunch is that you will be able to select from multiple targets that are displayed in a pop-up menu after you click a link. So, when you first click on a source resource for an extended link with multiple targets, a pop-up menu could appear with the available target links. To visit one of the links, you simply select the target from the menu. This is a reasonably intuitive way to implement the user interface portion of extended links with multiple targets, but it still isn't clear yet if browser vendors will employ this approach.

Another type of extended link is the arc, which is essentially a two-way link that connects two resources in such a way that the link can be traversed in either direction (forward or reverse). When you create an arc, you must first create locators for each resource involved in the link, and then you create the arc connections that connect the resources together. A Web ring is a good example of how arcs work—each Web page in a Web ring has a Forward and Back button that allows you to view more pages in the ring. The URI of a Web page in a Web ring would be identified in a locator, whereas the connections between each page in the ring would be established with arcs. The following is an example of an extended link that uses a few arcs to connect employee resources together:

```
<employees xmlns:xlink="http://www.w3.org/1999/xlink"
  xlink:type="extended"
  xlink:role="employees"
  xlink:title="Employee List">

  <employee xlink:type="locator" xlink:href="employee1.xml"
    xlink:role="employee1">
    Chuck Cinelli
  </employee>

  <employee xlink:type="locator" xlink:href="employee2.xml"
    xlink:role="employee2">
    Brian Briggs
  </employee>

  <employee xlink:type="locator" xlink:href="employee3.xml"
    xlink:role="employee3">
    Scott Kozicki
  </employee>

  <employeeconn xlink:type="arc" xlink:from="employee1" xlink:to="employee2"
    xlink:show="replace" xlink:actuate="user"/>

  <employeeconn xlink:type="arc" xlink:from="employee2" xlink:to="employee3"
    xlink:show="replace" xlink:actuate="user"/>
```

```
<employeeconn xlink:type="arc" xlink:from="employee3" xlink:to="employee1"
    xlink:show="replace" xlink:actuate="user"/>
</employees>
```

In this code, arcs are used to link several employee resources together. Notice that the employee resources are first referenced using employee elements. Although these elements have their `href` attributes set, they don't include any information about how the link is traversed. This information is specified in the `employeeconn` elements, which are of link type `arc`. The arc elements specify the 'From' and 'To' parts of the arc using the `from` and `to` attributes, which match up with the `role` attributes of the `employee` elements. The arcs effectively establish a ring of links that allows the program to navigate through the employees in a sequence.

Keep in mind that the examples shown in this section reveal only a couple of ways to use extended links. In truth, it has yet to be revealed exactly how XLink will impact XML, and what kinds of innovative linking applications people will dream up. Once there is support for XLink in Web browsers, we will likely see a revolution of sorts when it comes to how links are used and perceived.

Summary

Although many people associate Web browsers with the success of the Web, the true killer technology that made the Web possible is the linking of documents. Without links, documents on the Web would be islands of information with no connections between each other. Linking has worked so well on the Web that not too many people have questioned how it could be improved, even though practically every other facet of the Web has undergone huge evolutionary changes. XML provides a good opportunity to rethink document linking and evolve it to provide interesting new solutions to long-standing problems.

This hour introduced you to XLink and XPointer, two XML technologies that bring advanced linking support to XML, and at some point to the Web. The hour began by explaining the theoretical underpinnings of XML linking and what it aims to accomplish. You then learned how to create expressions in XPointer, followed by links in XLink. Although you gained some practical knowledge of XLink and XPointer, there unfortunately isn't support for either technology in any major Web browser or XML application at the moment. Even so, the W3C is pushing both technologies pretty aggressively, so it's hopefully only a matter of time before you can start linking your XML documents using XLink and XPointer.

20

Q&A

Q Why bother learning about XLink since it still isn't supported in major Web browsers or XML applications?

A The reason for learning about XLink has to do with the fact that it quite likely represents the future of XML document linking. The W3C has been steadily developing XLink with the goal of it becoming a standard technology with wide support. Admittedly, it's difficult to get excited about a technology that is somewhat intangible at the moment, but that doesn't lessen the future significance of XLink.

Q Once XLink is adopted by Web browsers, how will it impact the HTML anchor link?

A The HTML anchor link is a unique element (a) in HTML that has special meaning to Web browsers. In terms of XML, the HTML a element is just another element that happens to be interpreted as a linking element. When browsers add support for XLink, it will be very easy for them to support the a element for backward compatibility, while also supporting new XLink links. Keep in mind that with XLink you can create your own anchor links with very little effort.

Workshop

The Workshop is designed to help you anticipate possible questions, review what you've learned, and begin learning how to put your knowledge into practice.

Quiz

1. What is a link repository?

2. What are the three technologies that make XML linking possible?

3. What is a location path?

4. What is the difference between an inline link and an out-of-line link?

Quiz Answers

1. A link repository is a database of links that describe useful connections between resources on the Web.

2. The three technologies that make XML linking possible are XPath, XPointer, and XLink.

3. A location path is a construct used to describe the path that must be followed to arrive at a node within an XML document tree; location paths are the building blocks of XPointer expressions.

4. The content associated with an inline link serves as one of the link's participating resources, whereas the content associated with an out-of-line link does not.

Exercises

1. Modify the `tsali.xhtml` document from Hour 18 so that it uses XLink links instead of traditional HTML anchor links.

2. Create an XLink linking element named `searcher` that establishes a link for navigating some of the popular search engines. In other words, use XLink to create a search engine Web ring.

20

HOUR **21**

Going Wireless with WML

Don't you tell it to the trees
For they will tell the birds and bees.
Then everyone will know
Because you told the blabbering trees.

—Unknown

Wireless technologies promise to be the next wave of the Internet revolution—indeed, they may very well constitute a revolution in their own right. XML is well poised to take up the challenge of wireless communications. WML, Wireless Markup Language, strips a transmission down to its bare essentials by providing what is basically a pared down HTML for the wireless world. Paradoxically, it offers a remarkable amount of interactivity through its action elements, navigation controls, and scripting capabilities.

Although fairly crude in its current incarnation, wireless as an industry has taken the first giant step in making the World Wide Web infrastructure accessible to mobile users. The groundwork is laid for bringing full-fledged, and even broadband, Web experiences to the relentlessly busy. The plethora of new wireless devices, from intelligent phones to handheld computers to portable video games, is rapidly making wireless technologies a significant part of our culture.

In this hour, we'll cover

- How WML fits into the state of the wireless art
- Decks and cards—the anatomy of a WML document
- Formatting tags for WML text
- How to hook WML up to the microbrowser's controls
- How to provide for user entry in WML

XML and the Wireless Web

In a marketplace of competing standards vying for dominance, WML provides an effective solution to the needs of mobile users and developers. "Mobile devices" include any handheld or easily portable technology—cell phones, pagers, connected organizers, handheld PCs, and potentially others. WML is a component of WAP—Wireless Application Protocol. WAP is to WML as HTTP is to HTML; the WML markup language is a component of the larger WAP network protocol.

Although WAP and WML represent the lion's share of the American wireless market, other standards dominate in different geographical areas. In Japan, for instance, iMode has established cHTML—compact HTML, a subset of HTML—as the language of choice.

Compared to its competition, WML is compact and well tailored to the wireless environment. However, its current functionality is lagging behind that of cHTML or XHTML, and it also has the disadvantage of being yet another language for its developers to come up to speed on. On the other hand, the next major release of WAP, WAP 2.0, ups the ante considerably on wireless technologies by offering an impressive set of features. To be honest, it's still a little early to tell which wireless technology will win out in the end, but WAP and WML definitely offer a powerful punch that is slanted heavily toward XML.

It's important to understand that the Web is working just fine without WML, which means there must be a good reason to provide a wireless alternative to HTML. As an HTML alternative, WML addresses the issues of limited bandwidth and limited screen real estate, which are common limitations of wireless devices. Wireless connections are typically quite slow, and the display space accommodates a relatively small number of text characters—depending on the device—and 1-bit (straight black-and-white) monochrome graphics. WML documents are extremely simple, created with a small selection of tags. WML's deck-and-card metaphor subdivides a WML document—envisioned as a "deck"—into components—"cards." This allows the document to be transmitted all at once (if desired, and space allowing), without the need for the browser to display it all at once. However, it's ultimately up to the specific browser as to how a WML document is downloaded.

The wireless Web lends itself especially well to location-based services, LBSs, which rely on global positioning technologies to submit the user's geographical coordinates to a satellite that reports them onward to the server, which can use these data to determine what material to present to the user. This is some pretty high-tech stuff for a simple markup language, which is what makes WML so exciting.

Later in the hour, we will create a series of WML documents that display local movie and theatre information based on the user's location.

WML Essentials

WAP and its components, like WML, are stewarded by the WAP Forum, an industry consortium of mobile device manufacturers and service providers. You can find all of the organization's pertinent documentation at

`http://www.wapforum.org/what/technical.htm`

The WAP Forum is important because it serves as a single source of information on WAP-related technologies. The WAP Forum is also responsible for creating and maintaining formal specifications that result in industry standards, such as the WML language.

Nuts and Bolts

Before jumping into WML code, it's worth going over a few fundamental issues that surround any XML-based markup language. More specifically, you need to know about the WML specification, which is the last word on WML, as well as the WML DTD and MIME types associated with WML. Following is the information you need to get started with WML:

- The WML specification can be found at `http://www.wapforum.org/what/technical.htm`
- The WML DTD is `"-//WAPFORUM//DTD WML 1.1//EN,"` and can be found at `http://www.wapforum.org/DTD/wml_1.1.xml`
- WML MIME types, which are of interest to Web servers

21

The WML Root Element

As any legitimate XML-based language must, WML defines a root element for conforming documents—wml. As such, the wml root element serves as the container for all other elements in WML documents. To help facilitate display and navigation in limited screen space, a WML document is conceived as a deck of cards, one of which is visible at any given time. Although the document is typically transmitted as a single unit, it is navigated piece-by-piece, or card-by-card.

The wml element is the parent of the card element, which in turn contains all other elements in the document. You can have an unlimited number of cards in each document (deck). A card is intended to, but doesn't necessarily, convey approximately a screenful of information. (To scroll beyond the screen's boundaries, the user can navigate with the arrow keys.)

> Although we speak liberally of "decks" in WML, there is no such thing as a deck tag. It is implied in the wml element. In this way, a WML document is effectively serving as a "deck" for the cards within it.

Navigation in WML

Since so little text fits on the screen of a mobile device, efficient navigation is critical in a WML document. WML provides numerous ways of getting around, from the anchor element, which is adopted from HTML, to the monitoring of user events. One of WML's solutions to the screen real estate crunch is its capability of mapping actions to the mobile device's *softkeys,* which are the mysterious blank buttons just below the screen. The labels (names) that appear on the screen just above them may vary from one device to another, but their intention is usually clear. For the most part, they appear only when WML code instructs them to do so.

The softkeys provide navigation controls beyond what you can fit on the screen in the content of a document. For instance, a Menu or Options key displays the equivalent of an HTML navigation bar, whereas a Reset key takes the user back to the first card in the deck. The Link button, as shown in the examples in this hour, appears when the text contains hyperlinks.

Besides anchors, WML provides a selection list tool that lets you display a series of choices as a numbered list. Thus, the user can select an option with a number key on the keypad, in addition to using the Link button.

WML offers a number of action elements (go, prev, refresh, etc.) that move the user from one card to another under specified contexts, such as the use of go href="*url*" in the anchor element (a href, and so forth, is a shorthand version of this). These elements are flexible in their implementation and can be associated with a number of parent elements in order to provide a considerable amount of mobility.

Events in WML are comparable to events in any scripting or programming language; you set up the document to wait for a specified event to happen, and when it does the program automatically carries out a designated task. Some events you can code for are onenterforward, onenterbackward, and ontimer, which indicate entering a card in the forward direction, entering a card backward, and the elapsed time of a timer that is associated with a card, respectively.

Content in WML

Given the nature of mobile devices, screen space is severely limited and bandwidth is precious. Thus, we can't afford to clog the airwaves with fancy formatting or layout directives, which is why WML offers only the simplest of formatting tags. WML does support tables, but they are very primitive, nothing like the sophisticated layout capabilities afforded by tables in HTML. The few text-formatting tags that do exist in WML have been adapted straight from HTML, making for a flat learning curve for traditional Web developers.

Graphics support in WML is restricted to the WBMP (Wireless BitMap Picture) format, a 1-bit bitmap format whose files end in a .wbmp extension. One bit means on-or-off, black-or-white, which is just two colors. Besides the color depth restriction, the size is limited as well; WML images can't measure more than 64 × 64 pixels. Since you probably aren't accustomed to storing images in the WBMP format, you'll need to use a graphics converter of some sort to convert other graphics formats to WBMP. You'll find sources for such software listed in the "Inserting WBMP Images" section later in this hour.

It's worth pointing out that not all WAP implementations support images. It ultimately depends on the specific device being targeted as to whether or not images are an option.

Creating WML Documents

This section discusses the basics of setting up a WML document and describes several of the most common tasks involved in authoring a document for the wireless Web. We'll develop components of a site we'll call FilmTime, which uses geographic coordinates to present a list of movies currently playing within 10 miles of the user's current position.

21

Menus navigate the user through a series of choices about theatres, show times, and film synopses. This example is similar to the current Web site `http://www.moviefone.com/` — in fact, maybe `moviefone.com` already **has** a wireless version!

For the sake of simplicity, we won't worry about where FilmTime gets the user's coordinates, how it maps coordinates to a zip code, or how it processes database queries. We also won't worry about how the components we're authoring fit into the larger scheme of things, as our main objective is to introduce you to the elements rather than coaching you in designing a full-fledged application. In other words, this example focuses on the wireless aspects of such a Web site, not on the technical details that don't directly involve WML.

> For information and inspiration about the advanced aspects of WML (and of course, WAP), you can really take the bull by the horns and visit the formal WAP specification at `http://www.wapforum.org/what/technical.htm`. Or, you can go someplace more conversational, but no less exhaustive, such as `http://www.wirelessdevnet.com/`.

Though this hour does not introduce you to the full range of WML elements and their attributes, you will learn how to carry out the following tasks in WML:

- Create a deck (WML container document) and a number of cards, or sections of the document
- Enter and format text
- Navigate around other cards in the deck
- Associate events with a `card` element
- Set up a field for user entry
- Insert an image

The next few sections get you going with the creation of your first WML document and guide you through the fundamental tasks required to develop complete WML documents.

Before You Start—Tools of the Trade

As with just about any kind of software development, tools can ultimately determine how likely you are to succeed in completing a project. WML is no different, although its tool requirements are fairly straightforward. You will need the following items to build a wireless Web site with WML:

- A text editor, such as the no-frills Windows Notepad or Simple Text, or a dedicated WML editor such as WAPtor by WAPtop (http://www.waptop.net)

- A mobile phone simulator—software that runs on your PC and displays content as the user sees and experiences it (on a "microbrowser"), complete with clickable buttons

- Debugging capabilities, optionally, which typically accompany the simulator

- An Internet connection for testing

The most important tool in any WML developer's arsenal is the mobile phone simulator because it is what allows you to test WML documents in the context of a wireless device. A mobile phone simulator acts as a *microbrowser*, which is a small-scale Web browser that is designed specifically for wireless devices. The wireless tool used throughout this hour is WinWAP, which actually looks more like a traditional HTML-based Web browser than a WML microbrowser. WinWAP is a good test browser for WML documents because it is so simple to use. You can download WinWAP at http://www.winwap.org/. For a more full-featured microbrowser and WML development environment, you might consider the Openwave SDK, which provides a highly useful microbrowser that resembles a virtual mobile phone. You can download the Openwave SDK for free at http://www.openwave.com/products/developer_products/.

 The online offerings, though numerous, are Windows-centric. You'll have to look harder to find resources for UNIX, Linux, or Macintosh.

Laying Down the Infrastructure

In order to transmit WML documents, you need a WML gateway and a Web server in place. The cell phone transmits the user's information to a WAP gateway, which sends it on to the Web server, which stores it as session information in the user profile.

Your Web server needs to know how to process the MIME types of the WML documents, as mentioned in the section "Nuts and Bolts" earlier in the hour. You'll need to take a look at your Web server's documentation to learn how to do that. Essentially, you need to introduce each MIME type to the server in a statement of its own. Following are the MIME types associated with WML:

- text/vnd.wap.wmlscript

- image/vnd.wap.wbmp

- text/vnd.wap.si

21

- `text/vnd.wap.sl`

- `application/vnd.wap.wbxml`

- `application/vnd.wap.wmlc`

- `application/vnd.wap.wmlscriptc`

The Basic WML Document

The WinWAP microbrowser was used in creating this hour's examples. In order to view the example WML documents, you'll need WinWAP, the Openwave SDK, or some other suitable WML tool that includes a microbrowser. With a microbrowser in hand, you're ready to begin creating your first WML document.

To begin creating a WML document, you must first enter the familiar XML declaration, and then reference the WML DTD. The WML root element, `wml`, is then added as a paired tag. Following is code for a skeletal WML document, which accomplishes these basic tasks:

```
<?xml version="1.0" encoding="UTF-8"?>

<!DOCTYPE wml PUBLIC "-//WAPFORUM//DTD WML 1.1//EN"
  "http://www.wapforum.org/DTD/wml_1.1.xml">

<wml>
</wml>
```

After entering this code into a text editor, you should save it with a `.wml` extension, which is standard for WML documents. Granted, some microbrowsers don't care about the file extension and will display documents OK regardless of the extension, but it's good programming practice to get it right and use the correct file extension.

> Microbrowsers for wireless content are much more proprietary than HTML browsers, which means that most major mobile device manufacturers have their own. Even so, the WAP standard is there to provide a high degree of consistency across different microbrowsers.

Setting Up Cards

The `card` element is the basic unit of content in WML and the parent of all lower-level elements in the document; that is to say, it is the only child of the `wml` element. One card and a small snippet of text get you to the tiny silver screen. Of course, most practical WML documents consist of multiple cards.

FIGURE 21.3

*A list of links,
HTML fashion.*

The `select>option` Setup

The previous example showed how to allow the user to select from a list of options using anchors. You can get almost the same effect by using the `select` element with its child, the `option` element. This results in a numbered menu that can be accessed from the keypad as well as from the OK softkey, which replaces the Link softkey as the activating mechanism. As with the anchor approach, the user can hit the physical Send key to jump to a link.

The `select` element itself is a child of the p (paragraph) element, which is in turn a child of the `card` element. In other words, you need to place the `select` element within a paragraph. Listing 21.4 illustrates the `select>option` construction in an example that allows you to select movie theatres from a list.

LISTING 21.4   Using WML to Select a Movie Theatre (`theatrelist.wml`)

```
 1: <?xml version="1.0" encoding="UTF-8"?>
 2:
 3: <!DOCTYPE wml PUBLIC "-//WAPFORUM//DTD WML 1.1//EN"
 4:    "http://www.wapforum.org/DTD/wml_1.1.xml">
 5:
 6: <wml>
 7:   <card>
 8:     <p align="center"><b>***FILMTIME!***</b></p>
 9:     <p><b>THUMBELINA NOW PLAYING AT...</b>
10:     <select>
11:       <option onpick="#rio">Rio</option>
12:       <option onpick="#apollo">Apollo</option>
13:       <option onpick="#crown">Crown</option>
14:     </select>
15:     </p>
16:   </card>
17:
18:   <card id="rio">
19:     <p><b>Rio Theatre</b></p>
```

21

continues

LISTING 21.4   Continued

```
20:     <p>455 River St., Anytown</p>
21:     <p>111.222.3333</p>
22:     <p>3:30, 5:30, 7:30</p>
23:   </card>
24:
25:   <card id="apollo">
26:     <p><b>Apollo Theatre</b></p>
27:     <p>779 Pax Romana Dr., Chesterton</p>
28:     <p>111.222.4444</p>
29:     <p>3:45, 5:50, 7:40</p>
30:   </card>
31:
32:   <card id="crown">
33:     <p><b>Crown Theatre</b></p>
34:     <p>83 Imperial Avenue, Kingston</p>
35:     <p>111.234.5566</p>
36:     <p>2:00, 4:30, 6:45</p>
37:   </card>
38: </wml>
```

In this example, a select element is used (line 10) to establish a list of theatres from which the user can select one. Each theatre option is represented by an `option` element accompanied by an onpick attribute (lines 11–13), which determines the destination of the option link. The link destinations correspond to card IDs that appear later in the document (lines 18, 25, and 32). The rest of the listing is exactly the same as that in the anchor example, and the result is shown in Figure 21.4.

FIGURE 21.4

The select>option *list makes it possible to easily select movies from a list.*

Unlike the a `href` construction, `select>option`'s output is a numerical list, which allows the user to make the selection from the numerical keypad. Nine options are allowed, since there are nine numbered keys, and the user must scroll to see options that don't fit on the screen.

mapping tasks to the microbrowser's softkeys, and inserting an image into a document. Moving up a little on the ladder, we then covered setting up the document for user input—useful for simple name or password entries.

Workshop

The Workshop is designed to help you anticipate possible questions, review what you've learned, and begin learning how to put your knowledge into practice

Quiz

1. WML is a component of what transmission protocol—and what does the acronym stand for?

2. What navigation technique—that is, which element and attribute—should you use if you want to present the user with a numbered list from which they can jump to other cards or documents?

3. How many bits are in a WBMP image?

4. The select element is a child of what parent element?

Quiz Answers

1. Wireless Markup Language is a component of WAP, or Wireless Access Protocol.

2. Use the select element with the option attribute.

3. Only one! That means you get a straight black-and-white image, with no shades of gray.

4. The p (paragraph) element.

Exercises

1. Using do>type, set up a Help card for the FilmTime site.

2. Design a short and simple animation sequence (suggested length 5–10 frames) played by using the ontimer event.

21

22

describe the appearance of a graphical object using some kind of inherently non-graphical scheme. The specifics of each scheme used to represent a graphical object are ultimately what determine the differences between graphics formats. Though not necessarily superior to bitmap, or raster, graphics, vector graphics have several characteristics that make them just the right tool for the job in many circumstances.

A bitmap image file is a list of instructions on how the monitor or printer should render each rectangular dot, or pixel, that comprises an image. If an image measures 64×64 pixels, that means a total of 4,096 separate instructions, each with its own recipe of red, green, and blue components. And this is a tiny graphic! Although it is very accurate at representing complex images, such as photographs, bitmap technology results in very large image files—slow to transmit, tedious to edit, and impossible to interact with. On the other hand, they remain the tool of choice for photographs or other images where subtle gradations of tone are critical.

Vector graphics are the result of mathematical equations instead of thousands of pixels. SVG stands for Scalable Vector Graphics—a redundant term because vector graphics are scalable by definition. They are composed of a series of mathematical equations that describe graphics objects. So, for instance, if you wanted to draw a red circle, you would simply specify the center point, the radius, and the color, and SVG takes care of the details of rendering the red circle on the screen. To modify your drawing, you'd simply go in and change the parameters of the graphical objects being drawn. To modify the same picture with bitmap technology, by contrast, you would have to change the instructions for every pixel affected, up to thousands or millions.

In the desktop and print world, Adobe Photoshop, which produces mainly bitmap graphics, and Adobe Illustrator, which handles vector formats, typify the two different graphics approaches. They are also referred to as painting and drawing applications, respectively. It is worthwhile to note that, although you can create SVG files in any text editor (like an XML file), many current graphics programs offer the capability of exporting an image to SVG without the need to get involved with the code. Please see the section "Creating an SVG Drawing" later in this hour for further discussion.

SVG and Related Technologies

Revolutionary as SVG is, it is not alone in its class of Web-based vector graphics applications. Microsoft's VML (Vector Markup Language) is another XML-based solution, and Flash is a proprietary format with capabilities comparable to SVG. Although VML enjoys the power of Microsoft's endorsement and Flash has enormous support across the Web, SVG is the vector graphics format being touted by the W3C, which means that it stands a good chance at becoming the Web standard for vector graphics at some point in the near future.

VML

Ever loyal to its longstanding tradition of "my way or the highway," Microsoft has developed its own XML application for creating graphics: VML, or Vector Markup Language. Its main advantage—at least, for existing Microsoft customers—is that it is well integrated with Microsoft Office 2000 products. Hence, you can use the drawing tools in Word, Excel, or PowerPoint without having to leave your current workspace and can draw a WYSIWYG graphic that can be embedded in an HTML document. VML is also supported in Internet Explorer, which means you can use it immediately to embed vector graphics directly in your Web pages as long as you know everyone visiting your pages is using Internet Explorer.

Macromedia Flash

Macromedia Flash provides a WYSIWYG environment for the creation and editing of vector graphics in the proprietary SWF format, with a sophisticated specialty in motion graphics. As this book goes to press, the latest wave of state-of-the-art Web sites features Flash graphics—stunning but at times bandwidth hungry—which put the Web on par with television as a venue for complex animations. Although Flash covers the full range of SVG capabilities, its main focus is animation, which might be considered overkill for simpler purposes. The other big distinction between Flash and SVG is that Flash relies on a proprietary binary file format, which means you can't just open up a Flash movie in a text file and modify it. It also means you can't generate Flash movies dynamically with script code as you can with SVG. Of course, SVG doesn't allow you to put together complex animations with relative ease, which is Flash's forte.

Inside the SVG Language

As is the case with most XML-based languages, there are some housekeeping issues associated with SVG that you must know about before diving into the creation of SVG documents. Following are some key pieces of information related to SVG that are helpful to know as you begin learning more about the SVG language:

- SVG has its own DTD (Document Type Definition), which is declared as follows:

```
<!DOCTYPE svg PUBLIC "-//W3C//DTD SVG 1.0//EN"
    "http://www.w3.org/TR/2001/REC-SVG-20010904/DTD/svg10.dtd">
```

- The SVG namespace is http://www.w3.org/TR/svg.
- For server considerations, the MIME type for SVG is image/svg+xml.

The SVG DTD is important for SVG document validation, whereas the SVG namespace is necessary for using elements and attributes within the SVG language. The SVG MIME type isn't quite as critical and really enters the picture only from a Web-server perspective when SVG documents are being served to Web browsers.

The Bare Bones of SVG

As with all XML documents, SVG documents are required to have a root element, which in the case of SVG is the svg element. Beneath the SVG element is where you place specific SVG content consisting of additional SVG elements and attributes. There are three fundamental types of graphical objects that can be used within SVG drawings:

- Primitive vector shapes (squares, circles, etc.)
- Vector text
- External bitmap images

Vector shapes are what you might typically think of as traditional vector graphics objects. Additionally, you can include vector text, which is basically any text rendered in a mathematical font, such as a Windows TrueType font. To style vector text, SVG makes use of CSS (Cascading Style Sheet) attributes. Please see Hours 10 and 11 for more information about using CSS to create style sheets and the section in this hour, "SVG Children," for specifics of style rule names and functions that have been adapted for use in SVG.

 In the wider scheme of things, you can also use XSL transformations and XSL formatting objects to broaden the reach of SVG or to broaden another application's access to SVG. See Hours 12 and 13 for an in-depth discussion of XSL technologies.

SVG Coordinate Systems

To render graphics on a page or monitor, a graphics application must refer to a system of coordinates that determines the size and units of measurement associated with the drawing surface. SVG supports a few different systems, depending on your specific needs. By default, SVG measures its drawing surface in arbitrary "non-dimensional local units." Whereas some shapes can be defined by pixels (px), points (pt), inches (in), or centimeters (cm), other elements can be described only in abstract units, which the browser maps to pixels on the screen. When you don't specify real-world units of measurement—for instance, when you say r="50" to indicate the radius of a circle—SVG uses these non-dimensional local units to determine how an object is drawn to the screen. Additionally, some graphical elements, like path and polygon, support only such units. If you have a need to work with real-world measurements, you must redefine the coordinate system, as discussed in the following section.

By default, the opening "canvas" of an SVG drawing is infinite, which means it has no width or height. It's generally a good idea to set the size of the canvas using the width and height attributes of the root svg element. You learn how this is accomplished in the next section when you start assembling your first SVG drawing. In fact, let's get started now.

Creating an SVG Drawing

As you now know, SVG is an XML-based markup language, which means that you create SVG documents in a text editor using markup tags. The astute observer may well ask, "Isn't it much easier for a user to create an image in a graphics application than in a text editor?" The answer, of course, is "yes." The latest versions of all of the major drawing programs do allow you to create SVG files, and even SVGZ, the compressed variety of the format. Moreover, Adobe Illustrator offers an SVG Interactivity Palette that enables you to wire various JavaScript actions to selected parts of your image. What more could you want?

Before you put away this book and go the graphical route, let me clarify that there are reasons it might be worth your while to learn the SVG language:

- You may not want to invest in an expensive drawing application, or may not have one handy.
- WYSIWYG tools are great, but there's nothing like getting down and dirty with the code for ultimate control. You can always create a graphic in a drawing application and edit as needed in the raw SVG file.
- For collaborative projects, an image's SVG file will be more readily accessible from the Web site than the original, say, Illustrator file.
- You may need to generate SVG code on the fly or import SVG code into an application, which means you have to understand how the SVG language works.

A longer list of applications that support SVG includes CorelDraw 10 from Corel and Trajectory Pro from Jasc, both available only in Windows versions at the moment. Batik, from the makers of Apache, is a dedicated Java-based SVG editor and viewer, available at http://xml.apache.org/batik

Before getting started creating SVG documents, it's a good idea to have a browser or viewer set up to check your work as you go. Creating SVG code is relatively straightforward, but finding a browser that will display it is a bit more of an undertaking. There are essentially three ways to view an SVG document:

- Web browser with native support
- Web browser with an existing plug-in
- Dedicated SVG viewer

As of this writing, only the Amaya browser provides native support for viewing SVG documents. You can download it from www.w3c.org/amaya, but the current implementation is available only for Windows and Unix platforms.

Recent versions of the Netscape and Internet Explorer browsers can use a plug-in SVG viewer available from Adobe, which is available for free download at www.adobe.com/svg/. Even though it is in a beta stage as of this writing, I encourage you to download and use version 3.0 of Adobe's SVG viewer for compatibility with the latest Web browsers.

The Root Element

Every SVG document begins with the root element, which is svg. The svg element has many attributes and children, the most fundamental of which are described throughout this section.

The width and height elements describe the size of the drawing canvas. If no width and height elements are specified, the canvas is assumed to stretch infinitely in both dimensions. You can define these dimensions in a number of real-world units, including inches (in), centimeters (cm), points (pt), or pixels (px). Or, you can specify a percentage of the display window. If you don't indicate a unit of measurement, SVG defaults to non-dimensional local units, an arbitrary designation that it maps as it sees fit to your monitor's pixels, and displays the image at 100% of the available window space.

SVG borrows the title element from HTML to provide a means of assigning a title to SVG documents. Listing 22.1 shows a basic SVG document with a circle element that uses the attributes r, cx, and cy to define the circle, which you learn about shortly.

LISTING 22.1 A Basic SVG Document That Creates a Circle

```
1: <?xml version="1.0" encoding="UTF-8" standalone="yes"?>
2:
3: <svg xmlns="http://www.w3.org/2000/svg">
4:   <title>Circle 1</title>
5:   <circle r="100px" cx="200px" cy="200px"/>
6: </svg>
```

Figure 22.1 shows this document as viewed in Internet Explorer. Since no width or height is specified for the canvas, the canvas is assumed to extend infinitely, and therefore no bounds are placed on the drawing surface.

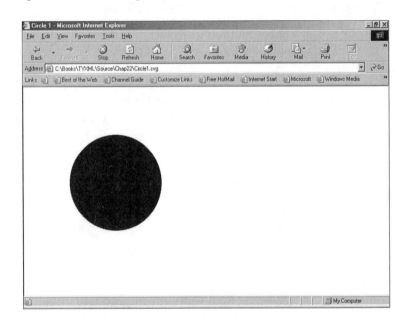

The width and height attributes define the space available to place your graphic. By setting the width and height attributes, you control the available drawing surface (Listing 22.2).

LISTING 22.2   An SVG Document with the Width and Height Set

```
1: <?xml version="1.0" encoding="UTF-8" standalone="yes"?>
2:
3: <svg xmlns="http://www.w3.org/2000/svg" width="200" height="200">
4:   <title>Circle 2</title>
5:   <circle r="100px" cx="200px" cy="200px"/>
6: </svg>
```

Figure 22.2 shows how the width and height of the canvas in this document aren't sufficient to allow the entire circle to fit. On the other hand, if you wanted to draw only a quarter circle, then this is one way to do it.

FIGURE 22.5

The ellipse *element allows you to create ellipses.*

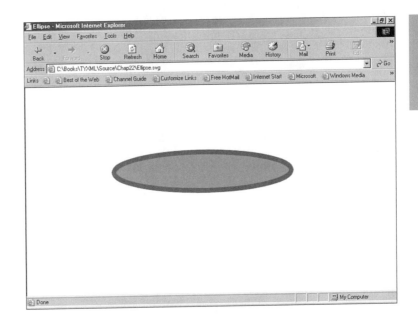

Lines

The line element speaks for itself in that it allows you to create lines; a line is defined by two connected endpoints. To define a line using the line element, you simply specify the coordinates of the two endpoints: (x1, y1) and (x2, y2). Listing 22.6 shows an example of how to create a line.

LISTING 22.6 A Simple SVG Line

```
1: <?xml version="1.0" encoding="UTF-8" standalone="yes"?>
2:
3: <svg xmlns="http://www.w3.org/2000/svg">
4:   <title>Line</title>
5:   <line x1="40" y1="40" x2="240" y2="120"
6:     style="stroke:green; stroke-width:5"/>
7: </svg>
```

Figure 22.6 shows the results of this code as viewed in Internet Explorer.

22

FIGURE 22.6

A simple line is drawn using the line *element.*

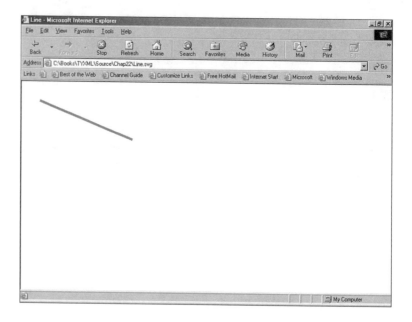

It's worth pointing out that you can use the line element to describe a polygon (a shape with multiple straight sides), but it is usually more economical to use the polygon element discussed in the next section or the path element, which is discussed a little later in the hour. The path element is interesting because it offers the capability of combining straight lines with arcs and Bezier curves in a single statement.

Incidentally, a Bezier curve is a curved line defined mathematically using special equations. The curve is named after the French engineer Pierre Bezier, who used the curve for the body design of the Renault automobile.

Compound Shapes

In addition to the simple graphical objects, such as circles, rectangles, and lines, there are also some additional shapes you can draw in SVG that are more flexible. I'm referring to shapes known as *compound shapes,* two of which are supported in SVG:

- polygon—A closed figure consisting of an unlimited number of sides
- polyline—An open figure consisting on an unlimited number of sides

Polygons

A polygon is considered a compound shape because it combines an unlimited number of straight lines to create a closed figure. A polygon may be convex or concave, typified

FIGURE 22.11

A hapless piece of mispositioned text.

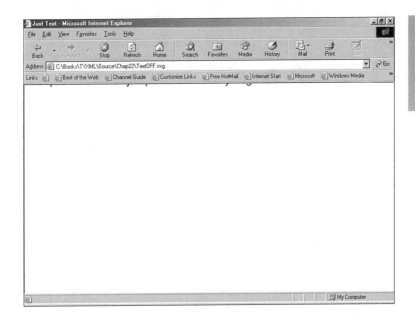

Text Along a Path

SVG also provides for text associated with a path, in which case the text is drawn along the path. The text and the path are created separately—that is, each in its own element statement—and joined together by an `xlink:href` attribute. To accomplish this, you give the path an `id` attribute, and reference it from the `textPath` element, which is a child of the text element.

Also, the `xlink` prefix needs to be mapped to the `w3.org` namespace. This can be done either on a containing element or on the `textPath` element itself. Listing 22.10 declares the `xmlns` attribute directly on the `textPath` element and references the path `id` as "path-demo" to associate the text with it. The stroke of the path disappears when you add text to the path in Illustrator, but we're going to leave that issue alone for the moment. We give the `path` element the `id` "newPath," and reference it from the `textPath` element that encloses the content.

LISTING 22.10   Text That Is Associated with a Path

```
1: <?xml version="1.0" encoding="iso-8859-1"?>
2:
3: <!-- Generator: Adobe Illustrator 9.0.1, SVG Export Plug-In  -->
4: <!DOCTYPE svg PUBLIC "-//W3C//DTD SVG 20000303 Stylable//EN"
5: "http://www.w3.org/TR/2000/03/WD-SVG-20000303/DTD/svg-20000303-
6:   stylable.dtd" [
```

continues

LISTING 22.10   Continued

```
 7: <!ENTITY st0 "fill:none;stroke-width:5.04;">
 8: <!ENTITY st1 "fill-rule:nonzero;clip-rule:nonzero;stroke:#000000;
 9:    stroke-miterlimit:4;">]>
10:
11: <svg width="254.989pt" height="104.255pt" viewBox="0 0 254.989 104.255"
12:    xml:space="preserve">
13:    <g id="Layer_x0020_1" style="&st1;">
14:      <path id="newPath" style="&st0;" d="M2.815,100.415c-0.147,0.822-0.159,
15:        1.598-0.354,2.401c9.705-13.879,14.356-30.552,
16:        24.381-44.408c9.544-13.191,22.468-24.158,38.313-28.809c21.493-6.308,
17:        43.011,4.355,64.516,1.717c15.429-1.893,28.255-17.305,
18:        41.55-24.599c8.506-4.667,17.982-4.18,27.42-4.185c18.782-0.011,37.527,
19:        1.272,56.301,1.606"/>
20:      <text x="40" y="100" font-family="palatino" font-size="18pt">
21:        <textPath xlink:href="#newPath"
22:          xmlns:xlink="http://www.w3.org/1999/xlink">
23:          The quick brown fox jumped over the lazy dog.
24:        </textPath>
25:      </text>
26:    </g>
27: </svg>
```

In this example, the path exported from Illustrator that you saw earlier is first assigned an ID of newPath (line 14). The sentence of text is then associated with the path by using the xlink:href attribute within the textPath element (line 22), where the path ID is referenced. Once this is done, the text is drawn along the path, as shown in Figure 22.12.

FIGURE 22.12

By linking text to a path, you can draw text along a path in SVG.

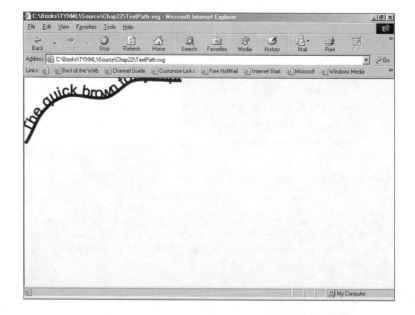

The `audio` Element

Whereas text and images are static media objects that are displayed over a specified period of time, audio represents a media type that is entirely time-dependent. In other words, audio must be played over a period of time. Interestingly enough, audio media types are used in SMIL presentations in a manner very similar to text and images. The `audio` element is used to play audio clips, and it does so using the familiar `region`, `src`, `type`, and `dur` attributes to define the parameters of the audio clip to be played. Unlike images, for which there are Web standards (GIF and JPEG) that govern the media types used, audio media types vary greatly. The audio types available for you to use are pretty much dependent on the SMIL player you are using to view a SMIL presentation; a SMIL player can be a Web browser plug-in, a Java applet, or a stand-alone application that supports the playback of SMIL presentations. One audio format that is popular on the Web is the AU format, which gained popularity with Java applets. The MIME type for the AU audio format is `audio/basic`. Following is an example of playing an AU audio clip using the `audio` element:

```
<audio src="music.au" region="background_audio" type="audio/x-au" dur="96s"/>
```

In this example, the `background.au` audio clip is played in the region with the ID `background_audio` for 96 seconds, which happens to be the length of the clip. As you may be guessing by its name and duration, this audio clip is actually a music clip that is intended to play throughout the duration of a SMIL presentation.

 The RealPlayer media player, which supports SMIL, is available for free download from the RealNetworks Web site at `http://www.real.com/`.

If you want to exert a little more control over how an audio clip is played, you can use the `begin` and `end` attributes of the `audio` element in lieu of the `dur` attribute. The `begin` and `end` attributes allow you to specify a portion of an audio clip to be played. Following is an example of how you would play a 10-second portion of an audio clip starting 5 seconds into the clip:

```
<audio src="music.au" region="background_audio" type="audio/x-au" begin="5s"
   end="15s"/>
```

The `video` Element

The last fundamental media type supported by the SMIL language is video, which enters the picture with SMIL documents thanks to the `video` element. The `video` element is used to play video clips and relies on the same `region`, `src`, `type`, and `dur` attributes that you've come to know and love. Similar to audio clips, video media types come in many different flavors, so you'll probably need to consult with the SMIL player that you intend to use to check and see which video media types are supported.

Similar to the `audio` element, the `video` element also supports the usage of the `begin` and `end` attributes, which allows you to play a portion of a video clip. This allows you to start playing a video clip anywhere within the clip for any period of time.

The `par` and `seq` Elements

Now that you have a feel for how media objects are placed in a SMIL presentation, you're probably wondering how exactly they are synchronized with each other. The `par` element is one of two elements that are used in SMIL to facilitate media synchronization. The `par` element is a container element in which you place media objects that you want to play in parallel with each other. Playing multiple media objects in parallel simply means that they are played at the same time. As an example, if you were to place an `img` element and an `audio` element inside of a `par` element, the image would be displayed as the audio clip is playing. In fact, the image would appear at exactly the same time that the audio clip starts playing. The following example demonstrates how to synchronize the start of a couple of media objects using the `par` element:

```
<par id="slide01">
  <img region="slide" src="skate01.jpg" type="image/jpeg" dur="16s"/>
  <text region="caption" src="skate01.txt" type="text/plain" dur="16s"/>
</par>
```

In this example, the `par` element is used to synchronize two media objects: an image and a string of text. Both media objects are set to a duration of 16 seconds, which means that they will appear at the same time and then disappear together 16 seconds later. If you were to shorten the duration of one of the objects, then it would disappear sooner than the other object. This code reveals that the `par` element supports an attribute named `id`, which allows you to uniquely identify a set of media objects that are being played.

 Although there is really no concept of "playing" a text or image media object because they are both static, I refer to all media objects as being "played" in this discussion to keep things simple.

The counterpart to the `par` element is the `seq` element, which is used to play media objects in series with each other. The `par` element plays media objects at the same time,

23

Summary

If you've ever been amazed by some of the online multimedia presentations made possible by technologies such as Flash, then you were hopefully impressed with the capabilities of SMIL (Synchronized Multimedia Integration Language), the XML-based markup language used to create synchronized multimedia presentations. SMIL allows you to combine a variety of different media types together in a single presentation and then carefully control the timing of each. SMIL is useful in creating animations, slide shows, educational courses, and virtually any kind of presentation where you need an efficient means of blending synchronized media objects, such as text, images, audio, and video.

This hour began by exploring the basics of SMIL and what it has to offer as an XML-based language. The details of the SMIL language were revealed, which include the most commonly used elements and attributes. The hour culminated in guiding you through the creation of a slide show complete with text captions and background music.

Q&A

Q Why would I want to use SMIL as opposed to just creating an animated GIF?

A It ultimately depends upon the kind of animation you're developing, but generally speaking, SMIL provides a much more efficient and flexible means of creating animations than that afforded by animated GIFs. Keep in mind that an animated GIF is essentially a single media object and therefore doesn't provide the flexibility of integrating several different types of objects, such as text, images, audio, and video. Additionally, if you decide to integrate text with a GIF animation, it becomes part of the image and therefore is more difficult to change and takes up more space than the SMIL approach.

Q How can I create SMIL presentations that can be viewed by the widest range of Web users?

A The best way to ensure that the widest range of Web users can view your SMIL presentations is to use very standard media objects. For example, you should attempt to stick with a very common audio format, such as AU or WAV, as well as common image formats, such as GIF and JPEG. You can also target a very popular media player such as RealPlayer; just keep in mind that some users will not yet have the player installed and may not take the time to download and install it just to see your SMIL presentation.

Workshop

The Workshop is designed to help you anticipate possible questions, review what you've learned, and begin learning how to put your knowledge into practice.

Quiz

1. What does the term "synchronized media" mean?
2. What is the purpose of the `smil` element in SMIL documents?
3. What is the purpose of the root layout in a SMIL presentation?
4. What is the difference between the `par` and `seq` elements?
5. What element do you use to establish the physical width and height of a SMIL presentation?

Quiz Answers

1. The term "synchronized media" refers to the arrangement of different static and time-based media objects so that they are played in a very precise manner.
2. The `smil` element serves as the root element in SMIL documents and therefore is the parent of all other SMIL elements.
3. The root layout of a SMIL presentation establishes the physical screen real estate set aside for the presentation.
4. The `par` element plays media objects at the same time (in parallel), whereas the `seq` element plays them one after the next (in series).
5. The `root-layout` element, in conjunction with the `width` and `height` attributes, is used to establish the physical width and height of a SMIL presentation.

Exercises

1. Using the skateboarding slide show SMIL document as a template, create your own slide show with digital photos of your own. Try viewing your slide show in the RealPlayer media player.
2. Create a Web page that uses the SOJA Java applet to allow your slide show to be viewed within a Web browser.

HOUR 24

Creating Virtual Worlds with 3DML

> Practical people would be more practical if they would take a little more time for dreaming.
>
> —J. P. McEvoy (writer)

I have to admit to being somewhat of a dreamer, and I have even dreamed of alternative worlds that aren't limited by the boundaries of our own. Believe it or not, there is a relationship between dream worlds and XML, and it's called 3DML. 3DML, which stands for 3-D Modeling Language, is a markup language used to create virtual worlds that can be viewed in the comfort of your Web browser. With 3DML you can create virtual walk-throughs for houses, imaginary fantasy worlds, and even 3-D games. I've even found a pretty neat usage of 3DML for creating conceptual designs for skateboard ramps, which you learn about in this hour. This hour introduces you to 3DML and reveals how amazingly easy it is to understand and use.

In this hour, you'll learn

- How 3DML allows you to create virtual worlds with relative ease
- The basics of the 3DML language
- How to create a practical virtual world in 3DML
- How to wire 3DML documents to Web pages for viewing in Web browsers

What Is 3DML?

3DML is a markup language that allows you to create virtual three-dimensional worlds in much the same way as you use HTML to create two-dimensional Web pages. 3DML was created by Flatland Online (`http://www.flatland.com/`) and works with Web browsers thanks to a free plug-in called Rover. Virtual 3DML worlds are known as *spots* and are created and stored in text files with a `.3dml` file extension. The main premise behind 3DML is simplicity, so it is extremely easy to create spots and put them online. For this reason, 3DML is designed to be somewhat simplistic, at least in comparison to other virtual reality technologies such as VRML (Virtual Reality Markup Language). However, the relative simplicity of 3DML allows it to be very efficient both in terms of graphics performance and bandwidth requirements. In other words, 3DML works surprisingly well on slow computers with modem connections, which is a very good thing.

VRML is a virtual reality language that is similar to 3DML, at least in general terms. VRML is actually more akin to a scripting language than a markup language and therefore is different than 3DML at the code level. VRML is more powerful than 3DML and also much more complex, which makes it more difficult to learn and use. The Web3D Consortium (`http://www.web3d.org/`) is currently in the process of adapting VRML to XML in a markup language known as X3D (eXtensible 3-D).

Since there is always a give and take when it comes to software performance, you're probably guessing that there is a drawback to the fact that 3DML spots are compact and efficient. 3DML's performance benefits are offset by limitations in graphical complexity. In other words, your 3DML spots will come closer to resembling Wolfenstein 3-D than they will Quake; if you aren't familiar with these games, just understand that Wolfenstein 3-D has considerably simpler 3-D graphics than Quake. The most obvious constraint of 3DML is the basic structure of spots. A spot in 3DML consists of an array

of cubes, or *blocks,* each of which is 256×256×256 pixels in size. When you define a
3DML spot, you specify how many blocks exist in each direction (X, Y, and Z). You can
think of a spot as a Rubik's cube, where each piece of the cube is a block. Another way
to express the structure of spots is to say that blocks in a spot are arranged in rows,
columns, and levels.

When you create a spot, you first specify how many blocks the spot contains. As an
example, a Rubik's cube spot would be 3×3×3 (rows × columns × levels). The inner
workings of the spot are determined by the specific kinds of blocks that reside in each
of the block spaces. The key point to understand about 3DML is that everything in a
3DML spot is made up of blocks. 3DML provides you with a set of building blocks,
also known as a *block set,* that is surprisingly flexible in allowing you to construct interesting spots. Flatland offers several different block sets that you can mix and match to
incorporate different kinds of blocks. For example, in addition to two basic block sets,
there is a village block set that includes blocks for physical structures, such as doors,
windows, and pathways, as well as an interior block set that includes blocks for furni-
ture, lighting, and so on.

Another interesting block set available for use with 3DML is the Islands
block set, which includes blocks for creating island worlds. There is also a
Tomb Raider block set that contains textures related to the popular Tomb
Raider video game. These block sets and all of the others are freely available
from the Flatland Web site at http://www.flatland.com/.

Not surprisingly, 3DML spots are not supported by default in any major Web browser; you
must use a browser plug-in to view them. The browser plug-in is known as Rover and is
freely available from Flatland Online at http://www.flatland.com/download/. Once
you've installed the Rover plug-in, you can immediately begin viewing 3DML spots. There
are several demonstration spots on the Flatland Web site (http://www.flatland.com/); I
encourage you to start there if you'd like to see 3DML in action before digging into
the specifics of the language. Figure 24.1 shows the Tomb Raider demo spot that is
available on the Flatland Web site as a showcase spot for 3DML.

FIGURE 24.1

The Tomb Raider demo spot is an excellent example of the capabilities of 3DML.

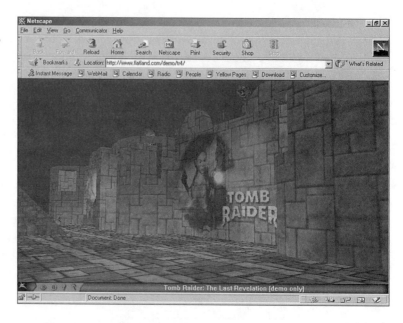

Inside the 3DML Language

Now that you're an expert in XML, you should be able to learn 3DML quickly and begin creating your own virtual worlds in a matter of minutes. You'll likely find that 3DML is surprisingly easy to learn, especially when you consider how interesting the end result can be. One thing worth pointing out is that Flatland Online doesn't offer a DTD or XSD for 3DML, so you'll have to do your best to adhere to the 3DML language as you code 3DML documents. Fortunately, the Rover plug-in does a pretty good job of validating 3DML spots when it processes them for display. So any mistakes you make will likely be revealed when you try to view your spot.

As with any XML-based language, the best place to start with 3DML is the core elements that make up the language, which are as follows:

- `spot`—the root element for 3DML documents
- `head`—contains header information about a spot
- `body`—contains the content of a spot

FIGURE 24.4

*A two-level 12×12
spot demonstrates
how to create multi-
level mazes.*

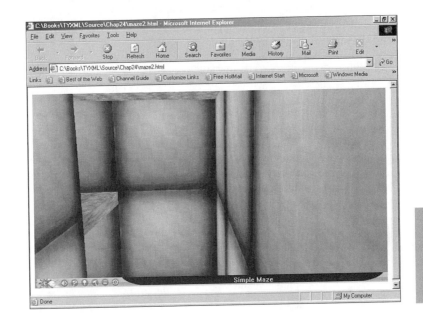

FIGURE 24.4

*A two-level 12×12
spot demonstrates
how to create multi-
level mazes.*

24

The `entrance` Element

Every spot must have at least one entrance, which determines where you start in the spot when it is first viewed in Rover. An entrance for a spot is determined by the `entrance` element, which is an empty element that includes three attributes: `location`, `name`, and `angle`. Following is the general syntax of the `entrance` element:

```
<entrance location="(column,row,level)" name="name" angle="degrees"/>
```

The `location` attribute specifies the location of the entrance, which is expressed as the column, row, and level of the block location. There is nothing special about the position of the entrance in a spot, and it doesn't look any different than other blocks. Block locations are always specified with respect to the upper left block in the first level of a spot. In other words, the upper left (northwest) block in level one of a spot has the location 1×1×1. If you moved the location over one block, down three blocks, and up two levels, the location would be specified as 2×4×3.

To assign a name to an entrance you use the `name` attribute. The `name` attribute is important because you may need to later link back to an entrance using the entrance name. Every spot is required to have one entrance named `default`, which is the default entrance for the spot. The `angle` attribute establishes the direction the users face when they are placed at the entrance. The origin of this angle is north (0 degrees), with values increasing in the clockwise direction. So, a value of `90` is east, a value of `180` is south, and a value of 270 is west. The angle attribute allows you to specify angles in whole number degrees, 0 through 359.

Following is an example of using the entrance element to specify a default entrance at the location 4×7×2 with an angle of 270 degrees:

```
<entrance location="(4,7,2)" NAME="default" ANGLE="270"/>
```

The exit Element

Spots are allowed to have *exits,* which are used to link individual blocks to other blocks in a spot or even to other spots entirely. Exits are created using the exit element, which is an empty element with the following five attributes: location, href, trigger, text, and target. Following is the syntax of the exit element:

```
<exit location="(column,row,level)" href="file_name#entrance_name"
  trigger="click on, step on" text="text" target="destination name"/>
```

The location attribute specifies the location of the exit, which is expressed as the column, row, and level of the block location. You can place an exit on any block in a spot, but it's common practice to associate an exit with a portal (@). This helps visitors to the spot know that the block will transport them to some other place. The destination of an exit is specified using the href attribute, which works much like the href attribute used in the HTML anchor element (a). In this case, the href attribute refers to a 3DML document filename and an entrance within that document. You can also leave the filename off and simply specify an entrance within the same document.

The trigger attribute determines how the exit is activated and can be a combination of two values: click on and step on. You can specify either of these trigger values or both. The click on value means that you have to click the mouse on an exit to activate the exit, whereas the step on value means that you have to move on top of the exit to activate it. The text attribute specifies a text message that is displayed to the users next to the cursor when they approach the exit. The target attribute allows you to specify a frame or window in which the exit link is opened. You can leave off the target attribute if you want the link to be opened in the same browser window.

Following is an example of using the exit element to create an exit at the location 3×5×4 that links back to the default entrance:

```
<EXIT LOCATION="(3,5,4)" HREF="#default" TRIGGER="click on, step on"
  TEXT="Back to start!"/>
```

The create Element

Next to the level element, the create element is likely the most powerful element in 3DML. The create element is used to create and modify blocks and must be placed in

Other Related Titles

XML for ASP.NET Developers
Dan Wahlin
0-672-32039-8
$39.99 US/$59.95 CAN

Strategic XML
W. Scott Means
0-672-32175-0
$34.99 US/$52.95 CAN

XML Internationalization and Localization
Yves Savourel
0-672-32096-7
$49.99 US/$74.95 CAN

Sams Teach Yourself Visual Basic.NET Web Programming in 21 Days
Peter Aiken and Phil Syme
0-672-32236-6
$39.99 US/$59.95 CAN

Sams Teach Yourself ASP.NET in 24 Hours
Joseph Martin and Brett Tomson
0-672-32126-2
$39.99 US/$59.95 CAN

Sams Teach Yourself UML in 24 Hours, Second Edition
Joseph Schmuller
0-672-32238-2
$29.99 US/$44.95 CAN

Sams Teach Yourself Illustrator 10 in 24 Hours
Peter Bauer and Mordy Golding
0-672-32313-3
$24.99 US/$37.95 CAN

Microsoft FrontPage 2002 Unleashed
William Stanek
0-672-32205-6
$49.99 US/$74.95 CAN

Sams Teach Yourself Adobe Acrobat 5 in 24 Hours
Christopher Smith and Sally Cox
0-672-32314-1
$24.99 US/$37.95 CAN

Sams Teach Yourself Adobe Photoshop 6 in 24 Hours
Carla Rose
0-672-31955-1
$24.99 US/$37.95 CAN

How to Use Adobe Premiere 6
Douglas Dixon
0-672-32166-1
$29.99 US/$44.95 CAN

How to Use The Internet, 2002 Edition
Rogers Cadenhead
0-672-32215-3
$29.99 US/$44.95 CAN

Sams Teach Yourself Web Publishing with HTML and XHTML in 21 Days, Professional Reference Edition
Laura Lemay
0-672-32204-8
$49.99 US/$74.95 CAN

Sams Teach Yourself Macromedia Flash 5 in 24 Hours
Phillip Kerman
0-672-31892-X
$24.99 US/$37.95 CAN

Sams Teach Yourself .NET XML Web Services in 24 Hours
Mark Augustyniak
0-672-32330-3
$29.99 US/$44.95 CAN

SAMS
www.samspublishing.com

All prices are subject to change.